Scala High Performance Programming

Leverage Scala and the functional paradigm to build performant software

Vincent Theron
Michael Diamant

BIRMINGHAM - MUMBAI

Scala High Performance Programming

First published: May 2016

Production reference: 1250516

Published by Packt Publishing Ltd.

Livery Place

35 Livery Street

Birmingham B3 2PB, UK.

ISBN 978-1-78646-604-4

www.packtpub.com

Credits

Authors

Vincent Theron

Michael Diamant

Reviewer

Nermin Šerifović

Commissioning Editor

Edward Gordon

Acquisition Editor

Chaitanya Nair

Content Development Editor

Nikhil Borkar

Technical Editor

Madhunikita Sunil Chindarkar

Copy Editor

Priyanka Ravi

Project Coordinator

Francina Pinto

Proofreader

Safis Editing

Indexer

Rekha Nair

Production Coordinator

Manu Joseph

Cover Work

Manu Joseph

About the Authors

Vincent Theron is a professional software engineer with 9 years of experience. He discovered Scala 6 years ago and uses it to build highly scalable and reliable applications. He designs software to solve business problems in various industries, including online gambling, financial trading, and, most recently, advertising. He earned a master's degree in computer science and engineering from Université Paris-Est Marne-la-Vallée. Vincent lives in the Boston area with his wife, his son, and two furry cats.

To everybody at Packt Publishing, thanks for working so hard to make this book a reality. To Chaitanya Nair, thanks for reaching out to me with this project. To Nikhil Borkar, thanks for providing us with guidance along the way. To Michael Diamant, my coauthor, coworker, and friend, thanks for the knowledge you have brought to this book and for being an inspiration every day. To my parents, thanks for your love and support and for buying me my first computer. And finally, to my wife, Julie, thanks for your constant encouragement and for giving me such a wonderful son.

Michael Diamant is a professional software engineer and functional programming enthusiast. He began his career in 2009 focused on Java and the object-oriented programming paradigm. After learning about Scala in 2011, he has focused on using Scala and the functional programming paradigm to build software systems in the financial trading and advertising domains. Michael is a graduate of Worcester Polytechnic Institute and lives in the Boston area.

The knowledge I am able to share in this book is the result of a lifetime of support and teaching from others. I want to recognize my coauthor, Vincent, for pushing me to take on this effort and for all the hours spent together developing the thoughts contained in our book. All of my current and former colleagues have helped me sharpen my engineering skills, and without their generosity of sharing their learning, I would not have been able to write this book. In addition to Vincent, I want to call out several colleagues that I feel particularly indebted to: Dave Stevens, Gary Malouf, Eugene Kolnick, and Johnny Everson. Thank you to my parents and my brother for supporting me and shaping me into the individual I am today. I am deeply appreciative of the support my girlfriend, Anna, gave me throughout the writing process. And last but not least, thank you to Packt Publishing for helping us write our first book.

About the Reviewer

Nermin Šerifović has been a Scala enthusiast since 2009, practicing it professionally since 2011. For most of his career, he has focused on building backend platforms using JVM technologies. Most recently, as VP Engineering at Pingup, he has been leading the development efforts of a local services booking system.

Nermin is an instructor at Harvard Extension School, where he co-teaches the Concurrent Programming in Scala course and has also given talks at various conferences.

An active Scala community member, Nermin organized the Boston Area Scala Enthusiasts user group and was part of the Northeast Scala Symposium founding team. He is a co-author of the *Scala Puzzlers* book and co-creator of the Scala Puzzlers website.

Nermin holds an M.Eng in computer science from Cornell University, and his areas of interest include distributed systems, along with concurrent, reactive, and functional programming.

www.PacktPub.com

For support files and downloads related to your book, please visit www.PacktPub.com.

eBooks, discount offers, and more

Did you know that Packt offers eBook versions of every book published, with PDF and ePub files available? You can upgrade to the eBook version at www.PacktPub.com and as a print book customer, you are entitled to a discount on the eBook copy. Get in touch with us at customercare@packtpub.com for more details.

At www.PacktPub.com, you can also read a collection of free technical articles, sign up for a range of free newsletters and receive exclusive discounts and offers on Packt books and eBooks.

https://www2.packtpub.com/books/subscription/packtlib

Do you need instant solutions to your IT questions? PacktLib is Packt's online digital book library. Here, you can search, access, and read Packt's entire library of books.

Why subscribe?

- Fully searchable across every book published by Packt
- Copy and paste, print, and bookmark content
- On demand and accessible via a web browser

Free access for Packt account holders

Get notified! Find out when new books are published by following @PacktEnterprise on Twitter or the Packt Enterprise Facebook page.

Table of Contents

Preface

Scala is an audacious programming language that blends object-oriented and functional programming concepts on the JVM. Scala has grown from relative obscurity to a top choice for developing robust and maintainable JVM applications. However, writing highly performant applications remains a challenge without a deep understanding of the language and the advanced features that it provides.

Since 2011, we have used Scala to solve complex business challenges with demanding performance requirements. In *Scala High Performance Programming*, we share the lessons that we have learned over the years and the techniques we apply when writing software. We explore the language and its ecosystem of tools and widely-used libraries in this book.

Our goal with this book is to help you understand the options that are made available to you by the language. We empower you to gather the information that is needed to make informed design and implementation decisions in your software systems. Rather than feed you a few Scala-fish and send you on your way, we help you learn how to fish and give you the tools to write more functional and more performant software. Along the way, we motivate technical discussions by concocting business problems that are reminiscent of real-world problems. We hope that by reading this book, you can come to appreciate the power of Scala, and find the tools to write more functional and more performant applications.

What this book covers

Chapter 1, *The Road to Performance*, introduces the concept of performance and the important terms for this topic.

Chapter 2, *Measuring Performance on the JVM*, details the tools that are available on the JVM to measure and evaluate performance, including JMH and Flight Recorder.

Chapter 3, *Unleashing Scala Performance*, provides a guided tour of various techniques and patterns to take advantage of the language features and improve program performance.

Chapter 4, *Exploring the Collection API*, discusses various collection abstractions that are provided by the standard Scala library. We focus on eagerly evaluated collections in this chapter.

Chapter 5, *Lazy Collections and Event Sourcing,* is an advanced chapter that discusses two types of lazy sequences: views and streams. We also give a brief overview of the event sourcing paradigm.

Chapter 6, *Concurrency in Scala,* discusses the importance of writing robust concurrent code. We dive into the Future API that is provided by the standard library, and introduce the Task abstraction from the Scalaz library.

Chapter 7, *Architecting for Performance,* this closing chapter combines deeper knowledge on previously covered topics and explores CRDTs as building blocks for distributed systems. This chapter also explores load control policies with the free monad to build systems with bounded latency characteristics when facing high throughput.

What you need for this book

You should install Java Development Kit version 8 or higher for your operating system to work through all code examples. This book discusses the Oracle HotSpot JVM, and it demonstrates tools that are included in Oracle JDK. You should also get the latest version of sbt (version 0.13.11, at the time of writing) from http://www.scala-sbt.org/download.html.

Who this book is for

You should possess a basic knowledge of the Scala programming language, have some familiarity with elementary functional programming concepts, and have experience of writing production-level JVM software. We recommend that readers who are new to Scala and functional programming spend some time studying other resources before reading this book in order to get the best out of it. Two excellent Scala-centric resources are *Programming in Scala, Artima Press* and *Functional Programming in Scala, Manning Publications*. The former is best suited for strong object-oriented Java programmers that are looking to understand the language first and the functional programming paradigm second. The latter focuses heavily on the functional programming paradigm and less so on language-specific constructs.

Conventions

In this book, you will find a number of text styles that distinguish between different kinds of information. Here are some examples of these styles and an explanation of their meaning.

Code words in text, database table names, folder names, filenames, file extensions, pathnames, dummy URLs, and user inputs are shown as follows: "The -XX:+FlightRecorderOptions accepts a parameter named settings, which, by default, points to $JAVA_HOME/jre/lib/jfr/default.jfc."

A block of code is set as follows:

```
def sum(l: List[Int]): Int = l match {
  case Nil => 0
  case x :: xs => x + sum(xs)
}
```

Any command-line input or output is written as follows:

```
    sbt 'project chapter2' 'set javaOptions := Seq("-Xmx1G")' 'runMain
highperfscala.benchmarks.ThroughputBenchmark
src/main/resources/historical_data 250000'
```

New terms and important words are shown in bold. Words that you see on the screen, for example, in menus or dialog boxes, appear in the text like this: "Let's start on the **Overview** tab of the **Code** tab group."

Warnings or important notes appear in a box like this.

Tips and tricks appear like this.

Reader feedback

Feedback from our readers is always welcome. Let us know what you think about this book—what you liked or disliked. Reader feedback is important for us as it helps us develop titles that you will really get the most out of.

To send us general feedback, simply e-mail feedback@packtpub.com, and mention the book's title in the subject of your message.

If there is a topic that you have expertise in and you are interested in either writing or contributing to a book, see our author guide at www.packtpub.com/authors.

Customer support

Now that you are the proud owner of a Packt book, we have a number of things to help you to get the most from your purchase.

Downloading the example code

You can download the example code files for this book from your account at http://www.packtpub.com. If you purchased this book elsewhere, you can visit http://www.packtpub.com/support and register to have the files e-mailed directly to you.

You can download the code files by following these steps:

1. Log in or register to our website using your e-mail address and password.
2. Hover the mouse pointer on the **SUPPORT** tab at the top.
3. Click on **Code Downloads & Errata**.
4. Enter the name of the book in the **Search** box.
5. Select the book for which you're looking to download the code files.
6. Choose from the drop-down menu where you purchased this book from.
7. Click on **Code Download**.

You can also download the code files by clicking on the **Code Files** button on the book's webpage at the Packt Publishing website. This page can be accessed by entering the book's name in the Search box. Please note that you need to be logged in to your Packt account.

Once the file is downloaded, please make sure that you unzip or extract the folder using the latest version of:

- WinRAR / 7-Zip for Windows
- Zipeg / iZip / UnRarX for Mac
- 7-Zip / PeaZip for Linux

The code bundle for the book is also hosted on GitHub at https://github.com/PacktPublishing/Scala-High-Performance-Programming. We also have other code bundles from our rich catalog of books and videos available at https://github.com/PacktPublishing/. Check them out!

Downloading the color images of this book

We also provide you with a PDF file that has color images of the screenshots/diagrams used in this book. The color images will help you better understand the changes in the output. You can download this file from `https://www.packtpub.com/sites/default/files/downloads/ScalaHighPerformanceProgramming_ColorImages.pdf`.

Errata

Although we have taken every care to ensure the accuracy of our content, mistakes do happen. If you find a mistake in one of our books—maybe a mistake in the text or the code—we would be grateful if you could report this to us. By doing so, you can save other readers from frustration and help us improve subsequent versions of this book. If you find any errata, please report them by visiting `http://www.packtpub.com/submit-errata`, selecting your book, clicking on the Errata Submission Form link, and entering the details of your errata. Once your errata are verified, your submission will be accepted and the errata will be uploaded to our website or added to any list of existing errata under the Errata section of that title.

To view the previously submitted errata, go to `https://www.packtpub.com/books/content/support` and enter the name of the book in the search field. The required information will appear under the Errata section.

Piracy

Piracy of copyrighted material on the Internet is an ongoing problem across all media. At Packt, we take the protection of our copyright and licenses very seriously. If you come across any illegal copies of our works in any form on the Internet, please provide us with the location address or website name immediately so that we can pursue a remedy.

Please contact us at `copyright@packtpub.com` with a link to the suspected pirated material.

We appreciate your help in protecting our authors and our ability to bring you valuable content.

Questions

If you have a problem with any aspect of this book, you can contact us at `questions@packtpub.com`, and we will do our best to address the problem.

1
The Road to Performance

We welcome you on a journey to learning pragmatic ways to use the Scala programming language and the functional programming paradigm to write performant and efficient software. Functional programming concepts, such as pure and higher-order functions, referential transparency, and immutability, are desirable engineering qualities. They allow us to write composable elements, maintainable software, and expressive and easy-to-reason-about code. However, in spite of all its benefits, functional programming is too often wrongly associated with degraded performance and inefficient code. It is our goal to convince you otherwise! This book explores how to take advantage of functional programming, the features of the Scala language, the Scala standard library, and the Scala ecosystem to write performant software.

Scala is a statically and strongly typed language that tries to elegantly blend both functional and object-oriented paradigms. It has experienced growing popularity in the past few years as both an appealing and pragmatic choice to write production-ready software in the functional paradigm. Scala code compiles to bytecode and runs on the **Java Virtual Machine (JVM)**, which has a widely-understood runtime, is configurable, and provides excellent tooling to introspect and debug correctness and performance issues. An added bonus is Scala's great interoperability with Java, which allows you to use all the existing Java libraries. While the Scala compiler and the JVM receive constant improvements and already generate well-optimized bytecode, the onus remains on you, the developer, to achieve your performance goals.

Before diving into the Scala and JVM specifics, let's first develop an intuition for the holy grail that we seek: performance. In this first chapter, we will cover performance basics that are agnostic to the programming language. We will present and explain the terms and concepts that are used throughout this book.

In particular, we will look at the following topics:

- Defining performance
- Summarizing performance
- Collecting measurements

We will also introduce our case study, a fictitious application based on real-world problems that will help us illustrate techniques and patterns that are presented later.

Defining performance

A performance vocabulary arms you with a way to qualify the type of issues at-hand and often helps guide you towards a resolution. Particularly when time is of the essence, a strong intuition and a disciplined strategy are assets to resolve performance problems.

Let's begin by forming a common understanding of the term, performance. This term is used to qualitatively or quantitatively evaluate the ability to accomplish a goal. The goal at-hand can vary significantly. However, as a professional software developer, the goal ultimately links to a business goal. It is paramount to work with your business team to characterize business domain performance sensitivities. For a consumer-facing shopping website, agreeing upon the number of concurrent app users and acceptable request response times is relevant. In a financial trading company, trade latency might be the most important because speed is a competitive advantage. It is also relevant to keep in mind nonfunctional requirements, such as "trade executions can never be lost," because of industry regulations and external audits. These domain constraints will also impact your software's performance characteristics. Building a clear and agreed upon picture of the domain that you operate in is a crucial first step. If you cannot define these constraints, an acceptable solution cannot be delivered.

 Gathering requirements is an involved topic outside the scope of this book. If you are interested in delving deeper into this topic, we recommend two books by Gojko Adzic: *Impact Mapping: Making a big impact with software products and projects* (http://www.amazon.com/Impact-Mapping-software-products-projects-ebook/dp/B009KWDKVA) and Fifty Quick Ideas to Improve Your User Stories (http://www.amazon.com/Fifty-Quick-Ideas-Improve-Stories-ebook/dp/B00OGT2U7M).

Performant software

Designing performant software is one of our goals as software engineers. Thinking about this goal leads to a commonly asked question, "What performance is good enough?" We use the term performant to characterize performance that satisfies the minimally-accepted threshold for "good enough." We aim to meet and, if possible, exceed the minimum thresholds for acceptable performance. Consider this: without an agreed upon set of criteria for acceptable performance, it is by definition impossible to write performant software! This statement illustrates the overwhelming importance of defining the desired outcome as a prerequisite to writing performant software.

 Take a moment to reflect on the meaning of performant for your domain. Have you had struggles maintaining software that meets your definition of performant? Consider the strategies that you applied to solve performance dilemmas. Which ones were effective and which ones were ineffective? As you progress through the book, keep this in mind so that you can check which techniques can help you meet your definition of performant more effectively.

Hardware resources

In order to define criteria for performant software, we must expand the performance vocabulary. First, become aware of your environment's resources. We use the term resource to cover all the infrastructure that your software uses to run. Refer to the following resource checklist, which lists the resources that you should collect prior to engaging in any performance tuning exercise:

- Hardware type: physical or virtualized
- CPUs:
  âۣۣۣۢNumber of cores
  âۣۣۣۢL1, L2, and L3 cache sizes
  âۣۣۣۢNUMA zones
- RAM (for example, 16 GB)
- Network connectivity rating (for example, 1GbE or 10GbE)
- OS and kernel versions
- Kernel settings (for example, TCP socket receive buffer size)
- JVM version

Itemizing the resource checklist forces you to consider the capabilities and limitations of your operating environment.

 Excellent resources for kernel optimization include Red Hat Performance Tuning Guide (`https://goo.gl/gDS5mY`) and presentations and tutorials by Brendan Gregg (`http://www.brendangregg.com/linuxperf.html`).

Latency and throughput

Latency and throughput define two types of performance, which are often used to establish the criteria for performant software. The illustration of a highway, like the following photo of the German Autobahn, is a great way to develop an intuition of these types of performance:

The Autobahn helps us think about latency and throughput. (image wikimedia, https://en.wikipedia.org/wiki/Highway#/media/File:Blick_auf_A_2_bei_Rastst%C3%A4tte_Lehrter_See_(2009).jpg. License Creative Commons CC BY-SA 3.0)

Latency describes the amount of time that it takes for an observed process to be completed. Here, the process is a single car driving down one lane of the highway. If the highway is free of congestion, then the car is able to drive down the highway quickly. This is described as a low-latency process. If the highway is congested, the trip time increases, which is characterized as a high-latency or latent process. Performance optimizations that are within your control are also captured by this analogy. You can imagine that reworking an expensive algorithm from polynomial to linear execution time is similar to either improving the quality of the highway or the car's tires to reduce road friction. The reduction in friction allows the car to cross the highway with lower latency. In practice, latency performance objectives are often defined in terms of a maximum tolerable latency for your business domain.

Throughput defines the observed rate at which a process is completed. Using the highway analogy, the number of cars traveling from point A to point B per unit of time is the highway's throughput. For example, if there are three traffic lanes and cars travel in each lane at a uniform rate, then the throughput is: (the number of cars per lane that traveled from point A to point B during the observation period) * 3. Inductive reasoning may suggest that there is a strong negative correlation between throughput and latency. That is, as latency increases, throughput decreases. As it turns out, there are a number of cases where this type of reasoning does not hold true. Keep this in mind as we continue expanding our performance vocabulary to better understand why this happens. In practice, throughput is often defined by the maximum number of transactions per second your software can support. Here, a transaction means a unit of work in your domain (for example, orders processed or trades executed).

Thinking back to the recent performance issues that you faced, how would you characterize them? Did you have a latency or a throughput problem? Did your solution increase throughput while lowering latency?

Bottlenecks

A bottleneck refers to the slowest part of the system. By definition, all systems, including well-tuned ones, have a bottleneck because there is always one processing step that is measured to be the slowest. Note that the latency bottleneck may not be the throughput bottleneck. That is, multiple types of bottleneck can exist at the same time. This is another illustration of why it is important to understand whether you are combating a throughput or a latency performance issue. Use the process of identifying your system's bottlenecks to provide you with a directed focus to attack your performance dilemmas.

From personal experience, we have seen how time is wasted when the operating environment checklist is ignored. Once, while working in the advertising domain on a high-throughput **real-time bidding** (**RTB**) platform, we chased a throughput issue for several days without success. After bootstrapping an RTB platform, we began optimizing for a higher request throughput goal because request throughput is a competitive advantage in our industry. Our business team identified an increase from 40,000 requests per second (RPS) to 75,000 RPS as a major milestone. Our tuning efforts consistently yielded about 60,000 RPS. This was a real head scratcher because the system did not appear to exhaust system resources. CPU utilization was well under 100%, and previous experiments to increase heap space did not yield improvements.

The "aha!" moment came when we realized that the system was deployed within AWS with the default network connectivity configured to 1 Gigabit Ethernet. The requests processed by the system are about 2KB per request. We performed some basic arithmetic to identify the theoretical maximum throughput rate. 1 Gigabit is equivalent to 125,000 kilobytes. 125,000 kilobytes / 2 kilobytes per request translates to a theoretical maximum of 62,500 RPS. This arithmetic was confirmed by running a test of our network throughput with a tool named iPerf. Sure enough, we had maxed out our network connectivity!

Summarizing performance

We properly defined some of the main concepts around performance, namely latency and throughput, but we still lack a concrete way to quantify our measurements. To continue with our example of cars driving down a highway, we want to find a way to answer the question, "How long a drive should I expect to go from point A to point B?" The first step is to measure our trip time on multiple occasions to collect empirical information.

The following table catalogs our observations. We still need a way to interpret these data points and summarize our measurements to give an answer:

Observed trip	Travel time in minutes
Trip 1	28
Trip 2	37
Trip 3	17
Trip 4	38
Trip 5	18

The problem with averages

A common mistake is to rely on averages to measure the performance of a system. An arithmetic average is fairly easy to calculate. This is the sum of all collected values divided by the number of values. Using the previous sample of data points, we can infer that on average we should expect a drive of approximately 27 minutes. With this simple example, it is easy to see what makes the average such a poor choice. Out of our five observations, only Trip 1 is close to our average while all the other trips are quite different. The fundamental problem with averages is that it is a lossy summary statistic. Information is lost when moving from a series of observations to the average because it is impossible to retain all the characteristics of the original observations in a single data point.

To illustrate how an average loses information, consider the three following datasets that represent the measured latency required to process a request to a web service:

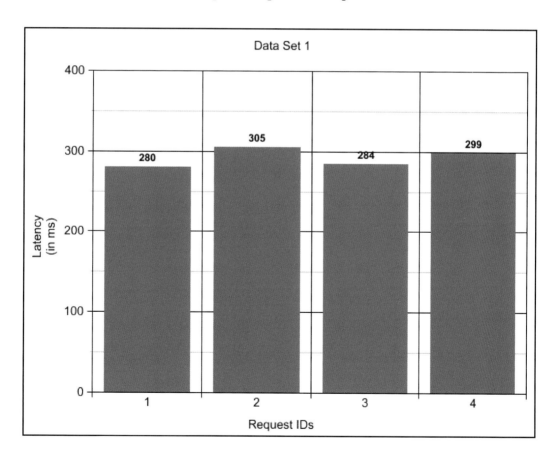

In the first dataset, there are four requests that take between 280 ms and 305 ms to be completed. Compare these latencies with the latencies in the second dataset, as follows:

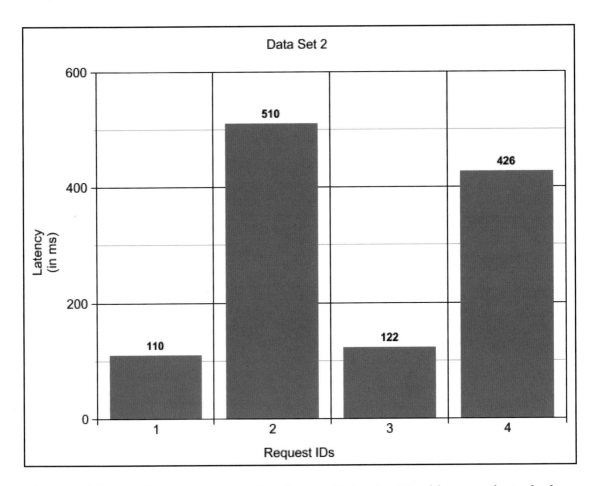

The second dataset shows a more volatile mixture of latencies. Would you prefer to deploy the first or the second service into your production environment? To add more variety into the mix, a third dataset is shown, as follows:

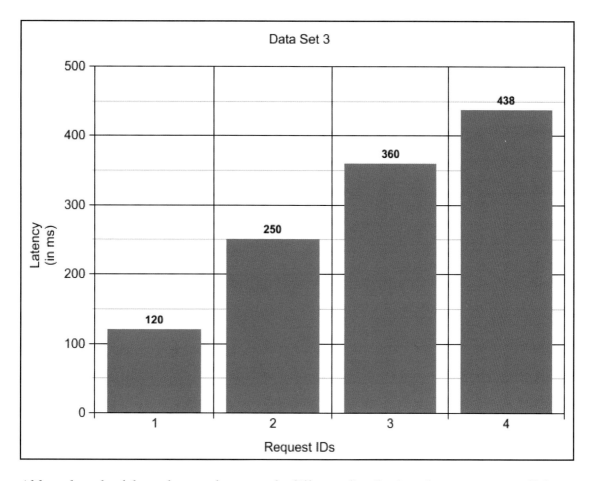

Although each of these datasets has a vastly different distribution, the averages are all the same, and equal 292 ms! Imagine having to maintain the web service that is represented by dataset 1 with the goal of ensuring that 75% of clients receive a response in less than 300 ms. Calculating the average out of dataset 3 will give you the impression that you are meeting your objective, while in reality only half of your clients actually experience a fast enough response (requests with IDs 1 and 2).

Percentiles to the rescue

The key term in the previous discussion is "distribution." Measuring the distribution of a system's performance is the most robust way to ensure that you understand the behavior of the system. If an average is an ineffective choice to take into account the distribution of our measurements, then we need to find a different tool. In the field of statistics, a percentile meets our criteria to interpret the distribution of observations. A percentile is a measurement indicating the following value into which a given percentage of observations in a group of observations falls. Let's make this definition more concrete with an example. Going back to our web service example, imagine that we observe the following latencies:

Request	Latency in milliseconds
Request 1	10
Request 2	12
Request 3	13
Request 4	13
Request 5	9
Request 6	27
Request 7	12
Request 8	7
Request 9	75
Request 10	80

The 20th percentile is defined as the observed value that represents 20% of all the observations. As there are ten observed values, we want to find the value that represents two observations. In this example, the 20th percentile latency is 9 ms because two values (that is, 20% of the total observations) are less than or equal to 10 ms (9 ms and 7 ms). Contrast this latency with the 90th percentile. The value representing 90% of the observations: 75 ms (as nine observations out of ten are less than or equal to 75 ms).

Where the average hides the distribution of our measurements, the percentile provides us with deeper insight and highlights that tail-end observations (the observations near the 100th percentile) experience extreme latencies.

If you remember the beginning of this section, we were trying to answer the question, "How long a drive should I expect to go from point A to point B?" After spending some time exploring the tools available, we realized that the original question is not the one we are actually interested in. A more pragmatic question is, "How long do 90% of the cars take to go from point A to point B?"

Collecting measurements

Our performance measurement toolkit is already filled with useful information. We defined a common vocabulary to talk about and explore performance. We also agreed on a pragmatic way to summarize performance. The next step in our journey is to answer the question, "In order to summarize them, how do I collect performance measurements?" This section introduces you to techniques to collect measurements. In the next chapter, we dive deeper and focus on collecting data from Scala code. We will show you how to use various tools and libraries designed to work with the JVM and understand your programs better.

Using benchmarks to measure performance

Benchmarks are a black-box kind of measurement. Benchmarks assess a whole system's performance by submitting various kinds of load as input and measuring latency and throughput as system outputs. As an example, imagine that we are working on a typical shopping cart web application. To benchmark this application, we can write a simple HTTP client to query our service and record the time taken to complete a request. This client can be used to send an increasing number of requests per second and output a summary of the recorded response times.

Multiple kinds of benchmark exist to answer different questions about your system. You can replay historical production data to make sure that your application is meeting the expected performance goals when handling realistic load. Load and stress test benchmarks identify the breaking points of your application, and they exercise its robustness when receiving exceptionally high load for an extended period of time.

Benchmarks are also a great tool to compare different iterations of the same application and either detect performance regression or confirm improvements. By executing the same benchmark against two versions of your code, you can actually prove that your recent changes yielded better performance.

For all their usefulness, benchmarks do not provide any insight into how each part of the software performs; hence, they are black-box tests. Benchmarks do not help us identify bottlenecks or determine which part of the system should be improved to yield better overall performance. To look into the black box, we turn to profiling.

Profiling to locate bottlenecks

As opposed to benchmarking, profiling is intended to be used to analyze the internal characteristics of your application. A profiler enables white-box testing to help you identify bottlenecks by capturing the execution time and resource consumption of each part of your program. By examining your application at runtime, a profiler provides you with great details about the behavior of your code, including the following:

- Where CPU cycles are spent
- How memory is used, and where objects are instantiated and released (or not, if you have a memory leak!)
- Where IO operations are performed
- Which threads are running, blocked, or idle

Most profilers instrument the code under observation, either at compile time or runtime, to inject counters and profiling components. This instrumentation imposes a runtime cost that degrades system throughput and latency. For this reason, profilers should not be used to evaluate the expected throughput and latency of a system in production (as a reminder, this is a use case for a benchmark).

In general, you should always profile your application before deciding to do any performance-driven improvement. You should make sure that the part of the code you are planning to improve actually is a bottleneck.

Pairing benchmarks and profiling

Profilers and benchmarks have different purposes, and they help us answer different questions. A typical workflow to improve performance should take advantage of both these techniques and leverage their strengths to optimize the code improvement process. In practice, this workflow looks like the following:

1. Run a benchmark against the current version of the code to establish a performance baseline.
2. Use a profiler to analyze the internal behavior and locate a bottleneck.
3. Improve the section causing a bottleneck.
4. Run the same benchmark from step 1 against the new code.
5. Compare the results from the new benchmark against the baseline benchmark to determine the effectiveness of your changes.

Keep in mind, it is important to run all benchmarking and profiling sessions in the same environment. Consult your resource checklist to ensure that your environment remains constant across tests. Any change in your resources invalidates your test results. Just like a science experiment, you must be careful to change only one part of the experiment at a time.

 What roles do benchmarking and profiling play in your development process? Do you always profile your application before deciding on the next part of the code to improve? Does your definition of "done" include benchmarking? Are you able to benchmark and profile your application in an environment as close to production as possible?

A case study

Throughout this book, we will provide code examples to illustrate the topics that are covered. To make the techniques that were described previously as useful as possible in your professional life, we are relating our examples to a fictitious financial trading company, named MV Trading. The company name originates from the combination of the first name initials of your dear authors. Coincidentally, the initials also form the Unix file move command, symbolizing that the company is on-the-move! Since inception one year ago, MV Trading has operated successful stock trading strategies for a small pool of clients. Software infrastructure has been rapidly built in the last twelve months to support various arms of the business. MV Trading built software to support real-time trading (that is, buying and selling) on various stock market exchanges, and it also built a historical trade execution analysis to create better performing trading algorithms. If you do not have financial domain knowledge, do not worry. With each example, we also define key parts of the domain.

Tooling

We recommend that you install all the necessary tooling up-front so that you can work through these examples without setup time. The installation instructions are brief because detailed installation guides are available on the websites that accompany each required tool. The following software is needed for all upcoming chapters:

- Oracle JDK 8+ using v1.8 u66 at the time of writing
- sbt v0.13+, using v0.13.11 at the time of writing, which is available at `http://www.scala-sbt.org/`

Detailed steps to download the code bundle are mentioned in the Preface of this book. Please have a look at it.

The code bundle for the book is also hosted on GitHub at `https://github.com/PacktPublishing/Scala-High-Performance-Programming`. We also have other code bundles from our rich catalog of books and videos available at `https://github.com/PacktPublishing/`. Check them out!

Summary

In this chapter, we focused on understanding how to talk about performance. We built a vocabulary to discuss performance, determined the best way to summarize performance with percentiles, and developed an intuition to measure performance. We introduced our case study, and then we installed the required tools to run the code samples and the source code provided with this book. In the next chapter, we will look at available tools to measure JVM performance and analyze the performance of our Scala applications.

2
Measuring Performance on the JVM

In the previous chapter, we introduced and defined important concepts that are related to performance. While extremely valuable, our journey so far has been somewhat academic, and you may grow impatient to exercise your newly acquired knowledge. Luckily, this second chapter does just this! We will take a close look at a real-world scenario and dive head first into the code to profile the application and measure its performance characteristics. This hands-on chapter focuses on one of MV Trading's most successful products: the order book. This is a critical piece of software that was developed to deliver high throughput while maintaining low latency. In this chapter, we will cover the following topics:

- Benchmarking the latency and throughput of an application
- Profiling a system with Flight Recorder
- Using JMH to microbenchmark our code

A peek into the financial domain

This month marks the one year anniversary for **MV Trading** (**MVT**). In the last year, the company delivered great returns to its clients by capitalizing on novel trading strategies. These strategies work most effectively when trades can be placed within milliseconds of receiving new price information. To support trading with low latency, the MVT engineering team directly integrated into a stock market exchange. Exchange integration involved datacenter work to collocate the trading system with the exchange and development effort to build the trading system.

A key component of the trading system, known as the order book, holds the state of the exchange. The goal of the exchange is to keep track of how many buyers and sellers have an active interest in a stock and at what price each side is willing to trade. As traders, such as MVT, submit orders to buy and sell a stock, the exchange determines when a trade happens and notifies the buyer and the seller about the transaction. The state managed by the exchange and by extension, MVT, is interesting because orders do not always execute when they reach the exchange. Instead, orders can remain in an open or pending state for up to the length of the trading day (on the order of six hours). This first version of the order book allows traders to place orders called limit orders. Limit orders include a constraint on the minimally-acceptable price. For buys, the limit represents the highest price that the trader wishes to pay, and for sells, this indicates the lowest price the trader wishes to receive in exchange for the stock. Another operation that is supported by the order book is the cancelation of an outstanding limit order, which removes its presence from the book. To help summarize the possible order states, the following table itemizes possible outcomes to support exchange actions:

Exchange action	Outcome
Limit order with a price worse than best bid or offer submitted.	The order rests on the book, meaning that the order remains in a pending state until an order from the opposing side generates a trade or the submitted order is canceled.
Limit order with a price better than or equal to best bid or offer submitted.	The order crosses the book. Crossing the book is industry jargon that indicates an order caused a trade to happen because its price matched one or more orders from the opposing side of the book. A trade consists of two executions, one per side.
Cancelation submitted for a resting order.	The resting order is removed from the book.
Cancelation submitted for an already executed or non-existent order.	The cancelation request is rejected.

Let's suppose that as a newly-hired MVT employee, you just joined the engineering team that is in charge of maintaining and improving the order book. Today is your first day, and you are planning to take most of the morning to calmly skim through the code and get familiar with the application.

After checking out the source code repository, you start with the domain model:

```
case class Price(value: BigDecimal)
case class OrderId(value: Long)

sealed trait LimitOrder {
  def id: OrderId
  def price: Price
}

case class BuyLimitOrder(id: OrderId, price: Price)
  extends LimitOrder
case class SellLimitOrder(id: OrderId, price: Price)
  extends LimitOrder

case class Execution(orderId: OrderId, price: Price)
```

The class and trait definitions in the preceding code represent the business concepts. We especially notice the two kinds of orders (`BuyLimitOrder` and `SellLimitOrder`) that are identified by their unique ID and the associated price assumed to be in USD.

You may wonder why we decided to create distinct class definitions for `Price` and `OrderId` while they only serve as mere wrappers for a unique attribute (respectively a `BigDecimal` for the price, and a `Long` for the unique ID). Alternatively, we can instead rely directly on the primitive types.

A `BigDecimal` could represent a lot of different things, including a price, but also a tax rate or a latitude on the globe. Using a specific type, named `Price`, gives contextual meaning to the `BigDecimal` and makes sure that the compiler helps us catch possible errors. We believe that it is good practice to always define explicit types to represent business concerns. This technique is part of the best practices known as domain-driven design, and we often apply these principles throughout the book. To learn more about this approach to software development, we recommend the excellent book *Domain-Driven Design: Tackling Complexity in the Heart of Software* (`http://www.amazon.com/Domain-Driven-Design-Tackling-Complexity-Software/dp/0321125215`) by Eric Evans.

The `OrderBook` module leverages the domain model to define the available commands and the resulting events that can be produced by the book:

```
object OrderBook {
  // all the commands that can be handled by the OrderBook module
  object Commands {
    sealed trait Command
    case class AddLimitOrder(o: LimitOrder) extends Command
    case class CancelOrder(id: OrderId) extends Command
  }

  // events are the results of processing a command
  object Events {
    sealed trait Event
    case class OrderExecuted(buy: Execution, sell: Execution)
      extends Event
    case object LimitOrderAdded extends Event
    case object OrderCancelRejected extends Event
    case object OrderCanceled extends Event
  }

  // the entry point of the module - the current book and
  // the command to process are passed as parameters,
  // the new state of the book and the event describing the
  // result of processing the command are returned
  def handle(book: OrderBook, command: Command): (OrderBook, Event) = //
omitted for brevity
}
```

Let's suppose that you are about to look at the implementation of the `handle` function in detail when you notice a message in your IM client from your technical lead, Alice: "Everybody in the conference room. We have a problem in production!"

Readers with financial domain expertise likely realize that the presented actions reflect a subset of the functionality of an actual financial exchange. One evident example is the absence of quantity from an order. In our examples, we assume each order represents a desire to buy an equal number of shares (for example, 100 shares). Experienced readers are aware that order volume further complicates order book state management, for example, by introducing the notion of partial executions. We are deliberately simplifying the domain to balance working on a realistic problem while minimizing the barrier to comprehension for readers who are new to the domain.

Unexpected volatility crushes profits

Alice and the head trader, Dave, kick off the meeting by summarizing the production problem. You digested a lot of insight into the problem from the meeting. You learned that currently, there is high market volatility and the rapid swings in prices amplify opportunities to generate profitable trades. Unfortunately for MVT, in recent weeks, the high volatility has brought with it unseen levels of order volume. Traders have been flooding the markets with limit orders and cancelations to react to the quickly changing price action. The MVT order book is certified via load testing to handle a maximum of 15,000 orders per second (OPS) with a 99th percentile latency of 10 milliseconds (ms). The current market conditions are producing sustained levels of 45,000 OPS, which is destroying tail-end order book latencies. In production, the deployed version of the order book is now producing 99th percentile latencies of up to 80 ms and maximum latencies reaching 200 ms. In the trading business, a slow reaction can quickly turn a profitable trade into a sizable loss. This is exactly what has been happening at MVT. Typically, in times of volatility, MVT is able to generate healthy returns, but in recent weeks, there have been staggering losses. Our goal is to apply the techniques that we learned in `Chapter 1`, *The Road to Performance*, to make inroads on the performance woes.

The traders at MVT are looking for a quick performance win to take advantage of the current market environment. The traders believe that the market volatility will persist for another week before subsiding. Once the volatility disappears, so do money-making opportunities. Therefore, it's been stressed to the engineering team that an incremental reduction in 99th percentile latency to 40 ms should halt trading strategy losses and actually produce small profits. Once the volatility subsides, more in-depth and extensive performance improvements are welcomed. For now, the clock is ticking, and we need to find a way to stop the losses by improving performance incrementally.

Reproducing the problem

This is not quite the first day you were expecting, but what an exciting challenge ahead of you! We start our investigation of the performance issue by reproducing the problem. As we mentioned in the previous chapter, it is always critical to properly benchmark an application to establish a baseline. The baseline is used to evaluate the effectiveness of any improvement that we may try to implement. We create two simple benchmarks to reproduce the load observed in production and measure the throughput and latency of the system.

But wait, I have not finished studying how `OrderBook` is actually implemented! You are correct! You still have no idea of the implementation of the module. However, production is broken, and we need to act fast! More seriously, this is our way of highlighting an important characteristic of benchmarking that we mentioned in `Chapter` 1, *The Road to Performance*. Benchmarks treat the application as a black box. You had time to study the module interface, and this is enough to write good benchmarks.

Throughput benchmark

Our first benchmark measures the throughput of our application. The operations team provided us with historical data that was logged from the production environment. This data contains several hundred thousand actual commands that were processed by the order book. We use this sample and replay these messages against a testing environment to get an accurate idea of the system's behavior.

Recall from `Chapter` 1, *The Road to Performance*, that it is important to run all benchmarks under the exact same environment to be able to compare them. To ensure consistency across tests, we created a command generator that is capable of outputting a static set of commands. We encourage you to review it.

Here is the code for our throughput benchmark, which you can find under the chapter subproject:

```
object ThroughputBenchmark {

  def main(args: Array[String]): Unit = {
    val commandSample = DataCodec.read(new File(args(0)))
    val commandCount = args(1).toInt

    jvmWarmUp(commandSample)

    val commands = generateCount(commandSample, commandCount)

    val start = System.currentTimeMillis()
    commands.foldLeft(OrderBook.empty)(OrderBook.handle(_, _)._1)
    val end = System.currentTimeMillis()
    val delayInSeconds = (end - start) / 1000.0

    println {
      s"""
```

```
              |Processed ${commands.size} commands
              |in $delayInSeconds seconds
              |Throughput: ${commands.size / delayInSeconds} operations/sec"""
              .stripMargin
        }
      }
    }
```

The code is fairly straightforward, so let's walk through it. First, we read our input arguments, the first one being the path to the file that contains our historical data, and the second one is the number of commands that we want to run. Note that in our implementation, if we ask for more commands than what is contained in our static file, the program will just loop through the provided commands. We then warm up the JVM by executing up to 100,000 commands without recording any throughput information. The point of a warm-up is to give the JVM the opportunity to exercise the code and find possible hotspots that can be optimized by the **just-in-time (JIT)** compiler.

 The JIT compiler is a compiler that runs after the application has been started. It compiles the bytecode (that is, the result of the first compilation by the `javac` compiler) on-the-fly into an optimized form, usually native instructions for the operating system. The JIT is able to optimize the code, based on runtime usage. This is something that the traditional compiler cannot do because it runs before the code can be executed.

The next part of the code is where we actually record the throughput. We save the starting timestamp, execute all the commands against an initially empty order book, and record the end timestamp. Our throughput in operations per second is easily calculated by dividing the command count by the elapsed time to execute them all. As our throughput is measured in seconds, millisecond precision is sufficient for our benchmarking needs. Lastly, we print out the interesting results. We can run this benchmark parameterized with 250,000 commands by issuing:

```
    sbt 'project chapter2' 'set javaOptions := Seq("-Xmx1G")' 'runMain
  highperfscala.benchmarks.ThroughputBenchmark
  src/main/resources/historical_data 250000'
```

Running the benchmark over a range of command counts yields the following results:

Command count	Processing time (seconds)	Throughput (operations per second)
250,000	2.2	112,309
500,000	6.1	81,886
750,000	12.83	58,456

1,000,000	22.56	44,328

We can see that when the command count increases, our throughput decreases. One explanation could be that the order book grows in size when receiving more orders, and thus becomes less efficient. At this point, we are able to evaluate the throughput of our application. In the next section, we focus on measuring the latency of the program.

Our benchmark and the ones that we will write later in this chapter are naive. It runs the test and the order book in the same JVM. A more realistic example would involve an order book with a server that maintains TCP connections to clients exchanging FIX messages (FIX being the most widely-used protocol in finance) to place or cancel orders. Our benchmark would impersonate one of these clients to simulate production load on our order book. For the sake of simplicity and to allow us to focus on more interesting subjects, we decided to leave this concern aside.

Latency benchmark

Recall from Chapter 1, *The Road to Performance*, that the latency is the time that it takes for an operation to happen, where the definition of an operation depends on your domain. In our case, we define an operation as the processing of a command from the time it is received to the time a new order book and a corresponding event are generated.

The first latency benchmark

The following listing shows a first version of our latency benchmark:

```
object FirstLatencyBenchmark {

  def main(args: Array[String]): Unit = {

    val commandSample = DataCodec.read(new File(args(0)))
    val (commandsPerSecond, iterations) = (args(1).toInt, args(2).toInt)
    val totalCommandCount = commandsPerSecond * iterations

    jvmWarmUp(commandSample)

    @tailrec
    def sendCommands(
      xs: List[(List[Command], Int)],
      ob: OrderBook,
      testStart: Long,
```

```
    histogram: HdrHistogramReservoir): (OrderBook, HdrHistogramReservoir)
    =
    xs match {
      case head :: tail =>
        val (batch, offsetInSeconds) = head
        val shouldStart = testStart + (1000 * offsetInSeconds)

        while (shouldStart > System.currentTimeMillis()) {
          // keep the thread busy while waiting for the next batch to be
          sent
        }

        val updatedBook = batch.foldLeft(ob) {
          case (accBook, c) =>
            val operationStart = System.currentTimeMillis()
            val newBook = OrderBook.handle(accBook, c)._1
            val operationEnd = System.currentTimeMillis()
            // record latency
            histogram.update(operationEnd - operationStart)
            newBook
        }

        sendCommands(tail, updatedBook, testStart, histogram)
      case Nil => (ob, histogram)
    }

  val (_, histogram) = sendCommands(
    // Organizes commands per 1 second batches
    generateCount(commandSample, totalCommandCount)
      .grouped(commandsPerSecond).zipWithIndex
      .toList,
    OrderBook.empty,
    System.currentTimeMillis(),
    new HdrHistogramReservoir())

  printSnapshot(histogram.getSnapshot)
  }
}
```

The beginning of this code is similar to what we had in our throughput benchmark. We use an HdrHistogram to record each operation's latency. The tail-recursive method sendCommands is where most of the interesting things happen (we take a closer look at tail-recursion in a later chapter). Our commands are grouped by batches of size and commandsPerSecond, meaning that we will send one batch per second. We record the current time before sending a command (operationStart) and after receiving a response (operationEnd). These timestamps are used to update the histogram.

HdrHistogram is an efficient implementation of a histogram. This is specifically designed to be used in latency and performance-sensitive applications. It maintains a fixed cost both in space and time. It does not involve memory allocation operations, and its memory footprint is constant. To learn more about HdrHistogram, visit `http://hdrhistogram.org/`.

At the end, after all batches have been processed, we take a snapshot of the state of the histogram and print interesting metrics. Let's give this a run:

```
sbt 'project chapter2' 'set javaOptions := Seq("-Xmx1G")' 'runMain
highperfscala.benchmarks.FirstLatencyBenchmark
src/main/resources/historical_data 45000 10'
... // removed for brevity
[info] Processed 450000 commands
[info] 99p latency: 1.0 ms
[info] 99.9p latency: 1.0 ms
[info] Maximum latency: 24 ms
```

We exercise our system with a rate of 45,000 operations per second for 10 seconds, and we see a latency of 1 ms for the 99.9th percentile. These are outstanding results! They are also completely wrong. In our hurry to write a latency benchmark, we overlooked a too often ignored issue: the coordinated omission problem.

The coordinated omission problem

Our benchmark is broken because we measure the time required to process a command without taking into account the time the command had to wait to be processed. This becomes a problem if the previous command took longer than expected to be processed. Take our previous example: we ran 45,000 commands per second, that is, 45 commands per millisecond. What if processing the first 45 commands takes longer than 1 millisecond? The next 45 commands have to wait before being picked up and processed. However, with our current benchmark, we ignore this waiting time. Let's take an example of a web application serving pages over HTTP. A typical benchmark may record request latency by measuring the elapsed time between the moment a request is handled by the web server and the time a response is ready to be sent back. However, this would not account for the time it took for the web server to read the request and actually send back the response. A better benchmark will measure the latency as the time between the moment the client sent the request and the moment it actually received a response. To learn more about the coordinated omission problem, refer to the discussion thread containing direct links to articles and presentations at `https://groups.google.com/forum/#!msg/mechanical-sympathy/icNZJejUHfE /BfDekfBEs_sJ`.

To fix this problem, we need to record `operationStart` not when we start processing a batch of commands, but when the batch of commands should have been processed, regardless of whether the system is late.

The second latency benchmark

In our second attempt, we make sure to start the clock to take into account when a command is meant to be sent, as opposed to when it is ready to be processed.

The benchmark code remains unchanged except for the recording of latency, which now uses `shouldStart` instead of `operationStart`:

```
histogram.update(operationEnd - shouldStart)
```

After this change, this is the new benchmark output:

```
    sbt 'project chapter2' 'set javaOptions := Seq("-Xmx1G")' 'runMain
highperfscala.benchmarks.SecondLatencyBenchmark
src/main/resources/historical_data 45000 10'
    ... // removed for brevity
    [info] Processed 450000 commands
    [info] 99p latency: 743.0 ms
    [info] 99.9p latency: 855.0 ms
    [info] Maximum latency: 899 ms
```

The results are very different when compared to our first benchmark. Actually, this new code also has a flaw. This assumes that all the requests sent in the same second are supposed to be processed at the very beginning of this second. While technically possible, it is more likely that these commands will be sent at different times during the second (a few during the first millisecond, some more during the second millisecond, and so on). Our current benchmark probably greatly overestimates our latency by starting the timer too soon for most commands.

The final latency benchmark

We will attempt to fix the latest issue and finally come up with a reliable benchmark. At this point, we are trying to address the problem of the distribution of the commands over each second. The best way to solve this issue would be to use real production data. If the recorded commands that we are using for our benchmark had a timestamp attached to them (that is, the moment they were received by the production system), we could replicate the distribution of commands observed in production.

Unfortunately, our current order book application does not record the timestamp when logging data. We could go different routes. One option is to randomly send the commands over a second. Another is to assume an even distribution of the commands (that is, the same amount is sent on each millisecond).

We choose to modify the benchmark assuming the latter. To accomplish this goal, we modify the generation of events. As our new strategy distributes commands over time rather than batching commands, for a single instant, the new command list return type changes from `List[(List[Command], Int)]` to `List[(Command, Int)]`. The logic to generate the command list changes to account for our new strategy, as follows:

```
generateCount(sampleCommands, totalCommandCount)
  .grouped(cps.value)
  .toList.zipWithIndex
  .flatMap {
    case (secondBatch, sBatchIndex) =>
      val batchOffsetInMs = sBatchIndex * 1000
      val commandIntervalInMs = 1000.0 / cps.value
      secondBatch.zipWithIndex.map {
        case (command, commandIndex) =>
          val commandOffsetInMs =
            Math.floor(commandIntervalInMs * commandIndex).toInt
          (command, batchOffsetInMs + commandOffsetInMs)
      }
  }
```

The creation of our set of commands is a bit more involved. We now calculate an offset for each command, taking into account the amount of milliseconds that should elapse between each command. Our final results with this benchmark are as follows:

```
sbt 'project chapter2' 'set javaOptions := Seq("-Xmx1G")' 'runMain
highperfscala.benchmarks.FinalLatencyBenchmark
src/main/resources/historical_data 45000 10'
    [info] Processed 450000 commands
    [info] 99p latency: 92.0 ms
    [info] 99.9p latency: 137.0 ms
    [info] Maximum latency: 145 ms
```

We finally established a good latency benchmark for our system, and sure enough, our results come close to what is currently being observed in production.

 Hopefully, this exercise made you reflect on your own production system and what kind of operation you may want to benchmark. The main thing to take away from this section is the importance of properly recording an operation's latency and taking into account the coordinated omission problem. What do you think would be the best way to measure the latency of your system? If you already have benchmarks in place, do they account for the coordinated omission effect?

Locating bottlenecks

Now that we are able to consistently reproduce the bad performance in production with our benchmark, we have confidence that the impact of any of the changes that we make can be accurately measured. The benchmarks treated the order book as a black box, meaning you have no insight into what areas of the order book are causing our performance woes. If you were previously familiar with this code, you could use your intuitions as a heuristic to make educated guesses about the subcomponents that require a deeper focus. As this is day one for you at MVT, you do not have previous intuition to rely on. Instead of guessing, we will profile the order book to gain deeper insights into various facets of our black box.

The JDK bundles an excellent profiler that is named Flight Recorder. Flight Recorder is free to use in nonproduction environments. Refer to Oracle's license, `http://docs.oracle.com/javacomponents/jmc-5-5/jfr-runtime-guide/about.htm`, to learn more about commercial usage. The existence of a great profiler is another reason that Scala is a pragmatic choice for production-quality functional programming. Flight Recorder works using internal JVM hooks to record events that are emitted by the JVM at runtime. The events that are captured by Flight Recorder cover memory allocation, thread state changes, IO activity, and CPU activity. To learn more about Flight Recorder internals, refer to Oracle's Flight Recorder documentation: `http://docs.oracle.com/javacomponents/jmc-5-5/jfr-runtime-guide/about.htm#sthref7`. In contrast to third-party profilers, which do not have access to JVM internals, Flight Recorder is able to access data outside of JVM safepoints. A JVM safepoint is a time when all threads are suspended from execution. Safepoints are necessary to coordinate global JVM activities, including stop-the-world garbage collection. To read more about JVM safepoints, check out this excellent blog article by Alexey Ragozin at `http://blog.ragozin.info/2012/10/safepoints-in-hotspot-jvm.html`. If a profiler is only able to inspect at safepoints, it is likely the profiler is missing useful data points because only a partial picture emerges.

Let's take our first look inside the order book by setting up a Flight Recorder trial. To expedite cycle time, we set up the profiler via `sbt` while we execute a run of `ThroughputBenchmark` replaying historical data. We set up Flight Recorder with the following JVM parameters:

```
sbt 'project chapter2' 'set javaOptions := Seq("-Xmx1G", "-
XX:+UnlockCommercialFeatures", "-XX:+FlightRecorder", "-
XX:+UnlockDiagnosticVMOptions", "-XX:+DebugNonSafepoints", "-
XX:FlightRecorderOptions=defaultrecording=true,dumponexit=true,dumponexitpa
th=/tmp/order-book.jfr")'
```

The max JVM heap size is set to match our benchmark runs, followed by four JVM parameters. The `-XX:+UnlockCommercialFeatures` and `-XX:+FlightRecorder` parameters are required to emit JVM events for Flight Recorder. The Flight Recorder documentation references `-XX:+UnlockDiagnosticVMOptions` and `-XX:+DebugNonSafepoints` to improve sampling quality. These options instruct the compiler to generate metadata that enables Flight Recorder to capture samples that are not at safepoints. The final argument configures Flight Recorder to begin recording as soon as the program starts and to dump profiling results to the provided path when the program exits. In our case, this means that the profile will begin when the benchmark starts and terminate when the benchmark concludes. Alternatively, it is possible to configure Flight Recorder to delay its start time and to record for a fixed time by the following configurations:

```
sbt 'project chapter2' 'set javaOptions := Seq("-Xmx1G", "-
XX:+UnlockCommercialFeatures", "-XX:+FlightRecorder", "-
XX:+UnlockDiagnosticVMOptions", "-XX:+DebugNonSafepoints", "-
XX:StartFlightRecording=delay=10s,duration=60s,name=Recording,filename=/tmp
/order-book.jfr")'
```

The preceding options configure Flight Recorder to start after five seconds (the `delay` option) and record for one minute (the `duration` option). The result is stored in `/tmp/order-book.jfr`.

We are now ready to generate profile results. Next, we run the benchmark configured to replay 2,000,000 requests. The more requests played back, the more opportunities there are for the profiler to capture JVM events. All other things equal, prefer longer profiles over shorter ones. The following output shows the benchmark invocation and the resulting output:

```
    sbt 'project chapter2' 'set javaOptions := Seq("-Xmx1G", "-
XX:+UnlockCommercialFeatures", "-XX:+FlightRecorder", "-
XX:+UnlockDiagnosticVMOptions", "-XX:+DebugNonSafepoints", "-
XX:FlightRecorderOptions=defaultrecording=true,dumponexit=true,dumponexitpa
th=/tmp/order-book.jfr")' 'runMain
highperfscala.benchmarks.ThroughputBenchmark
src/main/resources/historical_data 2000000'
    [info]
    [info] Processed 2000000 commands
    [info] in 93.276 seconds
    [info] Throughput: 21441.742784853555 commands/sec
```

To have a look at the profiling results, we use **Java Mission Control (JMC)**, a free, bundled GUI that supports, among other features, inspecting Flight Recorder results, and running Flight Recorder profile sessions. JMC exists in the same directory as the Java executable, which means that it is accessible on your path by just typing the following:

```
jmc
```

Once the GUI loads, open the profiler results by navigating to **File** | **Open**. Browse to the profile results and click on **OK** to load them. As we look at the results, we will build a checklist of questions to consider when reviewing profiler results. These probing questions are intended to make you critically analyze the results. These questions ensure that the experiment results truly address the hypothesis that led to the profile. At the end of this chapter, we will present the questions in a single checklist to make it easier to revisit later.

Did I test with the expected set of resources?

If the test environment was set up to use incorrect resources, the results are invalidated. For this reason, it makes sense to double-check the environment setup first. Fortunately, Flight Recorder captures much of this information for you.

The **General** and **System** tab groups are the areas to focus on for this checklist item. In **General**, click on **JVM Information** to identify key JVM facts. In this section, confirm the following:

Areas to focus on	Reason to focus on the area
JVM start time	This is a quick spot check that confirms that this test executed when you think it did. With a few profile results, ensuring that you are reviewing the correct results is trivial. As you collect more information and investigate additional hypotheses, this simple check ensures that you are not conflating results.
JVM version	Variations in JVM version can yield different results. Ensure that you are using the same JVM version as your production environment.
JVM command-line arguments and JVM flags	It is common to tune the JVM via command-line arguments. Often, the parameterization will change between runs, making it difficult to recall later on which run corresponded to which set of arguments. Reviewing this information provides useful context to review the results.
Java application arguments	Similar to the previous concern, the goal is to ensure that you are confident that you understand the inputs to your test.

To supplement confirmation of JVM configuration, view the **GC Configuration** tab under the **Memory** tab group. This tab details garbage collection configuration, which reflects a combination of user-supplied configuration and JVM defaults. As you are likely aware, small changes in the garbage collection configuration can yield significant runtime performance changes. Given the sensitivity of application performance to garbage collection configuration, you should reflect on each parameter in this tab. Questions to consider while reviewing are as follows:

- If I configured this parameter, did the configured value take effect?
- If I did not configure this parameter, what effect might tuning this value have? This question often helps you to create hypotheses for future profile runs.

Next, we focus on the **System** tab group. The **Overview** tab itemizes non-JVM resources to make it clear which resources were used to create this profile. Continuing with the theme of questions from the **General** tab group, the overarching goals are as follows:

- To confirm whether recorded information matches the resources that you expected to use (for example, does the amount of available RAM match how much you thought was present?)
- To look for unexpected differences between the test resources and a production environment (for example, my local machine uses kernel v3.18.x while

production is on an older minor version, v3.17.x)

If you are configuring your system via environment variables, there is an **Environment Variables** tab that should be reviewed. Like the **Overview** tab, you are looking to ensure your test resources are provisioned and configured as you intended. It bears repeating that any unexpected differences in your test resources always invalidate test results.

Was the system environment clean during the profiling?

Once you are comfortable that the appropriate resources were used, the next step is to confirm that only the application being profiled used resources. This is an important diagnostic step prior to reviewing test results because it ensures that the profiled application was truly isolated for the test. Fortunately, Flight Recorder catalogs useful information to answer this question. In the **System** tab group, the **Processes** tab captures all the processes running during the profiling. Scan this list with the following questions in mind:

- When I scan the list of processes, do I see anything that should not be running?
- When I filter by the command-line column and enter `java`, do I see the expected set of JVM applications running?
- When I scan the list of processes, do I see any duplicate processes?

Next, inspect the **Recording** tab under the **General** tab group. Flight Recorder provides the ability to create concurrent recordings. The profile results will contain the union of the concurrent recordings. If there are multiple recordings unexpectedly happening in only one of several runs, then you may not have an apples-to-apples results comparison between recordings.

The next area to focus on is system CPU usage over the duration of the profiling. Within the **General** tab group, select the **Overview** tab. This view displays the CPU usage panel, which provides you with the ability to inspect machine CPU usage throughout the recording. Here, you are looking for unexpected divergences between JVM and machine total CPU usage. The following screenshot depicts a scenario where there is a divergence worth investigating:

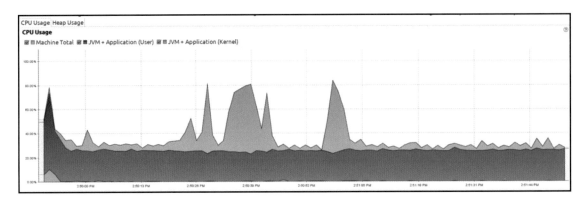

Unexpected non-JVM CPU usage highlighted by the CPU Usage panel

In the preceding screenshot, the combination of **JVM + Application (User)** and **JVM + Application (Kernel)** indicates the JVM-under-test's CPU usage, and **Machine Total** indicates machine (that is, JVM-under-test and all other processes) CPU usage. For the majority of this recording, the JVM-under-test CPU usage represents the majority of machine CPU usage. If your application should be the only process using system resources, then the small delta between the small delta between **JVM + Application (User)** and **Machine Total** represents the desired state. The divergences near the middle of the recording period indicate that another process or other processes were using CPU resources. These spikes suggest abnormal behavior that can negatively impact profiling results. It is worth considering what other processes are using system resources and whether or not your test results remain valid.

This is a good opportunity to introduce the range navigator, which is the small horizontal widget at the top of each tab containing red marks. The range navigator is a timeline that displays events from the current tab that happen over time with red marks. By default, the entire timeline is selected and the duration of the profiling is displayed above the center of the timeline. You can select a subset of the timeline to zoom in on an area of interest. For example, you may wish to zoom in on CPU usage when the machine CPU usage spikes up. When selecting a subset of the timeline and data is only available for a specific point in time (for example, at start of recording) or the data does not represent a time series (for example, the JVM version), then the data is hidden or replaced with N/A.

A final spot check is to check the used machine physical memory in the **Memory Usage** panel in the **Overview** tab under the **Memory** tab group. During this spot, check whether you are trying to assess if the amount of used machine physical memory is a sensible value. If there is little machine physical memory remaining and the reserved heap is a small fraction of the total machine physical memory, you should pause to consider what other processes are using memory. This scenario is illustrated in the following screenshot:

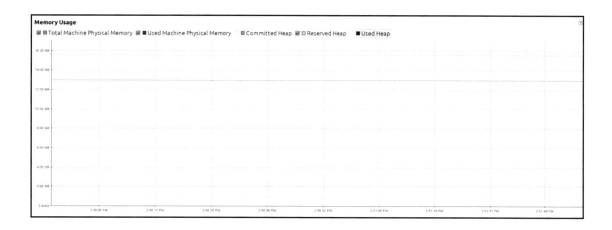

Non-JVM processes using most of the available memory captured by the Memory Usage panel

In the preceding example, the reserved heap space is 2 GB out of an available 16 GB system memory, and 13 GB of system memory is used. This implies that 11 GB of system memory is consumed by processes other than the profiled JVM. Unless you expect to have other processes running in your test environment, this type of memory-usage discrepancy warrants further investigation. For example, if your application makes use of off-heap memory, this discrepancy may invalidate your test results because your application may be unable to allocate memory as needed, or may result in excessive system swapping.

Are the JVM's internal resources performing to expectations?

We began our profiling checklist with the widest possible criterion by verifying that the resources are provisioned and configured correctly. We continue to tighten the scope of our checklist by focusing on JVM configuration to ensure that test results are created from valid configurations. Now, we introspect JVM internals to continue verifying that the profile has not been compromised.

Nearly all production applications involve multithreading to make better use of multiple CPU cores or to separate I/O intensive work from CPU-centric work. The **Threads** tab group helps you familiarize yourself with the division of labor within the application and provides hints for where it may make sense to look deeper. The following table outlines areas of focus within the **Threads** tab group and highlights questions that you need to consider when you are new or unfamiliar with the application that is being profiled and when you have several profile results to compare:

Focus area	New to the application	Familiar with the application
Thread Count panel in the **Overview** tab	How many total threads exist? Is this different than the count you might expect? For example, if the application is CPU-bound and there are ten times the number of threads than cores, this may be a warning sign that the application is poorly tuned.	Are there qualitative changes in the thread count across profiles? For example, a doubling or halving of the thread count could indicate a configuration error.
Hot Threads panel in the **Hot Threads** tab	Is the distribution of sample counts even, or are there a couple of threads that dominate the sample count? The hottest threads are likely indicative of threads to dive deeper into and also areas of the code you should be most familiar with.	Have there been significant changes in thread sample count distribution? If so, do these changes seem sensible to you?
Top Blocking Locks, **Top Blocked Threads**, and **Top Blocking Threads** in the **Contention** tab	Familiarize yourself with where locks exist and which threads block most often. This can be useful information to bear in mind when considering what factors are affecting critical path performance.	Compared to previous profile results, is there an increase in either the frequency or distribution of thread blocking? Are there new locks appearing in the results?
Latency Stack Traces in the **Latencies** tab	Familiarize yourself with the different maximum latencies per event type to better understand which operations affect the application most. Make mental notes to dive deeper into the more latent sections of the application.	Are maximum latencies qualitatively increasing, decreasing, or similar to previous profile results? When multiple top-level stack traces exist for an event type, consider the ones affecting critical path performance the most.

After thoroughly inspecting the **Threads** tab group, you should begin to have a mental picture forming about how this application functions and which areas are likely to be most interesting for further study. We now turn to a topic that links closely to JVM threading: **I/O**.

The **I/O** tab group provides valuable information about the profiled application's file and socket access. Like the review of the **Threads** tab group, this section may provide hints that your application has unexpected or undesirable behavior. Before diving into this tab group, pause to consider when or what causes disk reads and writes, and network reads and writes. As you review the **Overview** tab, do you see divergences between your thinking and the profiler results? If so, you should identify why this discrepancy exists and whether it invalidates your test results.

An example of unexpected I/O behavior could be excessive writes to standard out. This might happen accidentally when a debugging statement is left behind. Imagine if this side-effect occurs on the critical path of your application. This will negatively impact profile results and invalidates testing. In Flight Recorder, writes to standard out are captured by a blank write path. The following screenshot shows file write results from a simple, one-off application that repeatedly writes to standard out at a high frequency:

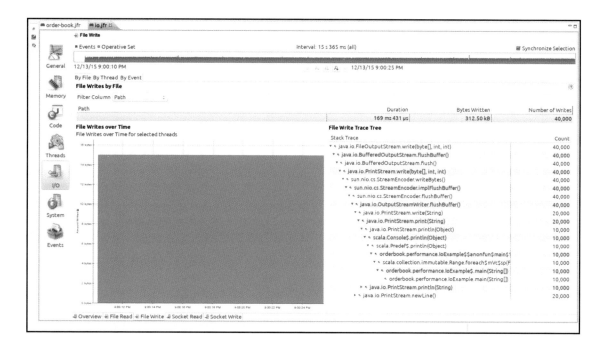

Identifying unexpected writes to standard out via the I/O tab group

This example is exaggerated for effect, which is why there is a continuous block of constant writes over time. By inspecting the **File Write** tab, we can also see how much time was spent writing to standard out, how much data was written, and how many writes occurred. In approximately 15 seconds of execution, a whopping 40,000 writes took place! The file write stack trace provides invaluable information, allowing us to backtrack to identify which parts of the application are responsible for the writes. Flight Recorder also allows you to view writes by thread. In a production application with dedicated writer threads, you can quickly isolate undesired I/O access.

Monitoring I/O reads and writes presents a good opportunity to discuss how to configure Flight Recorder recording parameters. The `-XX:+FlightRecorderOptions` accepts a parameter named `settings`, which, by default, points to `$JAVA_HOME/jre/lib/jfr/default.jfc`. You can either provide your own configuration file or modify the default file. In this configuration file, you can tweak the events that are recorded by Flight Recorder and the frequency at which to capture certain events. For example, by default, the `java/file_write` event has a threshold of 20 ms. This is a reasonable default, but you may wish to tune the value lower if you are focused on profiling file writes. Setting the threshold lower means that more event samples are captured. Tune carefully because more is not always better. A lower threshold implies higher overhead and more information to sift through.

A final area to investigate is the **Exceptions** tab under the **Code** tab group. Even if you are closely monitoring application logs during a profiling, you may not be persisting the logs for historical analysis. Fortunately, Flight Recorder captures exceptions and errors for review. Scanning the exceptions and errors, take note of how many total exceptions and errors occurred and which ones happen most frequently. Shrink the time horizon with the range navigator to better understand if exceptions and errors are concentrated at application startup, later in the profiling, or uniformly occurring. The timing at which exceptions and errors occur often provides insight into whether or not the root cause is misconfiguration or unexpected runtime behavior. As always, if you notice an alarming number of exceptions or errors, consider invalidating the profile results until you have a deeper understanding about why they are happening.

Where are the CPU bottlenecks?

At this stage, we have completed all checks necessary to maximize the likelihood that the profiler results are valid and worth investigating further. Now, we begin arguably the most fun part of the profiling process: identifying CPU bottlenecks. This is an enjoyable process because the profiler gives you a detailed look inside the black box of your application. It is an opportunity to objectively test your hypotheses and mental model of how the application works by comparing with the profiler results. Once you identify the bottlenecks, you will feel a sense of relief that you now know where to pinpoint your next set of changes to improve application performance.

Let's start on the **Overview** tab of the **Code** tab group. This view is useful to sensitize yourself from the bottom-up on which areas of the code are most expensive. The following figure displays the **Overview** tab for a sample run of the order book:

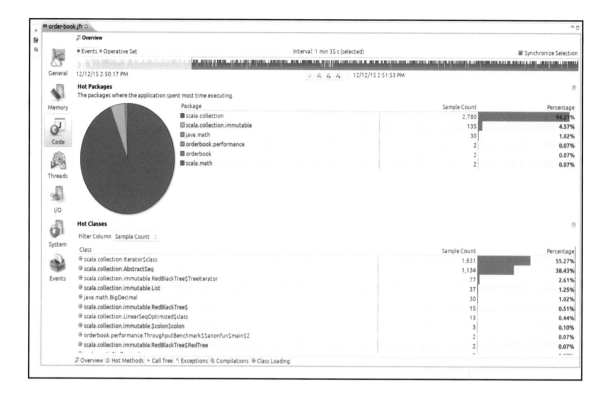

The Code Overview tab summarizing expensive packages and classes

In this view, the initial goal is to get a sense for the distribution of CPU time in the application. The **Hot Packages** panel quickly makes it clear to us that the order book is heavily reliant upon code from the `scala.collection` package. The **Hot Classes** panel shows that the order book is spending a significant amount of time, approximately 55% of the time, performing some type of iteration operations. In this screenshot, we also see that only a subset of the profile duration is selected with the range navigator. It is often helpful to view different subsets of the profile period to determine if hot spots remain constant over time. In this example, the early part of the profile results are excluded because they include time spent preparing requests to be sent to the order book. Selecting this subset allows us to focus purely on order book operations without pollution from test setup.

It is important to note that the percentage column indicates the amount of application time spent executing in the displayed package and class. This means that this view, along with the **Hot Methods** tab, are bottom-up views rather than top-down views. In a top-down view, the percentage column indicates the sum total amount of time spent in part of a stack trace. This view is captured in the **Call Tree** tab. This distinction is key because these two views help us answer different questions. The following table explores several topics from both perspectives to better understand when each view is most helpful:

Topic	Top-down view (Call Tree)	Bottom-up view (Overview/Hot Methods)
Point of view	This is from a macro picture to a micro picture	This is from a micro picture to a macro picture
Determining hot spots	These are areas of the code base that delegate to the most expensive function calls	These are the most expensive functions
Example questions best answered by each view	• Is the order book cancel operation more expensive than adding a resting limit order? • Where is CPU time spent on the critical path?	• Did switching from a `Double` price representation to a `BigDecimal` representation create any hot spots? • Relative to the rest of the application, which tree operations are most costly?

As a first-time profiler of the order book, you now know from the **Overview** tab that the order book makes heavy usage of Scala collections, but you do not yet have a feel for which order book operations are causing the performance to suffer. To deepen your understanding about the cost of different order book operations, you take a top-down view by investigating the **Call Tree** tab:

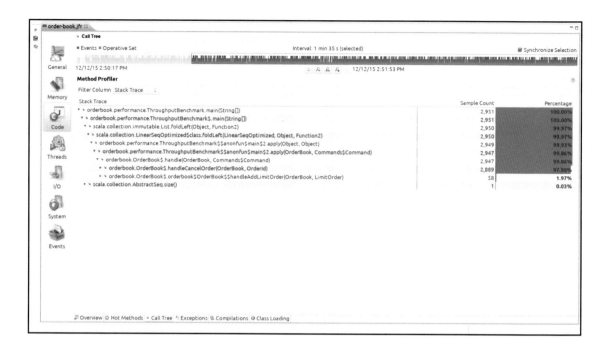

Investigating order book bottlenecks using Call Tree

Drilling down **Call Tree**, it becomes abundantly clear that the cancelation operation is the bottleneck. Overwhelmingly, CPU time is spent canceling orders rather than adding them. You call over the company's sharpest trader, Dave, to share this finding. Dave's eyes light up when you mention that cancelations are costly. As a trading domain expert, he is well aware that in volatile times, the frequency of cancelations increases significantly as compared to calmer market periods. Dave explains that traders frequently cancel orders in volatile markets to quickly adjust to swinging prices. Cancelations beget cancelations because traders are learning valuable pricing information. Ending the conversation, he tells you to cancel everything else that you are doing (no pun intended!) and focus on improving the performance of order canceling.

You walk away from the conversation feeling better knowing that you have identified the bottleneck that is likely to be the source of MVT trade losses. To get a better feel, you dig a bit deeper into the **Call Tree** to reveal which functions within **Cancel Order** are expensive. This is the process of moving from a macro view to a micro view. You end up looking at the **Call Tree** tab, which is displayed as follows:

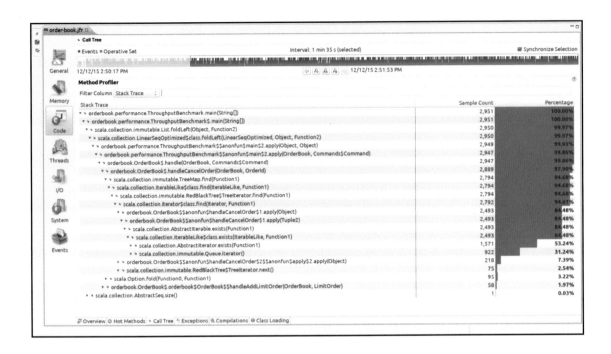

Understanding which cancel order functions are the slowest via Call Tree

The **Call Tree** shows that canceling an order involves an invocation of the RedBlackTree find() function and the exists() function. As you look deeper into the call, you also notice that the percentage column becomes smaller. This is because in a top-down view, the percentage column represents the sum total CPU time spent on a particular function and all the functions beneath it. According to the results, 84.48% of CPU time was spent executingOrderBook$$anonfun$handleCancelOrder$1.apply() and the functions deeper in the **Call Tree**. From this view, we also see that of the 84.48% of CPU time, 53.24% of the time is spent withinAbstractIterator.exists() and deeper function calls. This looks like the biggest bottleneck, with the invocation of Queue.iterator() in second place, taking 31.24% of CPU time.

Reflecting on this information, you are curious to start at the bottom, so-to-speak, with the most expensive functions, and work your way through the backtrace to identify affected order book operations. To address your curiosity, you investigate the **Hot Methods** tab and see the following view:

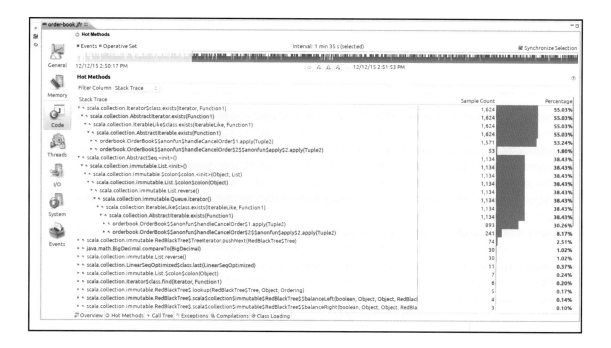

Going from the micro to the macro view with Hot Methods

By an order of magnitude, you discover the same two culprits from the **Call Tree** investigation are the hottest methods. This is a reassuring finding because it builds confidence that changes to the implementation of canceling an order are likely to yield qualitative benefits. As you have not spent any time studying the source code, there is still a significant amount of mystery about the implementation. Taking a step back to consider the situation, you think about the operations being modeled in the abstract. Canceling an order involves finding the existing order that could have any price and then once found, modifying the state of the order book to remove the order. Your intuition suggests that some of these operations are likely linear, or possibly logarithmic at best. As you begin considering what other implementation could be faster, Dave interrupts your thoughts.

In a rushed voice, you hear, "Have you fixed the order book? We need to get it deployed now!" Of course, you have no idea how to respond, and the thought of deploying code on day one makes you a bit uneasy. You share your findings with Dave, hoping that your findings will satisfy his appetite for progress and buy you more time to think. Unfortunately, Dave is not thrilled to hear the order book performance mystery remains unsolved, "We're losing money everyday because of this!" You acknowledge that you understand the gravity of the situation and that you are moving as fast as you can. It is your first day, after all! Dave sighs and acknowledges he is being a bit tough, and that his exasperation is causing him to overreact. As the conversation is winding down, Dave mentions his appreciation for how quickly you came up to speed, and he makes some small talk about how he cannot understand how his brand new smartphone, loaded with extra memory, still runs slowly. "Nothing seems to be working quickly anymore!" he exclaims. His mention of memory causes you to have an epiphany.

You remember that you have not yet reviewed memory usage results. You are hoping that there are some easy wins available by tuning the garbage collector to improve performance without making code changes. Before making any changes, you check out the **Memory** tab group for insight into memory allocation patterns.

What are the memory allocation patterns?

The **Memory** tab group is the final area that remains to dive into for our analysis. Even though we have not spent time looking at the order book source code, the **Code** tab group illustrated the relative costs of the different order of operations. Studying the **Hot Methods** provides insight into the types of objects that are used by various areas of the order book. Looking into the memory allocation patterns, we want to identify young and old generation garbage collection trends and which objects are most and least allocated.

The default Flight Recorder configuration settings do not track object allocations. For a more complete view of memory consumption, the following configuration settings should be enabled:

- Allocation-profiling-enabled
- Heap-statistics-enabled
- gc-enabled-all
- Allocation-profiling-enabled for both `java/object_alloc_in_new_TLAB` and `java/object_alloc_outside_TLAB` events

Once a profile is generated with all the preceding parameters enabled, you will get a first glimpse into application memory allocation patterns in the **Heap** panel on the **Garbage Collections** tab:

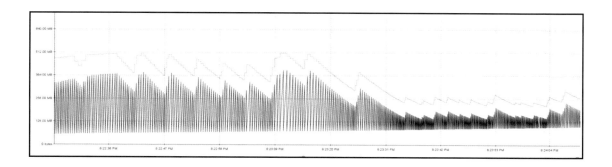

Visualizing memory allocation patterns via the Garbage Collections tab

This view shows a shape that is commonly referred to as a sawtooth pattern. There are frequent garbage collections creating a tooth-like pattern in the data as the JVM is constantly freeing young generation memory. Garbage collection tuning is a vast topic that is beyond the scope of this book. We encourage you to dig deeper into this area by reading through this well-written blog post entitled, "Understanding Java Garbage Collection" (`http://www.cubrid.org/blog/dev-platform/understanding-java-garbage-collection/`).

As shown in the following screenshot, Flight Recorder also provides summary metrics per garbage collection category in the **GC Times** tab:

Young Collection Total Time		Old Collection Total Time		All Collections Total Time	
GC Count	420	GC Count	0	GC Count	420
Average GC Time	2 ms 140 µs	Average GC Time	N/A	Average GC Time	2 ms 140 µs
Maximum GC Time	17 ms 461 µs	Maximum GC Time	N/A	Maximum GC Time	17 ms 461 µs
Total GC Time	898 ms 868 µs	Total GC Time	N/A	Total GC Time	898 ms 868 µs

Summarizing garbage per collection event type

The following are some questions worth considering when inspecting a visualization of heap usage and a breakdown of garbage collection per collection type:

Question	Thoughts to consider
On average, does memory usage remain constant, slope downwards, or slope upwards?	An upward slope in memory can point to a memory leak. In this scenario, the heap will grow until the old generation fills, causing an old generation collection. If there is a memory leak, old generation collections will not clear much memory and eventually cause an out of memory error. The order book's memory usage appears constant for the profiled period. When making this type of judgement, obtain the longest possible profile to ensure you are viewing as complete of a picture as possible.
Do outlier pause times correlate with other major events?	According to the garbage collection breakdown, the maximum collection time is an order of magnitude that is larger than the average collection time. Scan the **Heap** panel for collection pauses that are qualitatively larger than the average. Do you see a pattern among the outliers? Consider your application's interaction with external systems and the machine it is deployed onto. Could there be an explanation for the occurrence of extreme pauses? It may also be worthwhile to compare outliers across profiles to determine whether the pattern is specific to a single profile or appears to be systemic.
What is the frequency of collections and how long is a typical collection lasting?	All other things being equal, a lower collection count is preferable because it suggests garbage is generated at a slower rate. That said, a lower collection count can be the result of an increased heap size, which may cause an increase in the average collection time. The takeaway is that inspecting collection count and latencies should be taken with a grain of salt. For this reason, the total garbage collection time metric is insightful. The total collection time reflects the effects of collection frequency and duration. Additionally, this does not suffer from loss like the average collection duration.
What is the lifespan of an object for important use cases?	While studying these breakdowns of garbage collection performance, it is important to build an intuition for how memory is allocated for different use cases in your application. Understanding this relationship may help you figure out why certain allocation patterns occur. In volatile markets, we expect that the order book has a lot of short-lived objects because traders are frequently canceling orders. In less-volatile markets, we likely expect that the average age of an order resting on the book is higher, which implies more long-lived objects.

Studying these views of memory allocation provides a summary of memory allocation activity. Investigating the **Allocations** tab provides several different ways to see which parts of the application are applying memory pressure. Flight Recorder provides three allocation views: by class, by thread, and by profile:

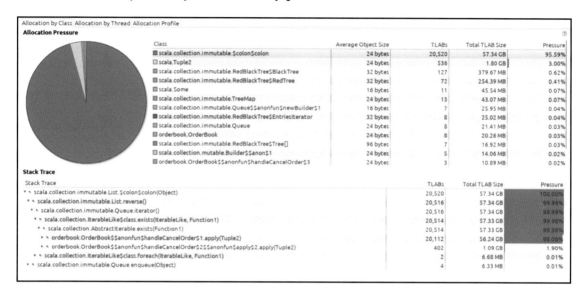

Correlating high-pressure List allocations via Allocations by Class

Class and profile allocations are shown in the preceding screenshot. Note that Allocations by Thread are skipped in this case because the order book is single-threaded.

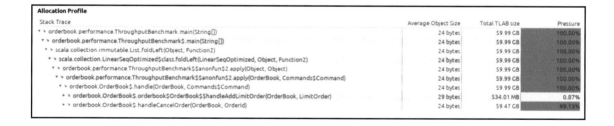

Confirming memory allocation pressure using top-down Allocation Profile view

When you are reviewing these allocation views, you should consider the following questions. As you read through these questions, reflect on how you would answer them to better understand how to improve order book performance:

Question	Thoughts to consider
When inspecting **Allocation by Class**, is there a positive correlation between classes with heavy collection pressure and classes that are referenced on the critical path?	If you determine that the classes creating the most garbage collection pressure are also often allocated on the critical path, then you have good reason to believe that if you optimize the critical path, there will be both algorithm speed and garbage collection benefits. The order book results indicate that List allocations is the worst offender. The backtrace shows that the allocations are almost entirely coming from handling **Cancel Orders**, which we know to be the bottleneck.
When inspecting **Allocation by Thread**, what does the distribution of garbage collection pressure look like?	Noting which threads are responsible for generating the most garbage collection pressure can direct you towards areas of the code to focus intently on. Ameliorating garbage collection pressure by the worst offenders will be reflected in the total pause time.
When drilling down the **Allocation Profile** stacktrace, do known CPU time bottlenecks correlate with high garbage collection pressure?	The order book shows that approximately 99% of garbage is generated when handling **Cancel Orders**. This is affirmation that handling **Cancel Orders** is computationally expensive and is further slowing down the system due to high object allocation rates. Establishing this correlation provides strong evidence that code changes to this section of the code will yield qualitative performance improvements.

Trying to save the day

Knowing that Dave will soon ask you again about improvements to order book performance, you take a few minutes to reflect on your findings. It is clear that handling **Cancel Orders** is both the CPU time and the memory allocation bottleneck. With more time to think about the problem, you are confident you can change the order book implementation to address either concern or possibly both. Unfortunately, time is one thing you do not currently have. One interesting observation from the memory allocations is that most garbage tends to be short-lived in a volatile market. Two inexpensive options to test come to mind:

JVM memory tuning options	Hypothesis
Switch from the default old generation collection, parallel old, to **Concurrent Mark Sweep (CMS)**.	The CMS collector is designed to keep your application responsive. Switching to the CMS collector may not improve order book throughput, but it may provide more consistent response latency during highly-volatile market movements.
Increase the new size from the default, approximately one-third of maximum heap size, to three-fourths of maximum heap size.	The order book has 1 GB of heap to store state, and it is currently only using approximately 380 MB to store young generation objects. You want to leverage the intuition that frequent cancels lead to frequent short-lived objects. Increasing the new generation size is a bet that there will be less than 250 MB of tenured objects and that an increased young generation heap improves order book throughput due to more infrequent collections.

The following table summarizes the results for each experiment:

Setup	Command	99th percentile in ms
Original	sbt 'project chapter2' 'set javaOptions := Seq("-Xmx1G")' 'runMain highperfscala.benchmarks.FinalLatencyBenchmark src/main/resources/historical_data 45000 10'	92
CMS collector	sbt 'project chapter2' 'set javaOptions := Seq("-Xmx1G", "-XX:+UseConcMarkSweepGC")' 'runMainhighperfscala.benchmarks.FinalLatencyBenchmark src/main/resources/historical_data 45000 10'	118
750M new size	sbt 'project chapter2' 'set javaOptions := Seq("-Xmx1G", "-XX:NewSize=750M")' 'runMain highperfscala.benchmarks.FinalLatencyBenchmark src/main/resources/historical_data 45000 10'	74
CMS collector and 750M new size	sbt 'project chapter2' 'set javaOptions := Seq("-Xmx1G", "-XX:NewSize=750M", "-XX:+UseConcMarkSweepGC")' 'runMain highperfscala.benchmarks.FinalLatencyBenchmark src/main/resources/historical_data 45000 10'	148

It looks like it will be more complicated than expected to improve the performance of the order book. At least one of the options, increasing the new size, seems to yield a better overall latency. We suggest that you take the time to go over this chapter again and repeat the process of benchmarking and profiling the application with these new sets of options. Observe what new behaviors these JVM options introduce, and try to understand the resulting increase or decrease in latency.

A word of caution

We want to take a moment to highlight some context about the profiling results that we interpreted in the previous section. We worked through an example that exhibited multiple real-world concerns. We laid out a pragmatic approach to working through the performance problem that has been applied by your authors at their day jobs. The point to be cautious of is that the order book is likely much simpler than most applications you work on day-to-day. We deliberately chose an example that was complicated enough to illustrate how to work through a performance problem, but also simple enough to understand without hours of code review. In practice, you will possibly need to repeat profiling numerous times, each time testing out a new hypothesis, in order to gain traction with your performance problem. Applying the structured approach that we walked through will ensure that you validate your results before analyzing them, and it will also ensure that you have well-founded evidence to pinpoint where to make changes.

A profiling checklist

We worked through each item on the profiling checklist throughout the chapter. We present the entire checklist for ease of reference, as follows:

1. Did I test with the expected set of resources?
2. Was the system environment clean during the profiling?
3. Are resources internal to the JVM performing as I would expect?
4. Where are the CPU bottlenecks?
5. What are the memory allocation patterns?

Taking big steps with microbenchmarks

In the coming chapters, we will share techniques from the functional paradigm and from the Scala language that enable you to write more performant software. However, you should not accept our prescriptions at face value. Measuring the performance is the objective way to determine whether the changes improve performance. A microbenchmark is a term used to describe a benchmark that exercises a small, isolated portion of a larger application. As microbenchmarks, by design, test a small piece of code, it is often easier to run a microbenchmark than to benchmark an entire application when a nuanced change is made.

Unfortunately, accurately observing the performance of nuanced changes is difficult, particularly on the JVM. Consider these order book-related examples of changes that warrant microbenchmarking.

- Replacing the data structure holding resting limit orders with one that handles cancels more efficiently
- Normalizing stock prices from a double representation to an integer representation to perform order matching with a lower overhead
- Determining the performance boost of reordering a set of branch statements to reflect the order you perceive to be accessed most frequently

How would you measure the performance before and after each change? You may try writing small benchmark programs, which are similar to the `ThroughputBenchmark`. This approach is likely to provide you with untrustworthy results due to the JVM's cleverness. The JVM applies a number of heuristics to make runtime optimizations. In a production environment, these changes are welcome because improved performance is always welcomed. However, in a microbenchmark, these changes are not welcomed because they decrease confidence that the microbenchmark is isolating only the nuanced change. Examples of changes the JVM is capable of making include the following:

- Dead-code elimination
- Just-in-time optimization (refer to our earlier sidebar regarding the JIT compiler)
- Constant folding (an optimization to avoid the evaluation on each call of a function with constant arguments and a return value dependent on these parameters)

We encourage you to read more about JVM optimizations by reading Oracle's *The Java HotSpot Performance Engine Architecture* (`http://www.oracle.com/technetwork/java/whitepaper-135217.html`). Given that this is a challenge to isolate small code changes, how can we write a proper microbenchmark? Fortunately, the OpenJDK team recognized these same challenges and introduced a library for this purpose named JMH, the Java microbenchmarking harness (`http://openjdk.java.net/projects/code-tools/jmh/`). JMH is designed for the express purpose of overcoming the limitations that we referenced in order to isolate the performance impact of your changes. The process to work with JMH is similar to other testing libraries. Similar to JUnit, JMH defines a set of annotations to control test setup and execution. Although tests can be run in several ways, we focus on executing tests via the sbt plugin, `sbt-jmh` (`https://github.com/ktoso/sbt-jmh`), for ease of use. Let's walk through the process of creating, running, and analyzing a microbenchmark with the order book. In future chapters, we will leverage our JMH knowledge to objectively measure the performance impact of prescribed changes.

 Are there changes that you made recently to your application that could benefit from microbenchmarking? If you did not microbenchmark the change, do you think microbenchmarking could have led you towards alternative solutions?

Microbenchmarking the order book

Having made progress towards improving performance by tweaking JVM memory settings, you set your eyes towards better understanding cancel performance. Based on the existence of a `scala.collection.immutable.Queue` in the profiler results, you hypothesize that there may be a linear time traversal of a FIFO queue to support order cancels. One way to test this hypothesis is to devise a microbenchmark that measures the cancelation performance in different scenarios. You brainstormed the following scenarios:

- Canceling a nonexistent order
- Canceling the first order in line for a price level
- Canceling the last order in line for a price level

Canceling a nonexistent order happens in the real world when a resting order is crossed before the cancel request arrives. This is an interesting scenario because you are unsure whether there is early termination logic to make this operation cheaper or whether canceling a nonexistent order requires inspecting the entire order book. The remaining two scenarios focus on the fill guarantees that are provided by stock exchanges. When multiple orders are placed at the same price, they are guaranteed to be filled on a first-come, first-served basis. You are speculating that the FIFO queue seen in the profile results is preserving the time ordering of resting orders for a price level. You expect canceling the first order in line to be faster by a linear factor than canceling the final order in line.

After reading through the excellent JMH examples at `http://hg.openjdk.java.net/code-tools/jmh/file/tip/jmh-samples/src/main/java/org/openjdk/jmh/samples/` and some deep thinking, you are able to put together the following tests that capture the scenarios that you are interested in. The code is in-full and is followed by a walkthrough, displayed as follows:

```
@BenchmarkMode(Array(Throughput))
@OutputTimeUnit(TimeUnit.SECONDS)
```

```scala
class CancelBenchmarks {

  @Benchmark
  def cancelLastOrderInLine(b: BookWithLargeQueue): (OrderBook, Event) =
OrderBook.handle(b.book, b.cancelLast)

  @Benchmark
  def cancelFirstOrderInLine(b: BookWithLargeQueue): (OrderBook, Event) =
OrderBook.handle(b.book, b.cancelFirst)

  @Benchmark
  def cancelNonexistentOrder(b: BookWithLargeQueue): (OrderBook, Event) =
OrderBook.handle(b.book, b.cancelNonexistent)
}

object CancelBenchmarks {

  @State(Scope.Benchmark)
  class BookWithLargeQueue {
    private val p = Price(BigDecimal(1.00))
    private val firstId: Int = 1
    private val defaultCancelLast = CancelOrder(OrderId(-1))

    @Param(Array("1", "100", "1000"))
    var enqueuedOrderCount: Int = 0

    var book: OrderBook = OrderBook.empty

    @Setup(Level.Trial)
    def setup(): Unit = {
      if (enqueuedOrderCount < 0)
        sys.error(s"Invalid enqueued order count = $enqueuedOrderCount")
      assert(book == OrderBook.empty)
      assert(cancelLast == defaultCancelLast)

      cancelLast = CancelOrder(OrderId(enqueuedOrderCount))
      book = {
        (firstId to enqueuedOrderCount).foldLeft(OrderBook.empty) {
          case (ob, i) =>
            OrderBook.handle(ob, AddLimitOrder(BuyLimitOrder(OrderId(i),
            p)))._1
        }
      }

      assert(cancelLast != defaultCancelLast)
      if (enqueuedOrderCount > 0)
        assert(book.bids.head._2.size == enqueuedOrderCount,
          s"Book built incorrectly! Expected book to contain " +
```

```
                 s"$enqueuedOrderCount bids for $p, but actual book is $book")
  }

    var cancelLast: CancelOrder = defaultCancelLast
    val cancelFirst: CancelOrder = CancelOrder(OrderId(firstId))
    val cancelNonexistent: CancelOrder = CancelOrder(OrderId(-1))
  }
}
```

Rather than duplicating JMH documentation, we will focus on the specific segments of interest and expect you to also investigate the JMH samples for additional context. Surveying the `CancelBenchmarks` class, you see the use of annotations to define benchmarks and control the benchmark outputs. Several benchmark modes exist. We are using the throughput mode to measure the number of times the benchmark completes in a fixed period of time. The implementation of each cancellation benchmark differs only by the ID of the order being canceled. Let's switch focus to the `CancelBenchmarks` object, which provides the necessary scaffolding to set up each benchmark.

The `CancelBenchmarks` object defines the `BookWithLargeQueue` state, which we observed is an argument to each benchmark. Defining the state that is required by the test is the first step towards parameterizing the benchmark. For this set of tests, we simplify the test setup by creating an order book with only a single price level at $1.00. We focus on sweeping the number of orders enqueued for the $1.00 price level in order to help identify the runtime behavior that we believe to be operating in linear time. The use of the `param` annotation supplies a set of default values to sweep for enqueued order count. We use the `setup` annotation to instruct JMH to prepare the state of the order book prior to invoking each of the three benchmarks. For each enqueued order count value, JMH invokes the `setup` method to create an order book with the desired number of resting orders at the $1.00 level.

Next, we run the benchmarks from sbt. JMH provides a number of command-line flags that control test configuration, which can be viewed from `sbt` using the following command:

```
sbt 'project chapter2' 'jmh:run -help'
```

All parameters that are configured as annotations can be overridden by supplying the associated command-line flag. The following is a sample invocation of `CancelBenchmarks`:

```
sbt 'project chapter2' 'jmh:run CancelBenchmarks -wi 3 -w 5s -i 30 -r
10s -jvmArgs "-Xmx1G -Xms1G" -gc true -foe true -p
enqueuedOrderCount=1,10,50,100'
```

In this invocation of JMH, we configure three warm-up iterations, each running for 5 seconds. Warm-up iterations do not count toward the output throughput result. We configure 30 recorded iterations, each lasting 10 seconds to compute throughput. We supply a 1 GB heap size for this test and switch on exiting the benchmark on uncaught exceptions to defend against a regression in the code. Lastly, we parameterize the enqueued order counts that we wish to sweep, indicating that we want to run three warm-up iterations and 30 recorded iterations for an enqueued order count of 1, 10, 50, and 100 orders.

With a single order in the book, we hypothesize that all operations should be approximately equally expensive. As we believe that cancel operations run in linear time, our expectation is that each benchmark should be approximately five times slower when the enqueued order count is 50 than when the count is 10. We cap testing at 100 enqueued orders because in discussion with Dave, we learned that in his experience, he has never analyzed a book with more than 85 orders in a level. Capping at 100 orders ensures that we understand performance characteristics at a level that we do not expect to see in production but could conceivably occur.

Imagine that you are writing a microbenchmark for the most performance-sensitive use case in your system. What variables would be important to sweep to have a complete understanding of how the system performs in this use case? How would you go about identifying a base case, step values, and a maximum value to parameterize your tests? Consider speaking with domain experts or using production data to guide decision making.

After executing the test, we see the following results summarized, as follows:

Benchmark	Enqueued order count	Throughput (ops per second)	Error (ops per second)	Error as percentage of throughput
Cancel first order	1	6,688,878.23	Â±351,518.041	Â±5.26
Cancel first order	10	2,202,233.77	Â±103,557.824	Â±4.70
Cancel first order	50	555,592.56	Â±18,632.547	Â±3.35
Cancel first order	100	305,615.75	Â±14,345.296	Â±4.69
Cancel last order	1	7,365,825.52	Â±284,773.895	Â±3.87
Cancel last order	10	1,691,196.48	Â±54,903.319	Â±3.25
Cancel last order	50	509,339.60	Â±15,582.846	Â±3.06
Cancel last order	100	242,049.87	Â±8,967.785	Â±3.70
Cancel nonexistent order	1	13,285,699.96	Â±374,134.340	Â±2.82

Cancel nonexistent order	10	3,048,323.44	Â±140,983.947	Â±4.62
Cancel nonexistent order	50	772,034.39	Â±16,535.652	Â±2.14
Cancel nonexistent order	100	404,647.90	Â±3,889.509	Â±0.96

From this result set, we can answer a number of interesting questions that help us characterize order book performance. Here are some questions for you to answer by inspecting the results:

- Does the base case of a single enqueued order result in qualitatively similar performance across the three benchmarks?
- Does each benchmark exhibit linear throughput degradation as enqueued order count increases?
- As enqueued order count increases, are there changes in relative performance between benchmarks (for example, between canceling the first and last order when the enqueued order count is 100 instead of 10)?
- Does it appear that there is early termination logic in place when evaluating nonexistent orders?

In addition to these questions that are specific to the order book, it is critical to ask yourself the following questions of any benchmark result:

- Do the results pass a test of reasonableness?
- What could have gone wrong with the test (that is, producing invalid results), and have we put in place safeguards to prevent these shortcomings from occurring?

Errors in measurement or test setup destroy the integrity of your results. These questions aim to make you critically analyze the microbenchmark results. The test of reasonableness requires you to develop a mental model for the executed test. Using the order book, we need to consider what is a plausible number of cancel operations per second. One way to answer this question is to take one of the throughput results, for example, cancel last order with 50 queued orders, and compute the average milliseconds per operation. This is useful because we have a sense for the cost on a per-operation basis from earlier benchmarks; 509,339.595 cancels per second translates to approximately 0.002 ms per operation. This result might be surprisingly low, but bear in mind these results do not account for coordinated omission because there is no targeted throughput rate (that is, the test attempts to send as many cancels per second as possible). The other reason the cost might be lower than expected is because there is only one price level in the book. Typically, the book contains numerous price levels on the buying and selling sides. This may direct us toward designing benchmarks that sweep the number of price levels to better inform our understanding of the cost of managing multiple price levels.

The second question forces us to critically analyze the test setup and the test methodology. For example, how do we know that the setup function produces the intended order book? One way to defend against this is to add assertions to enforce intended constraints. Another concern to verify is that each cancel invocation in the benchmark yields the intended event. Adding assertions to the benchmark for a single trial may address this concern. However, leaving assertions in the benchmark code is likely to affect performance, and this should be used sparingly, if at all. For added safety, it could make sense to write unit tests for the scenarios that are being tested to ensure that the desired behavior occurs and ensure that the unit test and performance test code are shared.

When interpreting JMH results, it is important to consider the significance of the computed error. JMH computes error by constructing a confidence interval from a benchmark's iterations. The confidence interval assumes that the results follow a normal distribution, and the error represents the range of the computed 99.9% confidence interval. This suggests that all other things being equal, running more benchmark iterations improves your confidence in the results. The final column in the results table is illustrative of the variability of the results. The lower the variability, the more inclined you should be to trust the results. High result variability suggests that there is an error in measurement or that there is something inhibiting your ability to measure true performance characteristics. This is often a warning sign that you need to revisit your testing methodology and that you should put little trust in the results.

 For our example, we ran 30 iterations to record throughput information. What do you think are the implications of running with fewer iterations? Alternatively, consider the effects of running fewer iterations with increased duration. For example, 10 iterations, each lasting 30 seconds. Build a hypothesis and then run JMH to see the results. Developing awareness for the sensitivity of different benchmark parameters is another way to build an intuition for how to approach future benchmarks.

As our JMH configuration does not account for coordinated omission and instead sends a firehose of cancel requests to the order book, we should focus on the relative results rather than the absolute throughput values. The order book-related questions that are posed after the results hone in on relative differences that should be visible independent of the testing environment (for example, available cores or RAM). There is value in focusing on relative concerns because the answers should be more robust to change. If future code changes cause significant relative changes, for example, causing an exponential instead of linear cancel performance degradation, you can have higher confidence that this degradation is due to a code change instead of an environmental change.

In this section, we saw how to set up, execute, and interpret a JMH microbenchmark. Along the way, we looked at the shortcomings of microbenchmarking without JMH, and the concerns to be aware of during benchmark result analysis. We've only scratched the surface of the capabilities of JMH. We will build on this introduction to JMH in future chapters.

Summary

Congratulations, in this chapter you helped improve MVT order book performance, which is going to directly translate to increased company profits and reduced losses! Along the way, you took an in-depth look at how to benchmark and profile on the JVM and what shortcomings to avoid. You also worked through a JMH microbenchmarking primer that will allow you to objectively assess performance improvements in future chapters. In the next chapter, we will look at how Scala language features can be used to write functional software, and we will assess their performance impacts using the skills that we learned in this chapter.

3
Unleashing Scala Performance

In this chapter, we will look at Scala-specific constructs and language features, and examine how they can help or hurt performance. Equipped with our newly-acquired performance measurement knowledge, we will analyze how to use the rich language features that are provided by the Scala programming language better. For each feature, we will introduce it, show you how it compiles to bytecode, and then identify caveats and other considerations when using this feature.

Throughout the chapter, we will show the Scala source code and generated bytecode that are emitted by the Scala compiler. It is necessary to inspect these artifacts to enrich your understanding of how Scala interacts with the JVM so that you can develop an intuition for the runtime performance of your software. We will inspect the bytecode by invoking the `javap` Java disassembler after compiling the command, as follows:

```
javap -c <PATH_TO_CLASS_FILE>
```

The minus `c` switch prints the disassembled code. Another useful option is `-private`, which prints the bytecode of privately defined methods. For more information on `javap`, refer to the manual page. The examples that we will cover do not require in-depth JVM bytecode knowledge, but if you wish to learn more about bytecode operations, refer to Oracle's JVM specification at `http://docs.oracle.com/javase/specs/jvms/se7/html/jvms-3.html#jvms-3.4`.

Periodically, we will also inspect a version of the Scala source code with Scala-specific features removed by running the following command:

```
scalac -print <PATH>
```

This is a useful way to see how the Scala compiler desugars convenient syntax into constructs that the JVM can execute. In this chapter, we will explore the following topics:

- Value classes and tagged types
- Specialization
- Tuples
- Pattern matching
- Tail recursion
- The `Option` data type
- An alternative to `Option`

Value classes

In `Chapter 2`, *Measuring Performance on the JVM*, we introduced the domain model of the order book application. This domain model included two classes, `Price` and `OrderId`. We pointed out that we created domain classes for `Price` and `OrderId` to provide contextual meanings to the wrapped `BigDecimal` and `Long`. While providing us with readable code and compilation time safety, this practice also increases the number of instances that are created by our application. Allocating memory and generating class instances create more work for the garbage collector by increasing the frequency of collections and by potentially introducing additional long-lived objects. The garbage collector will have to work harder to collect them, and this process may severely impact our latency.

Luckily, as of Scala 2.10, the `AnyVal` abstract class is available for developers to define their own value classes to solve this problem. The `AnyVal` class is defined in the Scala doc (`http://www.scala-lang.org/api/current/#scala.AnyVal`) as, "the root class of all value types, which describe values not implemented as objects in the underlying host system." The `AnyVal` class can be used to define a value class, which receives special treatment from the compiler. Value classes are optimized at compile time to avoid the allocation of an instance, and instead they use the wrapped type.

Bytecode representation

As an example, to improve the performance of our order book, we can define `Price` and `OrderId` as value classes:

```
case class Price(value: BigDecimal) extends AnyVal
case class OrderId(value: Long) extends AnyVal
```

To illustrate the special treatment of value classes, we define a dummy method taking a `Price` value class and an `OrderId` value class as arguments:

```
def printInfo(p: Price, oId: OrderId): Unit =
  println(s"Price: ${p.value}, ID: ${oId.value}")
```

From this definition, the compiler produces the following method signature:

```
public void printInfo(scala.math.BigDecimal, long);
```

We see that the generated signature takes a `BigDecimal` object and a `long` object, even though the Scala code allows us to take advantage of the types defined in our model. This means that we cannot use an instance of `BigDecimal` or `Long` when calling `printInfo` because the compiler will throw an error.

 An interesting thing to notice is that the second parameter of `printInfo` is not compiled as `Long` (an object), but `long` (a primitive type, note the lower case 'l'). `Long` and other objects matching to primitive types, such as `Int`, `Float` or `Short`, are specially handled by the compiler to be represented by their primitive type at runtime.

Value classes can also define methods. Let's enrich our `Price` class, as follows:

```
case class Price(value: BigDecimal) extends AnyVal {
  def lowerThan(p: Price): Boolean = this.value < p.value
}

// Example usage
val p1 = Price(BigDecimal(1.23))
val p2 = Price(BigDecimal(2.03))
p1.lowerThan(p2) // returns true
```

Our new method allows us to compare two instances of `Price`. At compile time, a companion object is created for `Price`. This companion object defines a `lowerThan` method that takes two `BigDecimal` objects as parameters. In reality, when we call `lowerThan` on an instance of `Price`, the code is transformed by the compiler from an instance method call to a static method call that is defined in the companion object:

```
public final boolean lowerThan$extension(scala.math.BigDecimal,
scala.math.BigDecimal);
    Code:
        0: aload_1
        1: aload_2
        2: invokevirtual #56  // Method
scala/math/BigDecimal.$less:(Lscala/math/BigDecimal;)Z
        5: ireturn
```

If we were to write the pseudo-code equivalent to the preceding Scala code, it would look something like the following:

```
val p1 = BigDecimal(1.23)
val p2 = BigDecimal(2.03)
Price.lowerThan(p1, p2)  // returns true
```

Performance considerations

Value classes are a great addition to our developer toolbox. They help us reduce the count of instances and spare some work for the garbage collector, while allowing us to rely on meaningful types that reflect our business abstractions. However, extending AnyVal comes with a certain set of conditions that the class must fulfill. For example, a value class may only have one primary constructor that takes one public val as a single parameter. Furthermore, this parameter cannot be a value class. We saw that value classes can define methods via def. Neither val nor var is allowed inside a value class. A nested class or object definitions are also impossible. Another limitation prevents value classes from extending anything other than a universal trait, that is, a trait that extends Any, only has defs as members, and performs no initialization. If any of these conditions are not fulfilled, the compiler generates an error. In addition to the preceding constraints that are listed, there are special cases in which a value class has to be instantiated by the JVM. Such cases include performing a pattern matching or runtime type test, or assigning a value class to an array. An example of the latter looks like the following snippet:

```
def newPriceArray(count: Int): Array[Price] = {
  val a = new Array[Price](count)
  for(i <- 0 until count){
    a(i) = Price(BigDecimal(Random.nextInt()))
  }
  a
}
```

The generated bytecode is as follows:

```
public
highperfscala.anyval.ValueClasses$$anonfun$newPriceArray$1(highperfscala.an
yval.ValueClasses$Price[]);
    Code:
        0: aload_0
        1: aload_1
        2: putfield      #29  // Field
a$1:[Lhighperfscala/anyval/ValueClasses$Price;
        5: aload_0
        6: invokespecial #80  // Method
```

```
scala/runtime/AbstractFunction1$mcVI$sp."<init>":()V
        9: return

public void apply$mcVI$sp(int);
    Code:
        0: aload_0
        1: getfield       #29  // Field
a$1:[Lhighperfscala/anyval/ValueClasses$Price;
        4: iload_1
        5: new            #31  // class
highperfscala/anyval/ValueClasses$Price
        // omitted for brevity
       21: invokevirtual #55  // Method
scala/math/BigDecimal$.apply:(I)Lscala/math/BigDecimal;
       24: invokespecial #59  // Method
highperfscala/anyval/ValueClasses$Price."<init>":(Lscala/math/BigDecimal;)V
       27: aastore
       28: return
```

Notice how `mcVI$sp` is invoked from `newPriceArray`, and this creates a new instance of `ValueClasses$Price` at the 5 instruction.

As turning a single field case class into a value class is as trivial as extending the `AnyVal` trait, we recommend that you always use `AnyVal` wherever possible. The overhead is quite low, and it generate high benefits in terms of garbage collection's performance. To learn more about value classes, their limitations, and use cases, you can find detailed descriptions at `http://docs.scala-lang.org/overviews/core/value-classes.html`.

Tagged types – an alternative to value classes

Value classes are an easy to use tool, and they can yield great improvements in terms of performance. However, they come with a constraining set of conditions, which can make them impossible to use in certain cases. We will conclude this section with a glance at an interesting alternative by leveraging the tagged type feature that is implemented by the `Scalaz` library (`https://github.com/scalaz/scalaz`).

The `Scalaz` implementation of tagged types is inspired by another Scala library, named `shapeless`. The `shapeless` library provides tools to write type-safe, generic code with minimal boilerplate. While we will not explore `shapeless`, we encourage you to learn more about the project at h ttps://github.com/milessabin/shapeless.

Tagged types are another way to enforce compile-type checking without incurring the cost of instance instantiation. They rely on the `Tagged` structural type and the `@@` type alias that are defined in the `Scalaz` library, as follows:

```
type Tagged[U] = { type Tag = U }
type @@[T, U] = T with Tagged[U]
```

Let's rewrite part of our code to leverage tagged types with our `Price` object:

```
object TaggedTypes {

  sealed trait PriceTag
  type Price = BigDecimal @@ PriceTag

  object Price {
    def newPrice(p: BigDecimal): Price =
      Tag[BigDecimal, PriceTag](p)

    def lowerThan(a: Price, b: Price): Boolean =
      Tag.unwrap(a) < Tag.unwrap(b)
  }
}
```

Let's perform a short walkthrough of the code snippet. We will define a `PriceTag` sealed trait that we will use to tag our instances, a `Price` type alias is created and defined as a `BigDecimal` object tagged with `PriceTag`. The `Price` object defines useful methods, including the `newPrice` factory function that is used to tag a given `BigDecimal` object and return a `Price` object (that is, a tagged `BigDecimal` object). We will also implement an equivalent to the `lowerThan` method. This function takes two `Price` objects (that is, two tagged `BigDecimal` objects), extracts the content of the tags that are two `BigDecimal` objects, and compares them.

Using our new `Price` type, we rewrite the same `newPriceArray` method that we previously looked at (the code is omitted for brevity, but you can refer to it in the attached source code), and print the following generated bytecode:

```
public void apply$mcVI$sp(int);
    Code:
       0: aload_0
       1: getfield       #29  // Field a$1:[Ljava/lang/Object;
       4: iload_1
       5: getstatic      #35  // Field
highperfscala/anyval/TaggedTypes$Price$.MODULE$:Lhighperfscala/anyval/Tagge
dTypes$Price$;
       8: getstatic      #40  // Field
scala/package$.MODULE$:Lscala/package$;
```

```
      11: invokevirtual #44   // Method
scala/package$.BigDecimal:()Lscala/math/BigDecimal$;
      14: getstatic      #49   // Field
scala/util/Random$.MODULE$:Lscala/util/Random$;
      17: invokevirtual #53   // Method scala/util/Random$.nextInt:()I
      20: invokevirtual #58   // Method
scala/math/BigDecimal$.apply:(I)Lscala/math/BigDecimal;
      23: invokevirtual #62   // Method
highperfscala/anyval/TaggedTypes$Price$.newPrice:(Lscala/math/BigDecimal;)L
java/lang/Object;
      26: aastore
      27: return
```

In this version, we no longer see an instantiation of `Price`, even though we are assigning it to an array. The tagged `Price` implementation involves a runtime cast, but we anticipate that the cost of this cast will be less than the instance allocations (and garbage collection) observed in the previous value class `Price` strategy. We will look at tagged types again later in this chapter, and use them to replace a well-known tool of the standard library: the `Option`.

Specialization

To understand the significance of specialization, it is important to first grasp the concept of object boxing. The JVM defines primitive types (`boolean`, `byte`, `char`, `float`, `int`, `long`, `short`, and `double`) that are stack-allocated rather than heap-allocated. When a generic type is introduced, for example, `scala.collection.immutable.List`, the JVM references an object equivalent, instead of a primitive type. In this example, an instantiated list of integers would be heap-allocated objects rather than integer primitives. The process of converting a primitive to its object equivalent is called boxing, and the reverse process is called unboxing. Boxing is a relevant concern for performance-sensitive programming because boxing involves heap allocation. In performance-sensitive code that performs numerical computations, the cost of boxing and unboxing can can create significant performance slowdowns. Consider the following example to illustrate boxing overhead:

```
List.fill(10000)(2).map(_* 2)
```

Creating the list via `fill` yields 10,000 heap allocations of the integer object. Performing the multiplication in `map` requires 10,000 unboxings to perform multiplication and then 10,000 boxings to add the multiplication result into the new list. From this simple example, you can imagine how critical section arithmetic will be slowed down due to boxing or unboxing operations.

As shown in Oracle's tutorial on boxing at `https://docs.oracle.com/javase/tutoria l/java/data/autoboxing.html`, boxing in Java and also in Scala happens transparently. This means that, without careful profiling or bytecode analysis, it is difficult to discern where you are paying the cost for object boxing. To ameliorate this problem, Scala provides a feature named specialization. Specialization refers to the compile-time process of generating duplicate versions of a generic trait or class that refer directly to a primitive type instead of the associated object wrapper. At runtime, the compiler-generated version of the generic class (or, as it is commonly referred to, the specialized version of the class) is instantiated. This process eliminates the runtime cost of boxing primitives, which means that you can define generic abstractions while retaining the performance of a handwritten, specialized implementation.

Bytecode representation

Let's look at a concrete example to better understand how the specialization process works. Consider a naive, generic representation of the number of shares purchased, as follows:

```
case class ShareCount[T](value: T)
```

For this example, let's assume that the intended usage is to swap between an integer or long representation of `ShareCount`. With this definition, instantiating a long-based `ShareCount` instance incurs the cost of boxing, as follows:

```
def newShareCount(l: Long): ShareCount[Long] = ShareCount(l)
```

This definition translates to the following bytecode:

```
  public
highperfscala.specialization.Specialization$ShareCount<java.lang.Object>
newShareCount(long);
    Code:
        0: new           #21  // class orderbook/Specialization$ShareCount
        3: dup
        4: lload_1
        5: invokestatic  #27  // Method
scala/runtime/BoxesRunTime.boxToLong:(J)Ljava/lang/Long;
        8: invokespecial #30  // Method
orderbook/Specialization$ShareCount."<init>":(Ljava/lang/Object;)V
       11: areturn
```

In the preceding bytecode, it is clear at instruction 5 that the primitive long value is boxed before instantiating the ShareCount instance. By introducing the @specialized annotation, we are able to eliminate the boxing by having the compiler provide an implementation of ShareCount that works with primitive long values. It is possible to specify which types you wish to specialize by supplying a set of types. As defined in the Specializables trait (http://www.scala-lang.org/api/current/index.html#scala.Specializable), you are able to specialize for all JVM primitives, as well as, Unit and AnyRef. For our example, let's specialize ShareCount for integers and longs, as follows:

```
case class ShareCount[@specialized(Long, Int) T](value: T)
```

With this definition, the bytecode now becomes the following:

```
    public
highperfscala.specialization.Specialization$ShareCount<java.lang.Object>
newShareCount(long);
    Code:
        0: new           #21  // class
highperfscala.specialization/Specialization$ShareCount$mcJ$sp
        3: dup
        4: lload_1
        5: invokespecial #24  // Method
highperfscala.specialization/Specialization$ShareCount$mcJ$sp."<init>":(J)V
        8: areturn
```

The boxing disappears and is curiously replaced with a different class name, ShareCount mcJsp. This is because we are invoking the compiler-generated version of ShareCount that is specialized for long values. By inspecting the output of javap, we see that the specialized class generated by the compiler is a subclass of ShareCount:

```
    public class highperfscala.specialization.Specialization$ShareCount$mcI$sp
    extends highperfscala.specialization.Specialization$ShareCount<java
    .lang.Object>
```

Bear this specialization implementation detail in mind as we turn to the *Performance considerations* section. The use of inheritance forces tradeoffs to be made in more complex use cases.

Performance considerations

At first glance, specialization appears to be a simple panacea for JVM boxing. However, there are several caveats to consider when using specialization. A liberal use of specialization leads to significant increases in compile time and resulting code size. Consider specializing `Function3`, which accepts three arguments as input and produces one result. To specialize four arguments across all types (that is, `Byte`, `Short`, `Int`, `Long`, `Char`, `Float`, `Double`, `Boolean`, `Unit`, and `AnyRef`) yields 10^4 or 10,000 possible permutations. For this reason, the standard library conserves the application of specialization. In your own use cases, consider carefully which types you wish to specialize. If we specialize `Function3` only for `Int` and `Long`, the number of generated classes shrinks to 2^4 or 16. Specialization involving inheritance requires extra attention because it is trivial to lose specialization when extending a generic class. Consider the following example:

```
class ParentFoo[@specialized T](t: T)
class ChildFoo[T](t: T) extends ParentFoo[T](t)

def newChildFoo(i: Int): ChildFoo[Int] = new ChildFoo[Int](i)
```

In this scenario, you likely expect that `ChildFoo` is defined with a primitive integer. However, as `ChildFoo` does not mark its type with the `@specialized` annotation, zero specialized classes are created. Here is the bytecode to prove it:

```
    public
highperfscala.specialization.Inheritance$ChildFoo<java.lang.Object>
newChildFoo(int);
    Code:
        0: new           #16  // class
highperfscala/specialization/Inheritance$ChildFoo
        3: dup
        4: iload_1
        5: invokestatic  #22  // Method
scala/runtime/BoxesRunTime.boxToInteger:(I)Ljava/lang/Integer;
        8: invokespecial #25  // Method
highperfscala/specialization/Inheritance$ChildFoo."<init>":(Ljava/lang/Obje
ct;)V
       11: areturn
```

The next logical step is to add the `@specialized` annotation to the definition of `ChildFoo`. In doing so, we stumble across a scenario where the compiler warns about the use of specialization, as follows:

```
    class ParentFoo must be a trait. Specialized version of class ChildFoo will
    inherit generic highperfscala.specialization.Inheritance.ParentFoo[Boolean]
```

```
class ChildFoo[@specialized T](t: T) extends ParentFoo[T](t)
```

The compiler indicates that you have created a diamond inheritance problem, where the specialized versions of `ChildFoo` extend both `ChildFoo` and the associated specialized version of `ParentFoo`. This issue can be resolved by modeling the problem with a trait, as follows:

```
trait ParentBar[@specialized T] {
  def t(): T
}

class ChildBar[@specialized T](val t: T) extends ParentBar[T]

def newChildBar(i: Int): ChildBar[Int] = new ChildBar(i)
```

This definition compiles using a specialized version of `ChildBar`, as we originally were hoping for, as seen in the following code:

```
  public
highperfscala.specialization.Inheritance$ChildBar<java.lang.Object>
newChildBar(int);
    Code:
      0: new            #32  // class
highperfscala/specialization/Inheritance$ChildBar$mcI$sp
      3: dup
      4: iload_1
      5: invokespecial #35  // Method
highperfscala/specialization/Inheritance$ChildBar$mcI$sp."<init>":(I)V
      8: areturn
```

An analogous and equally error-prone scenario is when a generic method is defined around a specialized type. Consider the following definition:

```
class Foo[T](t: T)

object Foo {
  def create[T](t: T): Foo[T] = new Foo(t)
}

def boxed: Foo[Int] = Foo.create(1)
```

Here, the definition of `create` is analogous to the child class from the inheritance example. Instances of `Foo` wrapping a primitive that are instantiated from the `create` method will be boxed. The following bytecode demonstrates how `boxed` leads to heap allocations:

```
  public
highperfscala.specialization.MethodReturnTypes$Foo<java.lang.Object>
```

```
    boxed();
      Code:
          0: getstatic      #19  // Field
highperfscala/specialization/MethodReturnTypes$Foo$.MODULE$:Lhighperfscala/
specialization/MethodReturnTypes$Foo$;
          3: iconst_1
          4: invokestatic  #25  // Method
scala/runtime/BoxesRunTime.boxToInteger:(I)Ljava/lang/Integer;
          7: invokevirtual #29  // Method
highperfscala/specialization/MethodReturnTypes$Foo$.create:(Ljava/lang/Obje
ct;)Lhighperfscala/specialization/MethodReturnTypes$Foo;
         10: areturn
```

The solution is to apply the @specialized annotation at the call site, as follows:

```
def createSpecialized[@specialized T](t: T): Foo[T] = new Foo(t)
```

One final interesting scenario is when specialization is used with multiple types and one of the types extends AnyRef or is a value class. To illustrate this scenario, consider the following example:

```
case class ShareCount(value: Int) extends AnyVal
case class ExecutionCount(value: Int)

class Container2[@specialized X, @specialized Y](x: X, y: Y)

def shareCount = new Container2(ShareCount(1), 1)

def executionCount = new Container2(ExecutionCount(1), 1)

def ints = new Container2(1, 1)
```

In this example, which methods do you expect to box the second argument to Container2? For brevity, we omit the bytecode, but you can easily inspect it yourself. As it turns out, shareCount and executionCount box the integer. The compiler does not generate a specialized version of Container2 that accepts a primitive integer and a value extending AnyVal (for example, ExecutionCount). The shareCount method also causes boxing due to the order in which the compiler removes the value class type information from the source code. In both scenarios, the workaround is to define a case class that is specific to a set of types (for example, ShareCount and Int). Removing the generics allows the compiler to select the primitive types.

The conclusion to draw from these examples is that specialization requires extra focus to be used throughout an application without boxing. As the compiler is unable to infer scenarios where you accidentally forgot to apply the `@specialized` annotation, it fails to raise a warning. This places the onus on you to be vigilant about profiling and inspecting bytecode to detect scenarios where specialization is incidentally dropped.

 To combat some of the shortcomings that specialization brings, there is a compiler plugin under active development, named miniboxing, at `http://scala-miniboxing.org/`. This compiler plugin applies a different strategy that involves encoding all primitive types into a long value and carrying metadata to recall the original type. For example, `boolean` can be represented in a `long` using a single bit to signal true or false. With this approach, performance is qualitatively similar to specialization while producing orders of magnitude fewer classes for large permutations. Additionally, miniboxing is able to more robustly handle inheritance scenarios and can warn when boxing will occur. While the implementations of specialization and miniboxing differ, the end user usage is quite similar. Like specialization, you must add appropriate annotations to activate the miniboxing plugin. To learn more about the plugin, you can view the tutorials on the miniboxing project site.

The extra focus to ensure specialization produces heap allocation free code is worthwhile because of the performance wins in performance-sensitive code. To drive home the value of specialization, consider the following microbenchmark that computes the cost of a trade by multiplying share count with execution price. For simplicity, primitive types are used directly instead of value classes. Of course, in production code this would never happen:

```
@BenchmarkMode(Array(Throughput))
@OutputTimeUnit(TimeUnit.SECONDS)
@Warmup(iterations = 3, time = 5, timeUnit = TimeUnit.SECONDS)
@Measurement(iterations = 30, time = 10, timeUnit = TimeUnit.SECONDS)
@Fork(value = 1, warmups = 1, jvmArgs = Array("-Xms1G", "-Xmx1G"))
class SpecializationBenchmark {

  @Benchmark
  def specialized(): Double =
    specializedExecution.shareCount.toDouble * specializedExecution.price

  @Benchmark
  def boxed(): Double =
    boxedExecution.shareCount.toDouble * boxedExecution.price
}

object SpecializationBenchmark {
```

```
    class SpecializedExecution[@specialized(Int) T1, @specialized(Double)
 T2](
      val shareCount: Long, val price: Double)
    class BoxingExecution[T1, T2](val shareCount: T1, val price: T2)

    val specializedExecution: SpecializedExecution[Int, Double] =
      new SpecializedExecution(101, 2d)
    val boxedExecution: BoxingExecution[Long, Double] = new
 BoxingExecution(101, 2d)
  }
```

In this benchmark, two versions of a generic execution class are defined.
`SpecializedExecution` incurs zero boxing when computing the total cost because of specialization, while `BoxingExecution` requires object boxing and unboxing to perform the arithmetic. The microbenchmark is invoked with the following parameterization:

```
sbt 'project chapter3' 'jmh:run SpecializationBenchmark -foe true'
```

 We configure this JMH benchmark via annotations that are placed at the class level in the code. This is different from what we saw in Chapter 2, *Measuring Performance on the JVM,* where we used command-line arguments. Annotations have the advantage of setting proper defaults for your benchmark, and simplifying the command-line invocation. It is still possible to override the values in the annotation with command-line arguments. We use the `-foe` command-line argument to enable failure on error because there is no annotation to control this behavior. In the rest of this book, we will parameterize JMH with annotations and omit the annotations in the code samples because we always use the same values.

The results are summarized in the following table:

Benchmark	Throughput (ops per second)	Error as percentage of throughput
boxed	251,534,293.11	±2.23
specialized	302,371,879.84	±0.87

This microbenchmark indicates that the specialized implementation yields approximately 17% higher throughput. By eliminating boxing in a critical section of the code, there is an order of magnitude performance improvement available through the judicious usage of specialization. For performance-sensitive arithmetic, this benchmark provides justification for the extra effort that is required to ensure that specialization is applied properly.

Tuples

First-class tuple support in Scala simplifies use cases where multiple values need to be grouped together. With tuples, you can elegantly return multiple values using a concise syntax without defining a case class. The following section shows how the compiler translates Scala tuples.

Bytecode representation

Let's look at how the JVM handles creating a tuple to understand how the JVM supports tuples better. To develop our intuition, consider creating a tuple with an arity of two, as follows:

```
def tuple2: (Int, Double) = (1, 2.0)
```

The corresponding bytecode for this method is as follows:

```
public scala.Tuple2<java.lang.Object, java.lang.Object> tuple2();
  Code:
     0: new           #36  // class scala/Tuple2$mcID$sp
     3: dup
     4: iconst_1
     5: ldc2_w        #37  // double 2.0d
     8: invokespecial #41  // Method scala/Tuple2$mcID$sp."<init>":(ID)V
    11: areturn
```

This bytecode shows that the compiler desugared the parenthesis tuple definition syntax into the allocation of a class named `Tuple2`. There is a tuple class that is defined for each supported arity (for example, `Tuple5` supports five members) up to `Tuple22`. The bytecode also shows at the 4 and 5 instructions that the primitive versions of `Int` and `Double` are used to allocate this `tuple` instance.

Performance considerations

In the preceding example, `Tuple2` avoids the boxing of primitives due to specialization on the two generic types. It is often convenient to tuple multiple values together because of Scala's expressive tupling syntax. However, this leads to excessive memory allocation because tuples with an arity larger than two are not specialized. Here is an example to illustrate this concern:

```
def tuple3: (Int, Double, Int) = (1, 2.0, 3)
```

This definition is analogous to the first tuple definition that we reviewed, except that there is now an arity of three. This definition produces the following bytecode:

```
public scala.Tuple3<java.lang.Object, java.lang.Object, java.lang.Object>
tuple3();
    Code:
        0: new           #45  // class scala/Tuple3
        3: dup
        4: iconst_1
        5: invokestatic  #24  // Method
scala/runtime/BoxesRunTime.boxToInteger:(I)Ljava/lang/Integer;
        8: ldc2_w        #37  // double 2.0d
       11: invokestatic  #49  // Method
scala/runtime/BoxesRunTime.boxToDouble:(D)Ljava/lang/Double;
       14: iconst_3
       15: invokestatic  #24  // Method
scala/runtime/BoxesRunTime.boxToInteger:(I)Ljava/lang/Integer;
       18: invokespecial #52  // Method
scala/Tuple3."<init>":(Ljava/lang/Object;Ljava/lang/Object;Ljava/lang/Objec
t;)V
       21: areturn
```

In this bytecode, the absence of specialization is clear because of the presence of integer and double boxing. If you are working on a performance-sensitive region of your application and find occurrences of tuples with an arity of three or larger, you should consider defining a case class to avoid the boxing overhead. The definition of your case class will not have any generics. This enables the JVM to use primitives instead of allocating objects on the heap for the primitive tuple members.

Even when using `Tuple2`, it is still possible that you are incurring the cost of boxing. Consider the following snippet:

```
case class Bar(value: Int) extends AnyVal
def tuple2Boxed: (Int, Bar) = (1, Bar(2))
```

Given what we know about the bytecode representation of Tuple2 and value classes, we expect the bytecode for this method to be two stack-allocated integers. Unfortunately, in this case, the resulting bytecode is as follows:

```
public scala.Tuple2<java.lang.Object,
highperfscala.patternmatch.PatternMatching$Bar> tuple2Boxed();
    Code:
        0: new           #18  // class scala/Tuple2
        3: dup
        4: iconst_1
        5: invokestatic  #24  // Method
scala/runtime/BoxesRunTime.boxToInteger:(I)Ljava/lang/Integer;
```

```
        8: new                #26  // class
highperfscala.patternmatch/PatternMatching$Bar
       11: dup
       12: iconst_2
       13: invokespecial #29  // Method
highperfscala.patternmatch/PatternMatching$Bar."<init>":(I)V
       16: invokespecial #32  // Method
scala/Tuple2."<init>":(Ljava/lang/Object;Ljava/lang/Object;)V
       19: areturn
```

In the preceding bytecode, we see that the integer is boxed and an instance of Bar is instantiated. This example is analogous to the final specialization example that we investigated involving `Container2`. Looking back at that example, it should be evident that `Container2` is a close analog to Tuple2. As before, due to how specialization is implemented by the compiler, the compiler is unable to avoid boxing in this scenario. If you are faced with performance-sensitive code, the workaround remains defining a case class. Here is proof that defining a case class erases the undesired value class instantiation and primitive boxing:

```
case class IntBar(i: Int, b: Bar)
def intBar: IntBar = IntBar(1, Bar(2))
```

This definition produces the following bytecode:

```
    public highperfscala.patternmatch.PatternMatching$IntBar intBar();
      Code:
        0: new                #18  // class
highperfscala.patternmatch/PatternMatching$IntBar
        3: dup
        4: iconst_1
        5: iconst_2
        6: invokespecial #21  // Method
highperfscala.patternmatch/PatternMatching$IntBar."<init>":(II)V
        9: areturn
```

Note that `IntBar` is not defined as a value class because it has two parameters. In contrast to the tuple definition, there is neither boxing nor any reference to the `Bar` value class. In this scenario, defining a case class is a performance win for performance-sensitive code.

Pattern matching

For programmers who are new to Scala, pattern matching is often one of the language features that is the simplest to understand, but it also unlocks new ways to think about writing software. This powerful mechanism enables you to match on disparate types with compile-time safety using an elegant syntax. Given how central this technique is to writing Scala in the functional paradigm, it is important to consider its runtime overhead.

Bytecode representation

Let's consider an example that involves order processing with an algebraic data type representing the possible sides of an order:

```
sealed trait Side
case object Buy extends Side
case object Sell extends Side
def handleOrder(s: Side): Boolean = s match {
  case Buy => true
  case Sell => false
}
```

 The terminology **algebraic data type (ADT)** is a more formal way of referring to a sealed trait and its cases. For example, Side, Buy, and Sell form an ADT. For our purposes, an ADT defines a closed set of cases. For Side, the enclosed cases are Buy and Sell. The sealed modifier provides closed set semantics because it disallows the extension of Side in separate source files. The closed set semantics implied by an ADT is what allows the compiler to infer whether or not a pattern match statement is exhaustive. If you are interested in studying another example of an ADT, view the order book commands defined in Chapter2, *Measuring Performance on the JVM*.

As shown in the following bytecode, pattern matching is desugared into a set of if statements:

```
  public boolean
handleOrder(highperfscala.patternmatch.PatternMatching$Side);
    Code:
        0: aload_1
        1: astore_2
        2: getstatic      #148  // Field
highperfscala.patternmatch/PatternMatching$Buy$.MODULE$:Lhighperfscala.patt
ernmatch/PatternMatching$Buy$;
```

```
    5: aload_2
    6: invokevirtual #152   // Method
java/lang/Object.equals:(Ljava/lang/Object;)Z
    9: ifeq           17
   12: iconst_1
   13: istore_3
   14: goto           29
   17: getstatic      #157   // Field
highperfscala.patternmatch/PatternMatching$Sell$.MODULE$:Lhighperfscala.pat
ternmatch/PatternMatching$Sell$;
   20: aload_2
   21: invokevirtual #152   // Method
java/lang/Object.equals:(Ljava/lang/Object;)Z
   24: ifeq           31
   27: iconst_0
   28: istore_3
   29: iload_3
   30: ireturn
   31: new            #159   // class scala/MatchError
   34: dup
   35: aload_2
   36: invokespecial #160   // Method
scala/MatchError."<init>":(Ljava/lang/Object;)V
   39: athrow
```

Inspecting the bytecode shows how the Scala compiler is able to desugar pattern match expressions into a set of efficient if statements with the `ifeq` instructions at the 9 and 24 indexes. This an illustrative example of how Scala is able to provide expressive and elegant first-class language features that retain efficient bytecode equivalents.

Performance considerations

Pattern matching against values that contain state (for example, a case class) imposes additional runtime costs that are not immediately clear when looking at the Scala source code. Consider the following extension to the previous example that introduces state:

```scala
sealed trait Order
case class BuyOrder(price: Double) extends Order
case class SellOrder(price: Double) extends Order
def handleOrder(o: Order): Boolean = o match {
  case BuyOrder(price) if price > 2.0 => true
  case BuyOrder(_) => false
  case SellOrder(_) => false
}
```

Here, the example is more complicated because the instance type must be identified for all three cases with the added complexity of a predicate on the `BuyOrder` price in the first case. In the following, we look at a snippet of the `scalac` output with all Scala-specific features removed:

```
case10(){
   if
(x1.$isInstanceOf[highperfscala.patternmatch.PatternMatching$BuyOrder]())
         {
           rc8 = true;
           x2 =
(x1.$asInstanceOf[highperfscala.patternmatch.PatternMatching$BuyOrder]():
highperfscala.patternmatch.PatternMatching$BuyOrder);
             {
               val price: Double = x2.price();
               if (price.>(2.0))
                 matchEnd9(true)
               else
                 case11()
             }
         }
      else
         case11()
   };
   case11(){
      if (rc8)
         matchEnd9(false)
      else
         case12()
   };
```

This desugaring illustrates several interesting points about the Scala compiler. Identifying the type of `Order` utilizes `isInstanceOf` from `java.lang.Object`, which maps to the `instanceOf` bytecode instruction. Casting, by way of `asInstanceOf`, coerces the `Order` into either a `BuyOrder` price or a `SellOrder`. The first takeaway is that pattern matching types carrying state incurs the runtime cost of type-checking and casting.

A second insight is that the Scala compiler is able to optimize away the instance checking for the second pattern match by creating a Boolean variable named `rc8` to determine whether a `BuyOrder` was discovered. This neat optimization is simple to handwrite, but it removes the elegance and simplicity of pattern matching. This is another example of how the compiler is able to produce efficient bytecode from expressive, high-level code.

From the preceding examples, it is now clear that pattern matches are compiled to if statements. One performance consideration for critical path code is the ordering of pattern match statements. If your code has five pattern match statements and the fifth pattern is the most frequently accessed, then your code is paying the price of always evaluating four other branches. Let's devise a JMH microbenchmark that estimates the linear access cost of pattern matching. Each benchmark defines ten pattern matches using different values (for example, the value class, the integer literal, the case class, and so on). For each benchmark, the matched index is swept to show the cost of accessing the first, the fifth, and the the tenth pattern match statement. Here is the benchmark definition:

```scala
class PatternMatchingBenchmarks {

  @Benchmark
  def matchIntLiterals(i: PatternMatchState): Int = i.matchIndex match {
    case 1 => 1
    case 2 => 2
    case 3 => 3
    case 4 => 4
    case 5 => 5
    case 6 => 6
    case 7 => 7
    case 8 => 8
    case 9 => 9
    case 10 => 10
  }

  @Benchmark
  def matchIntVariables(ii: PatternMatchState): Int = ii.matchIndex match {
    case `a` => 1
    case `b` => 2
    case `c` => 3
    case `d` => 4
    case `e` => 5
    case `f` => 6
    case `g` => 7
    case `h` => 8
    case `i` => 9
    case `j` => 10
  }

  @Benchmark
  def matchAnyVal(i: PatternMatchState): Int = CheapFoo(i.matchIndex) match
  {
    case CheapFoo(1) => 1
    case CheapFoo(2) => 2
    case CheapFoo(3) => 3
    case CheapFoo(4) => 4
```

```
      case CheapFoo(5)  => 5
      case CheapFoo(6)  => 6
      case CheapFoo(7)  => 7
      case CheapFoo(8)  => 8
      case CheapFoo(9)  => 9
      case CheapFoo(10) => 10
    }

  @Benchmark
  def matchCaseClass(i: PatternMatchState): Int =
    ExpensiveFoo(i.matchIndex) match {
      case ExpensiveFoo(1)  => 1
      case ExpensiveFoo(2)  => 2
      case ExpensiveFoo(3)  => 3
      case ExpensiveFoo(4)  => 4
      case ExpensiveFoo(5)  => 5
      case ExpensiveFoo(6)  => 6
      case ExpensiveFoo(7)  => 7
      case ExpensiveFoo(8)  => 8
      case ExpensiveFoo(9)  => 9
      case ExpensiveFoo(10) => 10
    }
}

object PatternMatchingBenchmarks {

  case class CheapFoo(value: Int) extends AnyVal
  case class ExpensiveFoo(value: Int)

  private val (a, b, c, d, e, f, g, h, i, j) = (1, 2, 3, 4, 5, 6, 7, 8, 9,
10)

  @State(Scope.Benchmark)
  class PatternMatchState {
    @Param(Array("1", "5", "10"))
    var matchIndex: Int = 0
  }
}
```

Performance was evaluated by running 30 trials, each lasting 10 seconds with three warm-up trials, each lasting 5 seconds. Here is the benchmark invocation:

```
sbt 'project chapter3' 'jmh:run PatternMatchingBenchmarks -foe true'
```

The results are summarized in the following table:

Benchmark	Index to match	Throughput (ops per second)	Error as percentage of throughput	Throughput change as percentage of base run
matchAnyVal	1	350,568,900.12	±3.02	0
matchAnyVal	5	291,126,287.45	±2.63	-17
matchAnyVal	10	238,326,567.59	±2.95	-32
matchCaseClass	1	356,567,498.69	±3.66	0
matchCaseClass	5	287,597,483.22	±3.50	-19
matchCaseClass	10	234,989,504.60	±2.60	-34
matchIntLiterals	1	304,242,630.15	±2.95	0
matchIntLiterals	5	314,588,776.07	±3.70	3
matchIntLiterals	10	285,227,574.79	±4.33	-6
matchIntVariables	1	332,377,617.36	±3.28	0
matchIntVariables	5	263,835,356.53	±6.53	-21
matchIntVariables	10	170,460,049.63	±4.20	-49

The last column takes the first trial of each benchmark when matching the first index as the base case. For trials matching the fifth and tenth indexes, the relative performance drop is displayed. In every case, except matching the fifth index of literal integers, throughput degrades nearly linearly as deeper indexes are matched. The one trial that defies this pattern is the trial matching literal integers. In this trial, performance improves relative to the first index when accessing the fifth index. Upon inspection of the bytecode, we discover that this scenario produces a jump table instead of a set of if statements. Here is a snippet from the generated bytecode:

```
6: tableswitch    { // 1 to 10
              1: 113
              2: 109
              3: 105
              4: 101
              5: 97
              6: 92
              7: 87
```

```
        8: 82
        9: 77
       10: 72
  default: 60
}
```

This bytecode snippet demonstrates that the JVM converts a pattern match on integer literals to a jump table using the `tableswitch` instruction. This is a constant time operation rather than a linear traversal of if statements. Given that the observed error is several percentage points and the observed differences across the three trials are roughly several percentage points, we can deduce that the linear access cost does not apply to this scenario. Instead, matching literal integers at the Nth index has a constant access cost due to the generated jump table. In contrast, matching an integer variable proves to be nearly twice as expensive at the tenth index. The clear takeaway from this experiment is that, for any pattern match that is generating a series of if statements, there is a linear cost to access the Nth pattern match statement. If you pattern match at least three cases in performance-sensitive code, consider reviewing the code to determine whether the statement order matches the access frequency.

Do you have examples of pattern matching containing only two patterns? In scenarios involving only two pattern match statements that directly match a value, the compiler is able to generate an efficient jump table. When matching primitive literals (for example, string literals or integer literals), the compiler is able to generate jump tables for larger pattern matches. Analogous to the `@tailrec` annotation, Scala defines a `@switch` annotation for you to indicate to the compiler that you expect this pattern match statement to be compiled to a jump table. If the compiler is unable to generate a jump table, and instead it produces a series of if statements, then a warning will be issued. Like the `@tailrec` annotation, the compiler will apply the jump table heuristic whether you provide the `@switch` annotation or not. In practice, we do not often use this annotation because of its limited applicability, but it is worthwhile to be aware of its existence. The following is an example of an annotated pattern match that compiles to a jump table:

```
def processShareCount(sc: ShareCount): Boolean =
(sc: @switch) match {
case ShareCount(1) => true
case _ => false
}
```

Tail recursion

A function is said to be recursive when it calls itself. Recursion is a powerful tool, and it is often used in functional programming. It allows you to break complex problems into smaller subproblems, making them easier to reason through and solve. Recursion also works well with the idea of immutability. Recursive functions provide us with a good way to manage changing state without using mutable structures or reassignable variables. In this section, we focus on the different shortcomings of using recursion on the JVM, and especially in Scala.

Let's take a look at a simple example of a recursive method. The following snippet shows a `sum` method that is used to calculate the sum of a list of integers:

```
def sum(l: List[Int]): Int = l match {
  case Nil => 0
  case x :: xs => x + sum(xs)
}
```

The `sum` method presented in the preceding code snippet performs what is called head-recursion. The `sum(xs)` recursive call is not the last instruction in the function. This method needs the result of the recursive call to compute its own result. Consider the following call:

```
sum(List(1,2,3,4,5))
```

It can be represented as:

```
1 + (sum(List(2,3,4,5)))
1 + (2 + (sum(List(3,4,5))))
1 + (2 + (3 + (sum(List(4,5)))))
1 + (2 + (3 + (4 + (sum(List(5))))))
1 + (2 + (3 + (4 + (5))))
1 + (2 + (3 + (9)))
1 + (2 + (12))
1 + (14)
15
```

Note how each time we perform a recursive call, our function is left hanging, waiting for the right side of the computation to finish to be able to return. As the calling function needs to complete its own computation after receiving the result of the recursive call, a new entry is added to the stack for each call. The stack has a limited size, and nothing prevents us from calling `sum` with a very long list. With a sufficiently long list, a call to `sum` would result in a `StackOverflowError`:

```
$ sbt 'project chapter3' console
scala> highperfscala.tailrec.TailRecursion.sum((1 to 1000000).toList)
```

```
java.lang.StackOverflowError
    at scala.collection.immutable.Nil$.equals(List.scala:424)
    at highperfscala.tailrec.TailRecursion$.sum(TailRecursion.scala:12)
    at highperfscala.tailrec.TailRecursion$.sum(TailRecursion.scala:13)
    at highperfscala.tailrec.TailRecursion$.sum(TailRecursion.scala:13)
    at highperfscala.tailrec.TailRecursion$.sum(TailRecursion.scala:13)
...omitted for brevity
```

The stack trace shows all the recursive calls piling up on the stack, waiting for the result from the following step. This proves that none of the calls to sum were able to complete without first completing the recursive call. Our stack ran out of space before the last call could be performed.

To avoid this problem, we need to refactor our method to make it tail-recursive. A recursive method is said to be tail-recursive if the recursive call is the last instruction performed. A tail-recursive method can be optimized to turn the series of recursive calls into something similar to a `while` loop. This means that only the first call is added to the stack:

```
def tailrecSum(l: List[Int]): Int = {
  def loop(list: List[Int], acc: Int): Int = list match {
    case Nil => acc
    case x :: xs => loop(xs, acc + x)
  }
  loop(l, 0)
}
```

This new version of sum is tail-recursive. Note that we create an internal `loop` method, which takes the list to sum, as well as an accumulator to compute the current state of the result. The `loop` method is tail-recursive because the recursive `loop(xs, acc+x)` call is the last instruction. By calculating the accumulator as we iterate, we avoid stacking recursive calls. The initial accumulator value is , as follows:

```
scala> highperfscala.tailrec.TailRecursion.tailrecSum((1 to
1000000).toList)
res0: Int = 1784293664
```

 We mentioned that recursion is an important aspect of functional programming. However, in practice, you should only rarely have to write your own recursive method, especially when dealing with collections such as `List`. The standard API provides already optimized methods that should be preferred. For example, calculating the sum of a list of integers can be written, as follows:

```
list.foldLeft(0)((acc, x) => acc + x)
```

Or when taking advantage of Scala sugar, we can use the following:

```
list.foldLeft(0)(+)
```
The `foldLeft` function is internally implemented with a `while` loop and will not cause a `aStackOverflowError` exception.

Actually, `List` has a `sum` method, which makes calculating the sum of a list of integers even easier. The `sum` method is implemented with `foldLeft` and is similar to the preceding code.

Bytecode representation

As a matter of fact, the JVM does not support tail-recursion optimization. To make this work, the Scala compiler optimizes tail-recursive methods at compile time and turns them into a `while` loop. Let's compare the bytecode that was generated for each implementation.

Our original, head-recursive `sum` method compiled into the following bytecode:

```
public int sum(scala.collection.immutable.List<java.lang.Object>);
    Code:
        0: aload_1
// omitted for brevity
        52: invokevirtual #41   // Method
sum:(Lscala/collection/immutable/List;)I
        55: iadd
        56: istore_3
        57: iload_3
        58: ireturn
// omitted for brevity
```

While the tail recursive `loop` method produced the following:

```
private int loop(scala.collection.immutable.List<java.lang.Object>, int);
    Code:
        0: aload_1
    // omitted for brevity
        60: goto            0
    // omitted for brevity
```

Note how the `sum` method calls itself with the `invokevirtual` instruction at the 52 index and still has to perform some instructions with the returned value. On the contrary, the `loop` method uses a `goto` instruction at the 60 index to jump back to the beginning of its block, thus avoiding stacking several recursive calls to itself.

Performance considerations

The compiler can only optimize simple tail-recursion cases. Specifically, only self-calling functions where the recursive call is the last instruction. There are many edge cases that could be described as tail-recursive, but they are too complex for the compiler to optimize. To avoid unknowingly writing a nonoptimizable recursive method, you should always annotate your tail-recursive methods with @tailrec. The @tailrec annotation is a way to tell the compiler, "I believe you will be able to optimize this recursive method; however, if you cannot, please give me an error at compile time." One thing to keep in mind is that @tailrec is not asking the compiler to optimize the method, it will do so anyway if it is possible. The annotation is for the developer to make sure the compiler can optimize the recursion.

> At this point, you should realize that all while loops can be replaced by a tail-recursive method without any loss in performance. If you have been using while loop constructs in Scala, you can reflect on how to replace them with a tail-recursive implementation. Tail recursion eliminates the use of mutable variables.

Here is the same tailrecSum method with the @tailrec annotation:

```
def tailrecSum(l: List[Int]): Int = {
  @tailrec
  def loop(list: List[Int], acc: Int): Int = list match {
    case Nil => acc
    case x :: xs => loop(xs, acc + x)
  }
  loop(l, 0)
}
```

If we attempted to annotate our first, head-recursive, implementation, we would see the following error at compile time:

```
[error]
chapter3/src/main/scala/highperfscala/tailrec/TailRecursion.scala:12: could
not optimize @tailrec annotated method sum: it contains a recursive call
not in tail position
[error]    def sum(l: List[Int]): Int = l match {
[error]                                  ^
[error] one error found
[error] (chapter3/compile:compileIncremental) Compilation failed
```

We recommend always using @tailrec to ensure that your methods can be optimized by the compiler. As the compiler is only able to optimize simple cases of tail-recursion, it is important to ensure at compile time that you did not inadvertently write a nonoptimizable function that may cause a StackOverflowError exception. We now look at a few cases where the compiler is not able to optimize a recursive method:

```
def sum2(l: List[Int]): Int = {

  def loop(list: List[Int], acc: Int): Int = list match {
    case Nil => acc
    case x :: xs => info(xs, acc + x)
  }
  def info(list: List[Int], acc: Int): Int = {
    println(s"${list.size} elements to examine. sum so far: $acc")
    loop(list, acc)
  }
  loop(l, 0)
}
```

The loop method in sum2 cannot be optimized because the recursion involves two different methods calling each other. If we were to replace the call to info by its actual implementation, then the optimization would be possible, as follows:

```
def tailrecSum2(l: List[Int]): Int = {
  @tailrec
  def loop(list: List[Int], acc: Int): Int = list match {
    case Nil => acc
    case x :: xs =>
      println(s"${list.size} elements to examine. sum so far: $acc")
      loop(list, acc)
  }

  loop(l, 0)
}
```

A somewhat similar use case involves the compiler's inability to take into account by-name parameters:

```
def sumFromReader(br: BufferedReader): Int = {
  def read(acc: Int, reader: BufferedReader): Int = {
    Option(reader.readLine().toInt)
      .fold(acc)(i => read(acc + i, reader))
  }
  read(0, br)
}
```

The `read` method cannot be optimized by the compiler because it is unable to use the definition of `Option.fold` to understand that the recursive call is effectively in the tail position. If we replace the call to fold by its exact implementation, we can annotate the method, as follows:

```
def tailrecSumFromReader(br: BufferedReader): Int = {
  @tailrec
  def read(acc: Int, reader: BufferedReader): Int = {
    val opt = Option(reader.readLine().toInt)
    if (opt.isEmpty) acc else read(acc + opt.get, reader)
  }
  read(0, br)
}
```

The compiler will also refuse to optimize a nonfinal public method. This is to prevent the risk of a subclass overriding the method with a non-tail-recursive version. A recursive call from the super class may go through the subclass's implementation and break the tail-recursion:

```
class Printer(msg: String) {
  def printMessageNTimes(n: Int): Unit = {
    if(n > 0){
      println(msg)
      printMessageNTimes(n - 1)
    }
  }
}
```

Attempting to flag the `printMessageNTimes` method as tail-recursive yields the following error:

```
[error]
chapter3/src/main/scala/highperfscala/tailrec/TailRecursion.scala:74: could
not optimize @tailrec annotated method printMessageNTimes: it is neither
private nor final so can be overridden
[error]      def printMessageNTimes(n: Int): Unit = {
[error]          ^
[error] one error found
[error] (chapter3/compile:compileIncremental) Compilation failed
```

Another case of recursive methods that cannot be optimized is when the recursive call is part of a try/catch block:

```
def tryCatchBlock(l: List[Int]): Int = {
  def loop(list: List[Int], acc: Int): Int = list match {
    case Nil => acc
    case x :: xs =>
```

```
    try {
      loop(xs, acc + x)
    } catch {
      case e: IOException =>
        println(s"Recursion got interrupted by exception")
        acc
    }
  }

  loop(l, 0)
}
```

In contrast to the prior examples, in this example the compiler is not to blame. The recursive call is not in the tail position. As it is surrounded by a try/catch, the method needs to be ready to receive a potential exception and perform more computations to address it. As proof, we can look at the generated bytecode and observe that the last instructions are related to the try/catch:

```
private final int loop$4(scala.collection.immutable.List, int);
    Code:
       0: aload_1
      // omitted for brevity
      61: new           #43  // class scala/MatchError
      64: dup
      65: aload_3
      66: invokespecial #46  // Method
scala/MatchError."<init>":(Ljava/lang/Object;)V
      69: athrow
      // omitted for brevity
     114: ireturn
    Exception table:
       from    to  target type
         48    61     70   Class java/io/IOException
```

We hope that these few examples have convinced you that writing a non-tail-recursive method is an easy mistake to make. Your best defense against this is to always use the @tailrec annotation to verify your intuition that your method can be optimized.

The Option data type

The Option data type is used pervasively throughout the Scala standard library. Like pattern matching, it is a language feature often adopted early by Scala beginners.
The Option data type provides an elegant way to transform and handle values that are not required, doing away with null checks often found in Java code. We assume you

understand and appreciate the value that Option brings to writing Scala in the functional paradigm, so we will not reiterate its benefits further. Instead, we focus on analyzing its bytecode representation to drive performance insights.

Bytecode representation

Inspecting the Scala source code, we see that Option is implemented as an abstract class with the possible outcomes, Some and None, extending Option to encode this relationship. The class definitions with implementations removed are shown for convenience in the following code snippet:

```
sealed abstract class Option[+A] extends Product with Serializable
final case class Some[+A](x: A) extends Option[A]
case object None extends Option[Nothing]
```

Studying the definitions, we can infer several points about the bytecode representation. Focusing on Some, we note the absence of extending AnyVal. As Option is implemented using inheritance, Some cannot be a value class due to limitations that we covered in the Value class section. This limitation implies that there is an allocation for each value wrapped as a Some instance. Furthermore, we observe that Some is not specialized. From our examination of specialization, we realize that primitives wrapped as Some instances will be boxed. Here is a simple example to illustrate both concerns:

```
def optionalInt(i: Int): Option[Int] = Some(i)
```

In this trivial example, an integer is encoded as a Some instance to be used as an Option data type. The following bytecode is produced:

```
public scala.Option<java.lang.Object> optionalInt(int);
   Code:
      0: new           #16  // class scala/Some
      3: dup
      4: iload_1
      5: invokestatic  #22  // Method
scala/runtime/BoxesRunTime.boxToInteger:(I)Ljava/lang/Integer;
      8: invokespecial #25  // Method
scala/Some."<init>":(Ljava/lang/Object;)V
     11: areturn
```

As we expected, there is an object allocation to create a Some instance, followed by the boxing of the provided integer to construct the Some instance.

The None instance is a simpler case to understand from the bytecode perspective. As None is defined as a Scala object, there is no instantiation cost to create a None instance. This makes sense because None represents a scenario where there is no state to maintain.

 Have you ever considered how the single value, None, represents no value for all the types? The answer lies in understanding the Nothing type. The Nothing type extends all other types, which allows None to be a subtype of any A type. For more insight into the Scala type hierarchy, view this useful Scala language tutorial at http://docs.scala-lang.org/tutorials/tour/unified-types.html.

Performance considerations

In any non-performance-sensitive environments, it is sensible to default to using Option to represent values that are not required. In a performance-sensitive area of the code, the choice becomes more challenging and less clear-cut. Particularly in performance-sensitive code, you must first optimize for correctness and then performance. We suggest always implementing the first version of the problem that you are modeling in the most idiomatic style, which is to say, using Option. Using the awareness gained from the bytecode representation of Some, the logical next step is to profile in order to determine whether or not Option use is the bottleneck. In particular, you are focusing on memory allocation patterns and garbage collection costs. In our experience, there are often other overhead sources present in the code that are more costly than Option use. Examples include inefficient algorithm implementation, a poorly constructed domain model, or inefficient use of system resources. If, in your case, you have eliminated other sources of inefficiency and are positive that Option is the source of your performance woes, then you need to take further steps.

An incremental step towards improved performance might include removing use of the Option higher-order functions. On the critical path, there can be significant cost savings by replacing higher-order functions with inlined equivalents. Consider the following trivial example that transforms an Option data type into a String data type:

```
Option(10).fold("no value")(i => s"value is $i")
```

On the critical path, the following change may yield substantive improvements:

```
val o = Option(10)
if (o.isDefined) s"value is ${o.get} else "no value"
```

Replacing the `fold` operation with an if statement saves the cost of creating an anonymous function. It bears repeating that this type of change should only ever be considered after extensive profiling reveals `Option` usage to be the bottleneck. While this type of code change is likely to improve your performance, it is verbose and unsafe due to usage of `o.get`. When this technique is used judiciously, you may be able to retain use of the `Option` data type in critical path code.

If replacing higher-order `Option` function use with inlined and unsafe equivalents fails to sufficiently improve performance, then you need to consider more drastic measures. At this point, profiling should reveal that `Option` memory allocation is the bottleneck, preventing you from reaching your performance goals. Faced with this scenario, you have two options (pun intended!) to explore, both of which involve a high cost in terms of time to implement.

One way to proceed is to admit that, for the critical path, `Option` is unsuitable and must be removed from the type signatures and replaced with null checks. This is the most performant approach, but it brings significant maintenance costs because you and all other team members working on the critical path must be cognizant of this modeling decision. If you choose to proceed this way, define clear boundaries for the critical path to isolate null checks to the smallest possible region of the code. In the next section, we explore a second approach that involves building a new data type that leverages the knowledge that we gained in this chapter.

Case study – a more performant option

If you are not yet ready to lose information that is encoded by the `Option` data type, then you may wish to explore alternative implementations of `Option` that are more garbage-collection-friendly. In this section, we present an alternative approach that also provides type-safety while avoiding boxing and instantiation of the `Some` instances. We leverage tagged types and specialization, and disallow null as a valid value for `Some` to come up with the following implementation:

```
sealed trait Opt

object OptOps {

  def some[@specialized A](x: A): A @@ Opt = Tag(x)
  def nullCheckingSome[@specialized A](x: A): A @@ Opt =
    if (x == null) sys.error("Null values disallowed") else Tag(x)
  def none[A]: A @@ Opt = Tag(null.asInstanceOf[A])

  def isSome[A](o: A @@ Opt): Boolean = o != null
  def isEmpty[A](o: A @@ Opt): Boolean = !isSome(o)
```

```
def unsafeGet[A](o: A @@ Opt): A =
  if (isSome(o)) o.asInstanceOf[A] else sys.error("Cannot get None")

def fold[A, B](o: A @@ Opt)(ifEmpty: => B)(f: A => B): B =
  if (o == null) ifEmpty else f(o.asInstanceOf[A])
}
```

This implementation defines factory methods to construct optional types (that is, some, nullCheckingSome, and none). In contrast to Scala's Option, this implementation uses tagged types to add type information to a value rather than creating a new value to encode optionality. The implementation of none takes advantage of null being a value in Scala rather than a language in keyword as is the case in Java. Remember, unless performance requirements required such extreme measures, we would not default to these more esoteric approaches. The tagged type returned by each factory method preserves type-safety, and it requires an explicit unwrapping to access the underlying type.

 If you would like to learn more about Scala's representation of the null value, we encourage you to check out these two StackOverflow posts at ht tp://stackoverflow.com/questions/8285916/why-doesnt-null-asinstanceofint-throw-a-nullpointerexception and http://sta ckoverflow.com/questions/10749010/if-an-int-cant-be-null-what-does-null-asinstanceofint-mean. In both posts, multiple responders provide excellent responses that will help you deepen your understanding.

The remaining methods in OptOps define methods that you would find in the implementation of Scala's Option. Rather than instance methods, we see that the methods are static because there are no new instances that are allocated by the factory methods. It is possible to define an implicit class that would provide a syntax emulating instance method invocation, but we avoid doing this because we are operating under the assumption of extreme performance sensitivity. Semantically, the operations that are defined in OptOps are equivalent to the Scala Option analogs. Instead of matching against a value representing no value (that is, None), we again take advantage of the ability to reference null as a value.

With this implementation, the runtime overhead consists of instance checking and invocations of scalaz.Tag. We lose the ability to pattern match, and instead we must either fold or, in extreme cases, use isSome and unsafeGet. To get a better understanding of runtime differences, we microbenchmarked Option creation using Scala's Option and the preceding tagged type implementation. The microbenchmark gives you a taste for the change in syntax. We encourage you to run javap to disassemble the bytecode in order to prove to yourself that this implementation avoids boxing and object creation:

```scala
class OptionCreationBenchmarks {

  @Benchmark
  def scalaSome(): Option[ShareCount] = Some(ShareCount(1))

  @Benchmark
  def scalaNone(): Option[ShareCount] = None

  @Benchmark
  def optSome(): ShareCount @@ Opt = OptOps.some(ShareCount(1))

  @Benchmark
  def optSomeWithNullChecking(): ShareCount @@ Opt =
    OptOps.nullCheckingSome(ShareCount(1))

  @Benchmark
  def optNone(): ShareCount @@ Opt = OptOps.none

  @Benchmark
  def optNoneReuse(): ShareCount @@ Opt = noShares
}

object OptionCreationBenchmarks {
  case class ShareCount(value: Long) extends AnyVal
  val noShares: ShareCount @@ Opt = OptOps.none
}
```

We run the test with the following familiar parameters:

```
sbt 'project chapter3' 'jmh:run OptionCreationBenchmarks  -foe true'
```

The results are summarized in the following table:

Benchmark	Throughput (ops per second)	Error as percentage of throughput
optNone	351,536,523.84	±0.75
optNoneReuse	344,201,145.90	±0.23
optSome	232,684,849.83	±0.37
optSomeWithNullChecking	233,432,224.39	±0.28
scalaNone	345,826,731.05	±0.35
scalaSome	133,583,718.28	±0.24

Perhaps the most impressive result here is that throughput increases approximately 57% when using the tagged type implementation of Some over the Scala-provided implementation. This is likely due to reduced memory allocation pressure. We see that None creation throughput is qualitatively similar. We also observe that there appears to be zero cost to add a null check in the construction of a tagged Some option. If you trust your team to avoid passing around null values, then the check is superfluous.

We also created a set of benchmarks to evaluate fold performance to get a sense of the relative cost of using this alternative Option implementation. Here is the source code for a simple fold benchmark:

```
class OptionFoldingBenchmarks {

  @Benchmark
  def scalaOption(): ShareCount =
    scalaSome.fold(ShareCount(0))(c => ShareCount(c.value * 2))


  @Benchmark
  def optOption(): ShareCount =
    OptOps.fold(optSome)(ShareCount(0))(c => ShareCount(c.value * 2))

}

object OptionFoldingBenchmarks {

  case class ShareCount(value: Long) extends AnyVal

  val scalaSome: Option[ShareCount] = Some(ShareCount(7))
  val optSome: ShareCount @@ Opt = OptOps.some(ShareCount(7))
}
```

This benchmark was run using the same set of parameters as before:

```
jmh:run OptionFoldingBenchmarks  -foe true
```

The results of this test are summarized in the following table:

Benchmark	Throughput (ops per second)	Error as percentage of throughput
optOption	346,208,759.51	±1.07
scalaOption	306,325,098.74	±0.41

In this benchmark we are hoping to prove that there is no significant throughput degradation when using the alternative tagged type-inspired implementation over the Scala `Option`. A significant degradation in performance would jeopardize the performance wins that we found in the creation benchmark. Fortunately, this benchmark suggests fold throughput actually increases approximately 13% over the Scala `Option` fold implementation.

It is a relief to see benchmarking yield results that confirm your hypothesis. However, it is equally important to understand why favorable results were produced, and to be able to explain this. Without an understanding of how these results happened, you are unlikely to be able to reproduce the results. How would you explain fold throughput improvement of the tagged type-inspired implementation over the Scala `Option` implementation? Consider the implementation and memory allocation differences that we covered.

The benchmarks suggest that the tagged type-inspired `Option` implementation yields qualitative performance improvements over the Scala `Option` implementation. If you are faced with a performance issue and profiling reveals the Scala `Option` to be the bottleneck, it may make sense to explore this alternative implementation. While the performance improves, realize that a tradeoff exists. When using the alternative implementation, you lose the ability to pattern match. This seems like a small price to pay because you are able to instead use the fold operation. The higher price to pay is integration with the standard library and third-party libraries. If your critical path code interacts heavily with the Scala standard library or a third-party library, you will be forced to rewrite significant chunks of code to use the alternative `Option` implementation. In this scenario, if you are under time pressure, it may make sense to reconsider whether or not modeling parts of the domain with `null` is sensible. If your critical path code avoids significant interaction with the Scala standard library or third-party libraries, then using the alternative `Option` implementation might be an easier decision.

Our case study is inspired by a novel approach Alexandre Bertails explores in his blog post at https://bertails.org/2015/02/15/abstract-algebraic-data-type/. He solves the same performance issues that we addressed by defining an approach that he refers to as abstract algebraic data types. Both approaches rely on using type constraints to model `Option` without instance allocation. By abstracting over the `Option` algebraic data type and its operations, he is able to devise an implementation free of allocations and boxing. We encourage you to explore this approach because it is another great example of how to achieve safety while still providing excellent performance.

Summary

In this chapter, we dived into the bytecode representation and performance considerations of commonly-used Scala language features. In our case study, you saw first-hand how you can combine several areas of knowledge about Scala language features in combination with the excellent Scalaz library to produce an `Option` implementation that is better suited for high-performance needs.

A consistent theme across all our examples is to promote type-safety and correctness while taking into account performance tradeoffs. As functional programmers, we value compile time correctness and referential transparency. Even with the usage of `null` in the tagged type `Option` implementation, we preserved correctness because the `null` value is an internal implementation detail. When you reflect on the strategies that we covered, consider how each one preserves referentially transparent (that is, side-effect-free) code while still enabling you to reach your performance goals.

At this point, you should feel more confident about the tradeoffs that are introduced by Scala's elegant language features. Through our analysis, you learned how to translate from concise Scala syntax to JVM bytecode. This is an invaluable skill to debug performance issues. As you practice your awareness by studying more examples, you will develop a stronger intuition for where potential problems lie. Over time, you can refer back to this chapter in order to review common remediation strategies to balance the tradeoff between elegance and safety with performance. In the next chapter, we will continue to grow our ability to leverage Scala to write performant, functional code by diving into collections.

4

Exploring the Collection API

In this chapter, we return to MVT in order to take on challenges that span multiple MVT teams. The market data team requires improved critical path order book performance to handle increased cancel request volume. The data science team wants better ad hoc data analysis tools to research trading strategies. Everyone has a problem that had to be solved yesterday. That's the start-up lifestyle!

We use the functional paradigm, our existing knowledge, and the Scala collections API to our advantage to solve these challenges. The power of the Scala language and its collections API allow you to approach problems in ways that you may not have thought possible before. As we work through these challenges and encounter new Scala collection usage, we detail collection implementation and tradeoffs to consider. We will consider the following collections in this chapter:

- List
- TreeMap
- Queue
- Set
- Vector
- Array

High-throughput systems – improving the order book

In `Chapter 1`, *The Road to Performance,* you met MVT's head trader, Dave, under tense circumstances. The financial markets underwent a period of extreme volatility that exposed a weakness in the order book design. After speaking to Dave, you learned that in volatile markets, order volume is dominated by cancels because traders are reacting to quickly changing market conditions. Through order book benchmarking and profiling, you confirmed the suspicion that under high volume, cancel performance causes high order book response latency.

Although the market volatility that caused trading losses has passed, Dave recognizes the risk that future volatility poses for MVT's returns. Dave wants to invest engineering effort into making the order book more performant when cancelations frequently occur. By working with the data science team, Dave analyzed historical order book activity over a three month period and discovered interesting market characteristics. He shares with you that in the three months analyzed, on a per trading day basis, cancels comprised, on average, 70% of order book commands. The analysis also revealed that on the most volatile market days, cancel activity represents about 85% of order book activity. Known for his puns, Dave concludes with, "Now, you know everything I know. Like the order book, we are counting on you to execute!"

Understanding historical trade-offs – list implementation

Excited to improve order book performance, your first step is to familiarize yourself with the order book implementation. As you open up the order book repository, you ping Gary, a fellow engineer who has prior order book development experience. As Gary knows the history of order book development, he tells you to check out `ListOrderBook`. "This was our first attempt at modeling the order book. I think you can learn from our design by seeing its first incarnation," he adds, "Once you understand the implementation, check out `QueueOrderBook`. That's the next version of the order book. You profiled an older iteration of this implementation when we had the volatility wave. Let me know if you have any questions!" After thanking him, you dig into the repository to find `ListOrderBook`.

The `ListOrderBook` class defines the following state to manage buys (bids) and sells (offers):

```
case class ListOrderBook(
  bids: TreeMap[Price, List[BuyLimitOrder]],
  offers: TreeMap[Price, List[SellLimitOrder]]) {
  def bestBid: Option[BuyLimitOrder] =
    ??? // hidden for brevity
  def bestOffer: Option[SellLimitOrder] =
    ??? // hidden for brevity
}
```

To refresh our memory, here are definitions of `Price`, `BuyLimitOrder`, and `SellLimitOrder`:

```
sealed trait LimitOrder {
  def id: OrderId
  def price: Price
}
case class BuyLimitOrder(id: OrderId, price: Price) extends LimitOrder
case class SellLimitOrder(id: OrderId, price: Price) extends LimitOrder
case class Price(value: BigDecimal)
```

The `LimitOrder` is an **algebraic data type (ADT)** that represents the two possible order sides. The `Price` class is a strongly-typed wrapper for `BigDecimal`. Recalling the performance boost that value classes provide, you modify the definition of `Price`, as follows:

```
case class Price(value: BigDecimal) extends AnyVal
```

The `ListOrderBook` class uses two Scala collection types to maintain its state: `List` and `TreeMap`. Let's have a deeper look at these data structures to understand the tradeoffs that they present.

List

Scala implements`List` as an immutable singly-linked list. A `List` is an ordered collection of elements of the same type. A `List` is a sealed abstract class with two implementations: `Nil`, which represents the empty list, and `::` (often called cons), which is used to represent an element and a tail. To make things more concrete, let's look at some pseudocode, which is close to the actual implementation:

```
sealed trait List[+A]
case object Nil extends List[Nothing]
case class ::[A](head: A, tail: List[A]) extends List[A]
```

A `List` of three integers can be constructed using the following notation:

```
val list = ::(1, ::(2, ::(3, Nil)))
```

> Note the plus sign in the definition of the `List` trait. The plus (+) sign indicates that `List` is covariant on its type parameter, `A`. Covariance allows you to express polymorphic constraints with generic types. To make this more concrete, consider the following definitions:
>
> ```
> sealed trait Base
> case class Impl(value: Int) extends Base
> ```
>
> Here, a relationship is expressed between `Base` and `Impl`. The `Impl` class is a subtype of `Base`. When used with `List`, covariance allows us to express that `List[Impl]` is a subtype of `List[Base]`. Expressed with an example, covariance is what allows the following snippet to compile:
>
> ```
> val bases: List[Base] = List[Impl](Impl(1))
> ```
>
> Covariance belongs to the broader topic of variances. If you wish to learn more about variances in Scala, refer to this excellent blog post by Andreas Schroeder at `https://blog.codecentric.de/en/2015/03/scala-type-system-parameterized-types-variances-part-1/`.

Unlike most other Scala collections, `List` supports pattern matching on its content. This is a powerful way to write expressive code that handles multiple scenarios while retaining compile-time safety that all possible cases are handled. Consider the following snippet:

```
List(1,2,3,4) match {
   case 1 :: x :: rest => println(s"second element: $x, rest: $rest")
}
```

In this simple pattern match, we are able to express several concerns. Here, 1 is 1, x is 2, and `rest` is `List(3,4)`. When compiled, this snippet elicits a compiler warning because the Scala compiler infers that there are possible `List` patterns that were unmatched (for example, empty `List`). Compiler-provided warnings minimize the chance of your forgetting to handle a valid input.

A `List` is optimized for prepend operations. Adding 0 to the previous list is as easy as doing this:

```
val list = ::(1, ::(2, ::(3, Nil)))
val listWithZero = ::(0, list)
```

This is a constant-time operation, and it has almost no memory cost, as `List` implements data sharing. In other words, the new list, `listWithZero`, is not a deep copy of `list`. Instead, it re-uses all its allocated elements and allocates only one new element, the cell containing `0`:

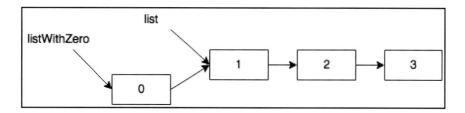

In contrast to prepend operations, append operations (that is, adding an element to the end of the list) are computationally expensive because the entire `List` must be copied:

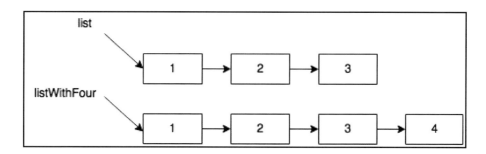

Given the poor append performance of List, you may wonder whether it is safe to use a `map` transform. A `map` transform occurs by applying a function to successive elements in the `List`, which can be logically represented by appending transformed values to a new `List`. To avoid this performance pitfall, `List.map` overrides the default implementation provided by the trait `TraversableOnce` to apply the transform using prepend operations. This provides improved `List.map` performance while retaining the same API. Overriding default behavior to provide a specialized implementation is a common Scala collections pattern. Constant time head operations make `List` ideal for algorithms involving last-in, first-out (LIFO) operations. For random access and first-in, first-out (FIFO) behaviors, you should employ `List` selectively.

In the next section, we investigate `TreeMap`. The `TreeMap` class is the implementation of the `SortedMap` trait that is used to maintain bids and offers.

TreeMap

The `TreeMap` class is a map that orders keys according to a provided ordering strategy. The following snippet of its class definition makes the ordering requirement clear:

```
class TreeMap[A, +B] private (tree: RB.Tree[A, B])(implicit val ordering:
Ordering[A])
```

The `Ordering` class is a type class that defines a contract for the natural ordering of elements of the `A` type.

 If type classes are a concept that is new to you, we encourage you to read Daniel Westheide's well-written blog post on the topic at `http://daniel westheide.com/blog/2013/02/06/the-neophytes-guide-to-scal a-part-12-type-classes.html`.

In `ListOrderBook`, we see that `Price` is the key. Looking at the companion object of `Price`, we see that the ordering is defined by delegating to the underlying `BigDecimal` type's ordering definition:

```
object Price {
  implicit val ordering: Ordering[Price] = new Ordering[Price] {
    def compare(x: Price, y: Price): Int =
      Ordering.BigDecimal.compare(x.value, y.value)
  }
}
```

The `TreeMap` class referenced by `ListOrderBook`, like `List`, is immutable. Immutability provides strong reasoning guarantees. We can be certain that there are no side effects because the effect of adding or removing a value from the map is always reflected as a new map.

The `TreeMap` class implementation is a special type of binary search tree, the red-black tree. This tree implementation provides logarithmic operation time for lookups, additions, and removals. You might be surprised to see `TreeMap` in place of `HashMap`. As documented in the Scala collections performance overview (`http://docs.scala-lang.org/overviews/collections/performance-character istics.html`), `HashMap` provides constant time lookups, additions, and removals, which is faster than `TreeMap`. However, `TreeMap` offers superior performance when performing ordered traversals. For example, finding the largest key in the map can be done in logarithmic time with `TreeMap`, while this is done in linear time for `HashMap`. This difference is an indicator that the order book implementation requires efficient ordered `Price` traversals.

Adding limit orders

Coming back to the `ListOrderBook` implementation, we see the following partial method definition reflects the heart of the order book:

```
def handle(
   currentTime: () => EventInstant,
   ob: ListOrderBook,
   c: Command): (ListOrderBook, Event) = c match {
   case AddLimitOrder(_, o) => ??? // hidden for brevity
   case CancelOrder(_, id) => ??? // hidden for brevity
}
```

It might seem curious that a function is supplied as an argument to retrieve the current time. A potentially simpler way to achieve the same effect is to invoke `System.currentTimeMillis()`. The shortcoming of this approach is that accessing the system clock is a side-effect, which means that the function is no longer referentially transparent. By providing a function to retrieve the current time, we are able to control how this side-effect happens and produce repeatable test cases.

Given a `Command`, an order book instance, and a way to obtain the current time for event timestamps, an `Event` and a new state are produced. To refresh our memory, here are the commands the order book can process:

```
sealed trait Command
case class AddLimitOrder(i: CommandInstant, o: LimitOrder) extends
Command
case class CancelOrder(i: CommandInstant, id: OrderId) extends Command
```

The following are the possible events created by processing commands:

```
sealed trait Event
case class OrderExecuted(i: EventInstant, buy: Execution,
   sell: Execution) extends Event
case class LimitOrderAdded(i: EventInstant) extends Event
case class OrderCancelRejected(i: EventInstant,
   id: OrderId) extends Event
case class OrderCanceled(i: EventInstant,
   id: OrderId) extends Event
```

Let's focus on supporting the `AddLimitOrder` command to better understand the algorithmic properties of historical design choices. When adding a limit order, one of two outcomes is possible:

- The incoming order price crosses the book resulting in `OrderExecuted`

- The oncoming order rests on the book resulting in `LimitOrderAdded`

Deducing whether or not the order crosses the book requires looking at the best price on the opposing side. Returning to the definition of `LimitOrderBook` with complete implementation of `bestBid` and `bestOffer`, we see the following:

```
case class ListOrderBook(
  bids: TreeMap[Price, List[BuyLimitOrder]],
  offers: TreeMap[Price, List[SellLimitOrder]]) {
  def bestBid: Option[BuyLimitOrder] =
    bids.lastOption.flatMap(_._2.headOption)
  def bestOffer: Option[SellLimitOrder] =
    offers.headOption.flatMap(_._2.headOption)
}
```

The implementation shows that we are taking advantage of the logarithmic ordered search property of `TreeMap`. The best bid is the key with the highest price, which is the last value in the tree because the ordering is ascending. The best offer is the key with the lowest price, which is the first value in the tree.

Focusing specifically on the addition of a buy limit order and given the best offer, the following comparison occurs to determine whether the incoming buy order crosses the book or rests on the book:

```
orderBook.bestOffer.exists(buyOrder.price.value >= _.price.value)
  match {
        case true => ??? // cross the book
        case false => ??? // rest on the book
  }
```

Let's first assume that the incoming buy order's price is lower than the best offer, which means the order is added to the book (that is, rests on the book). The question we are trying to answer is, "where in the book should the order be added?" The order book performs a logarithmic search to find the price level associated with the order price. From the definition of `ListOrderBook`, you know that each value in the map (the price level) is represented as a `List` of orders. Recalling a discussion with the head trader, Dave, you remember that orders within a price level are executed based on time priority. The first order added to a price level is the first order to be executed. Conceptually, a price level is a first-in, first-out (FIFO) queue. The implication is that adding an order to a price level is a linear time operation because the order is appended to the end. The following snippet confirms your hypothesis:

```
val orders = orderBook.bids.getOrElse(buyOrder.price, Nil)
        orderBook.copy(bids = orderBook.bids + (buyOrder.price ->
orders.:+(buyOrder))) ->
```

```
LimitOrderAdded(currentTime())
```

The snippet shows that adding a resting limit order to the book involves a linear time append operation to `List` of `BuyLimitOrder`. In your mind, you are beginning to wonder how MVT was able to trade profitably at all with this order book. Before leaping to this harsh judgment, you consider how crossing the book is handled.

Assuming that the incoming buy order's price is greater than or equal to the best offer price, then the buy order crosses the book, causing an execution. Time priority dictates that the first sell order received is executed against the incoming buy order, which translates to taking the first sell order in the price level. When generating an execution, you realize that modeling a price level with a `List` provides constant time performance. The following snippet shows how a price level is modified on a buy execution:

```
        case (priceLevel, (sell :: Nil)) => (orderBook.copy(offers =
    orderBook.offers - sell.price),
            OrderExecuted(currentTime(), Execution(buy.id, sell.price),
                Execution(sell.id, sell.price)))
        case (_, (sell :: remainingSells)) => (orderBook.copy(offers =
    orderBook.offers + (sell.price -> remainingSells)),
            OrderExecuted(currentTime(),
                Execution(buy.id, sell.price), Execution(sell.id, sell.price)))
```

The `ListOrderBook` takes advantage of the `List` pattern matching to handle the two possible cross scenarios:

- The executed sell order is the only order available in the price level
- Additional sell orders remain at the price level

In the former scenario, the price level is removed from the book by removing the key from the offers `TreeMap`. In the latter scenario, the remaining orders form the new price level. Clearly, the order book is optimized for executions over adding resting orders. You wonder why this bias exists in the order book implementation. You wonder to yourself, "perhaps, executions are more much more prevalent than resting orders?" You are unsure and make a mental note to chat with Dave.

 Pause for a moment to consider biases in systems that you have designed. Did you optimize operations proportional to usage or latency constraints? Looking back, did your design choices lead you towards the best possible performance for the most important operations? Of course, hindsight makes it easy to call out suboptimal design choices. By reflecting on how you made these choices, you might be better able to avoid similar deficiencies in future systems.

Canceling orders

The `ListOrderBook` also supports the `CancelOrder` command to remove an existing order by ID. Cancel requests pose an algorithmic challenge to `ListOrderBook`. As only the order ID is provided, `ListOrderBook` cannot efficiently determine which side the order rests on (that is, buy or sell). To determine the side, the buy and sell price levels are swept to find the order ID. This is an operation that is proportional to the number of price levels per side and the length of each price level. The worst case scenario is submitting an order ID that does not exist in the order book. The entire book must be swept to identify the absence of the provided order ID. A malicious trader could slow down MVT order book operations by submitting a constant stream of nonexistent order IDs. You make a note to talk with Dave about malicious trading activities and what MVT can do to defend against them.

Assuming that the order referenced by the cancel request exists in the book and its price level is discovered, the act of removing the cancelled order from the book is also expensive. Canceling is a linear time operation that requires traversing the linked list of orders and removing the node with the matching order ID. The following snippet implements canceling a sell order in `ListOrderBook`:

```
orderBook.offers.find { case (price, priceLevel) => priceLevel.exists(_.id
== idToCancel) }
        .fold[(ListOrderBook, Event)](orderBook ->
        OrderCancelRejected(currentTime(), idToCancel)) {
        case (price, priceLevel) =>
          val updatedPriceLevel = priceLevel.filter(_.id != idToCancel)
          orderBook.copy(offers = updatedPriceLevel.nonEmpty match {
            case true => orderBook.offers + (price -> updatedPriceLevel)
            case false => orderBook.offers - price
          }) -> OrderCanceled(currentTime(), idToCancel)
```

Studying this snippet, it is unsurprising to you that cancelation performance is the least performant order book operation. There are two linear time passes performed per price level to cancel the order. First, `exists` traverses the list of price level orders to determine whether the ID to be canceled exists in the price level. Once the price level containing the ID is found, there is a second traversal via `filter` to update the state of the order book.

The cancelation implementation in `ListOrderBook` is an illustration of the double-edged sword of Scala's expressive collection API. By virtue of being expressive, the cancelation logic is simple to understand and to maintain. However, its expressiveness also makes it easy to hide that the runtime performance of removing an order from a price level is $2 * N$, where N is the number of orders in a price level. This simple example makes it clear that in a performance-sensitive environment, it is important to take a step back from the code to consider the runtime overhead of the data structure that is being used.

The current order book – queue implementation

You refrain from judging `ListOrderBook` too harshly because you know from your prior software development experiences that there were likely extenuating circumstances that led to this implementation. You turn your attention to the current order book implementation, which is in `QueueOrderBook`. Looking over the source code, you are surprised to discover the implementation appears to match `ListOrderBook` except for the price level data structure:

```
case class QueueOrderBook(
   bids: TreeMap[Price, Queue[BuyLimitOrder]],
   offers: TreeMap[Price, Queue[SellLimitOrder]])
```

The only difference between the two implementations is the use of `scala.collection.immutable.Queue` in place of `List` to represent a price level. From a modeling perspective, using a FIFO queue makes sense. As time priority dictates execution order, a FIFO queue is a natural fit to store resting orders. You begin wondering whether switching out `List` for `Queue` was done purely for modeling purposes. The question on your mind is, "how does replacing `List` with `Queue` improve order book performance?" Understanding this change requires digging deeper into Scala's `Queue` implementation.

Queue

This snippet of a `Queue` definition reveals an interesting insight:

```
class Queue[+A] protected(protected val in: List[A], protected val out:
List[A])
```

Without reading deeply into the `Queue` implementation, we see that it uses two `List`s to manage state. Given the usage of `List` to model a FIFO queue in `ListOrderBook`, it should not be surprising to see the usage of `List` to build an immutable FIFO queue data structure. Let's look at the enqueue and dequeue operations to understand how in and out impact `Queue` performance. The following snippet shows the implementation of enqueue:

```
def enqueue[B >: A](elem: B) = new Queue(elem :: in, out)
```

As the element is prepended to `in`, enqueueing is a constant time operation. Recall that the analogous `ListOrderBook` operation is adding a resting order, which has linear runtime performance. This is a clear performance win for `QueueOrderBook`. Next, we consider dequeue implementation:

```
def dequeue: (A, Queue[A]) = out match {
   case Nil if !in.isEmpty => val rev = in.reverse ; (rev.head, new
```

```
Queue (Nil, rev.tail))
      case x :: xs            => (x, new Queue(in, xs))
      case _                  => throw new NoSuchElementException("dequeue on
empty queue")
   }
```

 As the implementation shows, dequeue throws an exception when invoked with an empty `Queue`. The exception is an unexpected outcome to invoking `dequeue` and feels out of place in the functional programming paradigm. For this reason, `Queue` also provides `dequeueOption` that returns an `Option`. This makes the handling of an empty `Queue` explicit and easier to reason about. We recommend using `dequeueOption` in any situation where you cannot guarantee that `dequeue` will always be called on a nonempty `Queue`.

The `dequeue` operation is more involved than `enqueue` due to the interaction between `in` and `out`. To understand how the `Queue` state is managed with the `dequeue` operations, review the following table. This table walks through a series of the `enqueue` and `dequeue` operations, listing the state of `in` and `out` at each step. As you review the table, consider which `dequeue` patterns match statements that are invoked:

Operation	In	Out
enqueue(1)	List(1)	Nil
enqueue(2)	List(1, 2)	Nil
enqueue(3)	List(1, 2, 3)	Nil
dequeue	Nil	List(2, 3)
dequeue	Nil	List(3)
enqueue(4)	List(4)	List(3)
dequeue	List(4)	Nil
dequeue	Nil	Nil

As the `enqueue` and `dequeue` invocations are intermingled, both `in` and `out` retain state. In the final sequence displayed, the queue returns to its initial state (that is, both `in` and `out` empty). The key insight from this implementation is that `Queue` amortizes the cost of `dequeue` to be constant time by deferring transfers from `in` and `out`. Each element transfer from `in` and `out` is a linear time `reverse` operation to maintain first-in, first-out ordering. Deferring the cost of this expensive operation until `out` is empty is a form of lazy evaluation. This is an illustrative example of how lazy evaluation can be used to improve runtime performance.

Now that you have an understanding of how `Queue` is implemented, you can reason about the performance improvements delivered by `QueueOrderBook`. The following table itemizes the runtime performance of each scenario to modify a price level:

Scenario	ListOrderBook	QueueOrderBook
Add resting limit order	Linear	Constant
Generate execution	Constant	Amortized constant
Cancel order	Linear	Linear

This table illustrates how understanding the runtime characteristics of the Scala collection API can result in tangible performance wins with small changes to your implementation. Recall that when `QueueOrderBook` was introduced, it was noted that its implementation is identical to `ListOrderBook`, the module changes to replace `List` operations with analogous `Queue` operations. This is a comparatively simple change for the performance boost shown previously.

You are excited to see the performance win to handle limit orders with `QueueOrderBook`, but you are left wondering about what can be done about cancelation performance. It remains unsettling to you that `QueueOrderBook` retains the same cancelation performance. In particular, because of the recent market volatility that exposed order book cancelation performance's weakness that caused MVT to trade unprofitably. Lazy evaluation was a big performance win to handle limit orders. Can this principle also be applied to cancel requests?

Improved cancellation performance through lazy evaluation

Queue provides high-performance `enqueue` and `dequeue` operations using the additional state, the second `List`, to defer and to batch expensive operations. This principle can be applied to the order book. When canceling an order, there are two expensive operations:

- Identifying the price level containing the order-to-be-canceled
- Traversing a `Queue` or `List` to remove the canceled order

Focusing on the second operation, the motivating question is, "how can the order book defer the cost of linear traversal to modify internal state?" To answer this question, it is often helpful to consider the strengths of your implementation. With either order book implementation, we know there is excellent execution performance. One strategy that takes advantage of this insight is to defer cancellation until order execution occurs. The approach is to use additional state to maintain the intent to cancel without removing the order from order book state until it is performant to do so. This approach could look like the following:

```
case class LazyCancelOrderBook(
  pendingCancelIds: Set[OrderId],
  bids: TreeMap[Price, Queue[BuyLimitOrder]],
  offers: TreeMap[Price, Queue[SellLimitOrder]])
```

The `LazyCancelOrderBook` class adds additional state in the form of a `scala.collection.immutable.Set` to manage the IDs of canceled requests that have not been reflected into the the state of `bids` and `offers`. Before diving into how `pendingCancelIds` is used, let's investigate the Scala implementation of `Set`.

Set

Scala's implementation of `Set` is neither an ADT, such as `List`, nor a concrete implementation, such as `TreeMap`. Instead, it is a trait, as shown in this snippet of its definition:

```
trait Set[A]
```

The reason the standard library defines it is as a trait is to support specific implementations depending upon the element count. The `Set` companion object defines five implementations for sizes zero to four. Each implementation contains a fixed number of elements, as shown in `Set3`, as follows:

```
class Set3[A] private[collection] (elem1: A, elem2: A, elem3: A)
```

When the number of elements is small, the runtime performance is faster with hand-rolled `Set` implementations. With this technique, additions and removals point to the next or previous hand-rolled implementation. For example, consider + and – from `Set3`:

```
def + (elem: A): Set[A] =
  if (contains(elem)) this
  else new Set4(elem1, elem2, elem3, elem)

def - (elem: A): Set[A] =
  if (elem == elem1) new Set2(elem2, elem3)
  else if (elem == elem2) new Set2(elem1, elem3)
```

```
        else if (elem == elem3) new Set2(elem1, elem2)
        else this
```

After Set 4, the standard library uses an implementation named HashSet. This is visible when adding an element to Set 4:

```
    def + (elem: A): Set[A] =
        if (contains(elem)) this
        else new HashSet[A] + (elem1, elem2, elem3, elem4, elem)
```

The HashSet is analogous to TreeMap because it is backed by an efficient data structure to manage internal state. For HashSet, the backing data structure is a hash trie. The hash trie provides amortized constant time performance for additions, removals, and contains operations as per the Scala collections performance overview
(http://docs.scala-lang.org/overviews/collections/performance-character istics.html). If you want to dig deeper into how a hash trie works, the Scala hash trie overview
(http://docs.scala-lang.org/overviews/collections/concrete-immutable-co llection-classes.html#hash-tries) is a good starting point.

Returning to the LazyCancelOrderBook, we now know that common set operations with pendingCancelIds are completed in amortized constant time. Provided that we focus on additions and removals, and contains operations, this suggests there will be minimal overhead as the size of the set increases. We can use pendingCancelIds to represent the intent to remove an order from the order book without paying the cost of performing the removal. This simplifies the handling of a cancel order to be a constant time addition to pendingCancelIds:

```
    def handleCancelOrder(
        currentTime: () => EventInstant,
        ob: LazyCancelOrderBook,
        id: OrderId): (LazyCancelOrderBook, Event) =
        ob.copy(pendingCancelIds = ob.pendingCancelIds + id) ->
          OrderCanceled(currentTime(), id)
```

The implementation of handleCancelOrder becomes trivial because the work to remove the order from the book is deferred. While this is a performance win, this implementation suffers from a serious deficiency. This implementation is no longer able to identify order IDs that are absent from the order book, which result in OrderCancelRejected. One way to account for this requirement is to maintain an additional Set containing order IDs actively resting on the book. Now, the LazyCancelOrderBook state looks like the following:

```
    case class LazyCancelOrderBook(
```

```
    activeIds: Set[OrderId],
    pendingCancelIds: Set[OrderId],
    bids: TreeMap[Price, Queue[BuyLimitOrder]],
    offers: TreeMap[Price, Queue[SellLimitOrder]]])
```

With this definition, we can rewrite `handleCancelOrder` to account for nonexistent order IDs:

```
def handleCancelOrder(
    currentTime: () => EventInstant,
    ob: LazyCancelOrderBook,
    id: OrderId): (LazyCancelOrderBook, Event) =
    ob.activeIds.contains(id) match {
      case true => ob.copy(activeIds = ob.activeIds - id,
        pendingCancelIds = ob.pendingCancelIds + id) ->
        OrderCanceled(currentTime(), id)
      case false => ob -> OrderCancelRejected(currentTime(), id)
    }
```

This implementation involves three amortized, constant time operations when the order ID exists in the book. First, there is an operation to identify whether or not the order ID exists in the order book. Then, the provided order ID is removed from the active ID set and added to the pending cancel set. Previously, this scenario required two linear runtime operations. The degenerate scenario of handling a nonexistent order ID now shrinks to a single amortized constant time operation.

Before celebrating performance wins, bear in mind that we still need to remove canceled orders from the book. To reduce the cost of cancelations, two potentially large sets were added to the order book, which increases the size of the memory footprint and garbage collection pressure. Additionally, benchmarking is needed to prove that theoretical performance improvements translate to real-world performance.

To complete `LazyCancelOrderBook` implementation, we need to account for `activeIds` when handling a limit order and `pendingCancelIds` when generating an execution. As you may recall, handling a limit order involved two scenarios:

- Adding a resting limit order
- Crossing the book to generate an execution

Here is a partially implemented snippet that prepares us to handle these two scenarios for a `BuyLimitOrder`:

```
orderBook.bestOffer.exists(_.price.value <= buy.price.value) match {
        case true => ??? // crossing order
        case false => ???  // resting order
```

To support resting buy orders, the provided buy order must be enqueued and additionally, the buy order ID must be added to the `activeOrderIds` set:

```
def restLimitOrder: (LazyCancelOrderBook, Event) = {
   val orders = orderBook.bids.getOrElse(buy.price, Queue.empty)
   orderBook.copy(bids = orderBook.bids + (buy.price ->
orders.enqueue(buy)),
      activeIds = orderBook.activeIds + buy.id) ->
LimitOrderAdded(currentTime())
   }

orderBook.bestOffer.exists(_.price.value <= buy.price.value) match {
      case true => ??? // crossing order
      case false => restLimitOrder
```

The logic to add a resting limit order is shown in the preceding code and extracted into a method named `restLimitOrder`. This logic resembles the analogous scenario for `ListOrderBook` with the added amortized constant time active order ID addition operation. This change is straightforward and adds little processing time overhead. Finally, we consider the more complicated order crossing scenario. This scenario is analogous to `Queue.dequeue` in that this implementation pays the cost of the deferred action. The first dilemma to solve is identifying which order can be executed and which orders must be removed because they are canceled. `findActiveOrder` supplies this functionality and is shown with the assumption that `orderBook` is lexically in scope, as follows:

```
@tailrec
def findActiveOrder(
   q: Queue[SellLimitOrder],
   idsToRemove: Set[OrderId]): (Option[SellLimitOrder],
Option[Queue[SellLimitOrder]], Set[OrderId]) =
   q.dequeueOption match {
      case Some((o, qq)) => orderBook.pendingCancelIds.contains(o.id)
match {
         case true =>
            findActiveOrder(qq, idsToRemove + o.id)
         case false =>
            (Some(o), if (qq.nonEmpty) Some(qq) else None, idsToRemove +
o.id)
      }
      case None => (None, None, idsToRemove)
   }
```

`findActiveOrder` recursively inspects a sell price level until an executable order is found or the price level is empty. In addition to optionally resolving a sell order that can be executed, the method returns the remaining price level. These order IDs have been canceled and must be removed from `pendingCancelIds`. Here, we see the bulk of the canceled work deferred when the cancel request was handled. Execution is now amortized to be a constant time operation when executions occur repeatedly without a cancelation in-between. The worst case scenario is a linear runtime that is proportional to the number of canceled orders in the price level. Let's look at how `findActiveOrder` is used to update the state of the order book:

```
orderBook.offers.headOption.fold(restLimitOrder) {
        case (price, offers) => findActiveOrder(offers, Set.empty) match {
            case (Some(o), Some(qq), rms) => (orderBook.copy(
                offers = orderBook.offers + (o.price -> qq), activeIds =
orderBook.activeIds -- rms),
                OrderExecuted(currentTime(),
                    Execution(buy.id, o.price), Execution(o.id, o.price)))
            case (Some(o), None, rms) => (orderBook.copy(
                offers = orderBook.offers - o.price, activeIds =
orderBook.activeIds -- rms),
                OrderExecuted(currentTime(),
                    Execution(buy.id, o.price), Execution(o.id, o.price)))
            case (None, _, rms) =>
                val bs = orderBook.bids.getOrElse(buy.price,
Queue.empty).enqueue(buy)
                (orderBook.copy(bids = orderBook.bids + (buy.price -> bs),
                    offers = orderBook.offers - price,
                    activeIds = orderBook.activeIds -- rms + buy.id),
                    LimitOrderAdded(currentTime()))
        }
    }
```

Order crossing implementation is now arguably more complicated than in `ListOrderBook` or `QueueOrderBook` due to the work to remove canceled orders and to remove the removed order IDs from `pendingCancelIds`. In all three pattern match statements, the set of returned order IDs returned as the final tuple member is removed from `pendingCancelIds` to indicate that the order is now removed from the book. The first two pattern match statements handle the distinction between finding an active order with one or more remaining orders in the price level and finding an active order with zero remaining orders in the price level. In the latter scenario, the price level is removed from the book. The third pattern match statement accounts for the scenario where an active order is not found. If an active order is not found because all orders were pending cancelation, then, by definition, the entire price level was searched, and it is, therefore, now empty.

Benchmarking LazyCancelOrderBook

As a rigorous performance engineer, you realize that although your code compiles and your tests pass, your work is not yet complete. You begin pondering how to benchmark `LazyCancelOrderBook` to determine whether or not your changes have improved real-world performance. Your first idea is to test cancelation in isolation to confirm that this operation has indeed been optimized. To do this, you rework `CancelBenchmarks`, which was introduced in `Chapter 2`, *Measuring Performance on the JVM*, to work with `QueueOrderBook` and `LazyCancelOrderBook`. This benchmark sweeps different price level sizes canceling the first order, the last order, and a nonexistent order. We omit the source code because it is identical to the previous implementation and instead consider the results. These results were produced by running the following:

```
sbt 'project chapter4' 'jmh:run CancelBenchmarks -foe true'
```

The benchmark provides us with the following results:

Benchmark	Enqueued order count	Throughput (ops per second)	Error as percentage of throughput
eagerCancelFirstOrderInLine	1	6,912,696.09	± 0.44
lazyCancelFirstOrderInLine	1	25,676,031.5	± 0.22
eagerCancelFirstOrderInLine	10	2,332,046.09	± 0.96
lazyCancelFirstOrderInLine	10	12,656,750.43	± 0.31
eagerCancelFirstOrderInLine	1	5,641,784.63	± 0.49
lazyCancelFirstOrderInLine	1	25,619,665.34	± 0.48
eagerCancelFirstOrderInLine	10	1,788,885.62	± 0.39
lazyCancelFirstOrderInLine	10	13,269,215.32	± 0.30
eagerCancelFirstOrderInLine	1	9,351,630.96	± 0.19
lazyCancelFirstOrderInLine	1	31,742,147.67	± 0.65
eagerCancelFirstOrderInLine	10	6,897,164.11	± 0.25
lazyCancelFirstOrderInLine	10	24,102,925.78	± 0.24

This test demonstrates that `LazyCancelOrderBook` consistently outperforms `QueueOrderBook` when canceling the first order, the last order, and a nonexistent order across order queue sizes of one and ten. This is exactly as expected because `LazyCancelOrderBook` defers the most expensive work until an order is executed. We see constant performance independent of the position of the order-to-be-canceled, which is further proof that the removal work is deferred. Also as expected, we see that canceling a nonexistent order results in improved performance because a linear traversal is no longer required to ascertain the absence of an order. However, we notice the performance hit as the enqueued order count increases from one to ten for `LazyCancelOrderBook`. We can hypothesize that the nearly 50% throughput reduction is due to the overhead of managing the state of active and pending cancel order IDs.

This result is a promising sign that your changes are indeed improving the real-world performance. As the new implementation passed the initial litmus test, you think about how to representatively simulate a combination of executions and cancelations. You decide to focus on creating a microbenchmark that combines executions and cancelations to exercise `LazyCancelOrderBook` in scenarios that more closely resemble production. You think back to a recent lunch conversation you had with Dave about market trading flows and recall that he said it is common to see about two cancelations per execution. Running with this idea, you create a benchmark that interleaves trades and cancelations. For both order book implementations, you want to test performance when during the following scenarios:

- Two trades per cancelation
- One trade per cancelation
- Two cancelations per trade

These three scenarios will help reveal shortcomings in `LazyCancelOrderBook` by focusing on production-like order book activities. The benchmark requires initializing each order book with a set of resting orders to be canceled or executed against. The following snippet demonstrates how to initialize the order books in a JMH test:

```scala
@State(Scope.Benchmark)
  class InterleavedOrderState {
    var lazyBook: LazyCancelOrderBook = LazyCancelOrderBook.empty
    var eagerBook: QueueOrderBook = QueueOrderBook.empty

    @Setup
    def setup(): Unit = {
      lazyBook = (1 to maxOrderCount).foldLeft(LazyCancelOrderBook.empty) {
        case (b, i) => LazyCancelOrderBook.handle(
          () => EventInstant.now(), b, AddLimitOrder(
            CommandInstant.now(), BuyLimitOrder(OrderId(i), bidPrice)))._1
```

```
        }
        eagerBook = (1 to maxOrderCount).foldLeft(QueueOrderBook.empty) {
          case (b, i) => QueueOrderBook.handle(
            () => EventInstant.now(), b, AddLimitOrder(
              CommandInstant.now(), BuyLimitOrder(OrderId(i), bidPrice)))._1
        }
      }
    }
```

Before each trial, both order books will be filled with `maxOrderCount` (defined to be 30) resting bids. As there are three scenarios to test and two order books, there are six benchmarks defined for this test. Each set of three scenarios is the same per order book implementation. To avoid duplication, the following snippet shows the three benchmarks implemented for `LazyCancelOrderBook`:

```
@Benchmark
  def lazyOneToOneCT(state: InterleavedOrderState): LazyCancelOrderBook = {
    val b1 = LazyCancelOrderBook.handle(() => EventInstant.now(),
      state.lazyBook, firstCancel)._1
    LazyCancelOrderBook.handle(() => EventInstant.now(),
      b1, firstCrossSell)._1
  }

@Benchmark
  def lazyTwoToOneCT(state: InterleavedOrderState): LazyCancelOrderBook = {
    val b1 = LazyCancelOrderBook.handle(() => EventInstant.now(),
      state.lazyBook, firstCancel)._1
    val b2 = LazyCancelOrderBook.handle(() => EventInstant.now(),
      b1, secondCancel)._1
    LazyCancelOrderBook.handle(() => EventInstant.now(),
      b2, firstCrossSell)._1
  }

@Benchmark
  def lazyOneToTwoCT(state: InterleavedOrderState): LazyCancelOrderBook = {
    val b1 = LazyCancelOrderBook.handle(() => EventInstant.now(),
      state.lazyBook, firstCancel)._1
    val b2 = LazyCancelOrderBook.handle(() => EventInstant.now(),
      b1, firstCrossSell)._1
    LazyCancelOrderBook.handle(() => EventInstant.now(),
      b2, secondCrossSell)._1
  }
```

These benchmarks follow the convention of denoting the cancelation frequency ("C") first and the trade frequency ("T") second. For example, the final benchmark implements the scenario that represents one cancelation for every two trades. The commands are defined as values out-of-scope to avoid generating garbage during benchmark invocation. The benchmark invocation looks like the following:

```
sbt 'project chapter4' 'jmh:run InterleavedOrderBenchmarks -foe true'
```

This invocation produces the following results:

Benchmark	Throughput (ops per second)	Error as percentage of throughput
eagerOneToTwoCT	797,339.08	± 2.63
lazyOneToTwoCT	1,123,157.94	± 1.26
eagerOneToOneCT	854,635.26	± 2.48
lazyOneToOneCT	1,469,338.46	± 1.85
eagerTwoToOneCT	497,368.11	± 0.72
lazyTwoToOneCT	1,208,671.60	± 1.69

Across the board, LazyCancelOrderBook outperforms QueueOrderBook. The relative difference between lazy and eager performance shows an interesting relationship. The following table captures the relative performance difference:

Benchmark	LazyCancelOrderBook percentage performance improvement
OneToTwoCT	141.00%
OneToOneCT	172.00%
TwoToOneCT	243.00%

Studying the preceding table, we observe that LazyCancelOrderBook shows the greatest performance win when there are two cancelations per trade. This result demonstrates the benefit of deferring the cost of processing a cancelation request. The next trend that we see is that as the frequency of trades increases and the frequency of cancelations decreases, QueueOrderBook performance improves relative to LazyCancelOrderBook. This result makes sense because LazyCancelOrderBook incurs extra costs when performing a trade. In addition to searching for canceled orders, LazyCancelOrderBook must update activeIds. The QueueOrderBook avoids these costs, but we see the overwhelming cost of cancelation processing continues to overshadow `QueueOrderBook` performance. Summarizing these results, we have more confidence that `LazyCancelOrderBook` is a stand-in replacement for `QueueOrderBook`. In scenarios involving heavy volumes of cancelations, it appears to be a clear winner, and in other scenarios, it appears to maintain parity with `QueueOrderBook`.

Lessons learned

In this section, we leveraged Scala collections, in conjunction with the judicious use of lazy evaluation, to improve the performance of a critical component in MVT's infrastructure. By working through several order book implementations, you learned first-hand how a well-suited data structure can improve performance while a less optimal choice can derail performance. This exercise also exposed you to how Scala implements several of its collections, which you can now use to your advantage when working on a performance problem.

`LazyCancelOrderBook` illustrates how valuable deferred evaluation can be in a performance-sensitive environment. When faced with a performance challenge, ask yourself the following questions to see whether it is possible to defer work (CPU work, not your actual work!). The following table lists each question and how it was answered with the order book:

Question	Application to order book example
How can I decompose into smaller discrete chunks?	The act of canceling was decomposed into identifying the event that was sent to the requester and removing the canceled order from the book state.
Why am I performing all of these steps now?	Originally, order removal happened eagerly because it was the most logical way to model the process.
Can I change any constraints to allow me to model the problem differently?	Ideally, we would have liked to remove the constraint requiring rejection of nonexistent orders. Unfortunately, this was out of our control.
What operations in my system are most performant?	Executing an order and resting an order on the book are the most performant operations. We leveraged fast execution time to perform removals of canceled orders from the book.

Like any approach, deferred evaluation is not a panacea. Diligent benchmarking and profiling are necessary to validate the benefit delivered by the change. Arguably the implementation of `LazyCancelOrderBook` is more complicated than `QueueOrderBook`, which will increase the cost to maintain the system. In addition to making implementation more complicated, it is now more difficult to reason about runtime performance due to the variable cost of order execution. For the scenarios that we tested, `LazyCancelOrderBook` remained at parity with or better than `QueueOrderBook`. However, we only exercised a few of the many possible scenarios, and we did so with only a single price level in the order book. In a real-world environment, additional benchmarking and profiling are needed to build enough confidence that this new implementation delivers better performance.

Historical data analysis

You have done great work with the order book, and we hope, have learned valuable skills along the way! It is now time to explore a new facet of MVT's activities. A group of expert traders and data scientists are constantly studying historical market data to design performant trading strategies. Until now, the company has not had the luxury of allocating technical resources to this team. As a result, this group has been using clunky, unreliable, and under-performing tools to analyze market data and build elaborate trading strategies. With a performant order book, the top priority is to focus on improving the strategies implemented by the company. Your new best friend, Dave, has explicitly asked for you to join the team and help them modernize their infrastructure.

Lagged time series returns

The main tool used by the team is a simple program designed to compute lagged time series returns from historical trade execution data. So far, this tool has been a big disappointment. Not only does it return mostly invalid results, it is also slow and fragile. Before diving into the code, Dave gives you a short presentation of the business rules involved. Return time series are derived from midpoint time series. A midpoint is calculated on each minute, and it is based on the bid and ask prices of each trade execution. Consider the following table as a simple example:

Execution time	Bid price	Ask price	Midpoint
01/29/16 07:45	2.3	2.5	2.55
01/29/16 07:46	2.1	2.4	2.25
01/29/16 07:47	2.9	3.4	3.15

| 01/29/16 07:48 | 3.2 | 3.4 | 3.3 |
| 01/29/16 07:49 | 3.1 | 3.3 | 3.2 |

The formula to calculate a midpoint is *(bid_price + ask_price) / 2*. For example, the midpoint at 01/29/16 07:47 is *(2.9 + 3.4) / 2*, that is, 3.15.

 In the real world, a midpoint would be weighed by the volume of the transaction, and the time series would use a more fine-grained time unit, such as seconds or even milliseconds. To keep the example simple, we disregard the volume dimension by assuming a volume of 1 for all executions. We also focus on calculating one data point per minute instead of a more granular time series that would use seconds or even milliseconds.

A series of midpoints is used to compute a series of returns. A series of returns is defined for a certain rollup value in minutes. To calculate the three minute return at time t_3, the formula is: $(midpoint\_at\_t_3 - midpoint\_at\_t_0) / midpoint\_at\_t_0$. We also multiply the result by 100 to use percentages. If we use the previous midpoint series to calculate a three minute return series, we obtain the following table:

Time	Midpoint	3 minute return
01/29/16 07:45	2.55	N/A
01/29/16 07:46	2.25	N/A
01/29/16 07:47	3.15	N/A
01/29/16 07:48	3.3	22.73
01/29/16 07:49	3.2	29.69

Note that the first three midpoints do not have a corresponding three minute return as there is no midpoint that is old enough to be used.

You are now familiar with the domain and can have a look at the existing code. Starting with this model:

```
case class TimestampMinutes(value: Int) extends AnyVal {
  def next: TimestampMinutes = TimestampMinutes(value + 1)
}
```

```
case class AskPrice(value: Int) extends AnyVal
case class BidPrice(value: Int) extends AnyVal
case class Execution(time: TimestampMinutes, ask: AskPrice, bid: BidPrice)

case class Midpoint(time: TimestampMinutes, value: Double)
object Midpoint {
  def fromAskAndBid(time: TimestampMinutes,askPrice: AskPrice,
    bidPrice: BidPrice): Midpoint =
    Midpoint(time, (bidPrice.value + askPrice.value) / 2D)
}

case class MinuteRollUp(value: Int) extends AnyVal
case class Return(value: Double) extends AnyVal

object Return {
  def fromMidpoint(start: Midpoint, end: Midpoint): Return =
    Return((end.value - start.value) / start.value * 100)
}
```

Everything looks straightforward. Note that prices, midpoints, and returns are represented as `Int` and `Double`. We assume that our system is able to normalize the prices as integers instead of decimals. This simplifies our code, and also improves the performance of the program since we use primitive `Double` instead of, for example, `BigDecimal` instances. `TimestampMinutes` is similar to the more commonly used Epoch timestamp, but only down to the minute (see `https://en.wikipedia.org/wiki/Unix_time`).

After studying the model, we look at the existing implementation of the `computeReturnsWithList` method:

```
def computeReturnsWithList(
  rollUp: MinuteRollUp,
  data: List[Midpoint]): List[Return] = {
  for { i <- (rollUp.value until data.size).toList} yield
Return.fromMidpoint(data(i - rollUp.value), data(i))
  }
```

This method assumes that the list of midpoint received as input is already sorted by execution time. This randomly accesses various indices of the list to read the midpoints that are required to compute each return. To compute the second return value (index 1 in the returned list) with a rollup value of three minutes, we access elements at index 4 and 1 in the input list. The following diagram provides a visual reference for how returns are computed:

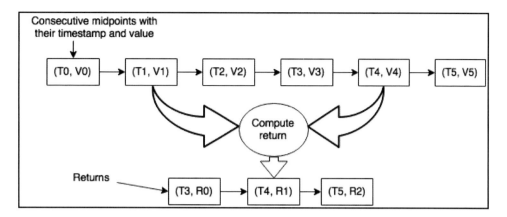

You have been warned that this method is slow, but it is also incorrect. Dave has verified many times that it returns incorrect results. Before tackling the performance issue, you have to handle the correctness problem. Optimizing an incorrect approach would not be a good use of your time and, therefore, of the company's money! Rapidly, you realize that this method puts too much trust in the data that it is fed. For this algorithm to work, the input list of midpoints has to do the following:

- This has to be properly sorted by execution time, from the oldest to the newest execution
- This has to have no more than one midpoint per minute
- This has to not contain any minutes without a midpoint, that is, it has no missing data points

You bring this up to Dave to better understand how the midpoint series is generated. He explains that it is loaded from sequential logs that are recorded by the order book. It is certain that the list is sorted by execution time. Also, he assures you that considering the large volume of trades handled by the order book, it is impossible to have a minute without a single execution. However, he acknowledges that it is more than likely that more than one midpoint is computed for the same execution time. It looks like you have found the problem causing invalid returns. Fixing it should not be too complicated, and you think that it is now time to reflect on the performance issue.

We spent time studying the structure of a singly-linked list in the previous section. You know that it is optimized for operations involving the head and the tail of the list. On the contrary, randomly accessing an element by its index is an expensive operation requiring linear time. To improve midpoint execution performance, we turn to a data structure with improved random access performance: Vector.

Vector

To improve the performance of our system, we should reconsider the data structure that stores `Midpoint` values. A good option is to replace `List` with `Vector`, another Scala collection provided by the standard library. The `Vector` is an efficient collection that provides effectively constant time random access. The cost of random access operations depends on various assumptions, such as, the maximum length of the `Vector`. The `Vector` is implemented as an ordered tree data structure called a trie. In a trie, the keys are the indices of the values stored in the `Vector` (to learn more about tries and their use cases, see `https://en.wikipedia.org/wiki/Trie`). As `Vector` implements the `Seq` trait, just like `List`, modifying the existing method is straightforward:

```
def computeReturnsWithVector(
  rollUp: MinuteRollUp,
  data: Vector[Midpoint]): Vector[Return] = {
  for {
    i <- (rollUp.value until data.size).toVector
  } yield Return.fromMidpoint(data(i - rollUp.value), data(i))
}
```

Changing the type of the collection is enough to switch to a more performant implementation. To make sure that we actually improved the performance, we devise a simple benchmark that is designed to use a few hours of historical trade executions and measure the throughput of each implementation. The results are as follows:

Benchmark	Return rollup in minutes	Throughput (ops per second)	Error as percentage of throughput
computeReturnsWithList	10	534.12	± 1.69
computeReturnsWithVector	10	49,016.77	± 0.98
computeReturnsWithList	60	621.28	± 0.64
computeReturnsWithVector	60	51,666.50	± 1.64
computeReturnsWithList	120	657.44	± 1.07
computeReturnsWithVector	120	43,297.88	± 0.99

Not only does `Vector` yield significantly better performance, it delivers the same throughput regardless of the size of the rollup. As a general rule, it is better to use `Vector` as a default implementation for immutable indexed sequences. Vector effectively provides constant time complexity not only for element random access but also for head and tail operations, as well as to append and prepend elements to an existing `Vector`.

The implementation of `Vector` is a tree structure of parity 32. Each node is implemented as an array of size 32, and it can store either up to 32 references to child nodes or up to 32 values. This 32-ary tree structure explains why the complexity of `Vector` is "effectively constant" instead of "constant". The real complexity of the implementation is log(32, N), where N is the size of the vector. This is considered close enough to actual constant time. This collection is a good choice to store very large sequences because the memory is allocated in chunks of 32 elements. These chunks are not preallocated for all levels of the tree, but only allocated as needed.

Until Scala 2.10, one downside of `Vector` as compared to `List` was the lack of pattern matching support. This is now fixed and you can pattern-match an instance of `Vector` in the same way you pattern match a `List`. Consider this short example of a method pattern matching a `Vector` to access and return its third element or return `None` if it contains fewer than three elements:

```scala
def returnThirdElement[A](v: Vector[A]): Option[A] = v match {
  case _ +: _ +: x +: _ => Some(x)
    case _ => None
}
```

Invoking this method in the REPL demonstrates that pattern matching can be applied, as follows:

```scala
scala> returnThirdElement(Vector(1,2,3,4,5))
res1: Option[Int] = Some(3)
```

Data clean up

The return algorithm is now blazingly fast. That is, blazingly fast to return incorrect results! Remember that we still have to handle some edge cases and clean up the input data. Our algorithm only works if there is exactly one midpoint per minute, and Dave informed us that we are likely to see more than one midpoint computed for the same minute.

To handle this problem, we create a dedicated `MidpointSeries` module and make sure that an instance of `MidpointSeries`, wrapping a series of `Midpoint` instances, is properly created without duplicates:

```scala
class MidpointSeries private(val points: Vector[Midpoint]) extends AnyVal
object MidpointSeries {

  private def removeDuplicates(v: Vector[Midpoint]): Vector[Midpoint] = {
    @tailrec
    def loop(
      current: Midpoint,
```

```scala
      rest: Vector[Midpoint],
      result: Vector[Midpoint]): Vector[Midpoint] = {
      val sameTime = current +: rest.takeWhile(_.time == current.time)
      val average = sameTime.map(_.value).sum / sameTime.size

      val newResult = result :+ Midpoint(current.time, average)
      rest.drop(sameTime.size - 1) match {
        case h +: r => loop(h, r, newResult)
        case _ => newResult
      }
    }

    v match {
      case h +: rest => loop(h, rest, Vector.empty)
      case _ => Vector.empty
    }
  }

  def fromExecution(executions: Vector[Execution]): MidpointSeries = {
    new MidpointSeries(removeDuplicates(
      executions.map(Midpoint.fromExecution)))
  }
```

Our `removeDuplicates` method uses a tail recursive method (Refer to `Chapter 3`, *Unleashing Scala Performance*). This groups all the midpoints with the same execution time, calculates the average value of these data points, and builds a new series with these average values. Our module provides a `fromExecution` factory method to build an instance of `MidpointSeries` from a `Vector` of `Execution`. This factory method calls `removeDuplicates` to clean up the data.

To improve our module, we add our previous `computeReturns` method to the `MidpointSeries` class. That way, once constructed, an instance of `MidpointSeries` can be used to compute any return series:

```scala
  class MidpointSeries private(val points: Vector[Midpoint]) extends AnyVal {

    def returns(rollUp: MinuteRollUp): Vector[Return] = {
      for {
        i <- (rollUp.value until points.size).toVector
      } yield Return.fromMidpoint(points(i - rollUp.value), points(i))
    }
  }
```

This is the same code that we previously wrote, but this time, we are confident that `points` does not contain duplicates. Note that the constructor is marked `private`, so the only way to instantiate an instance of `MidpointSeries` is via our factory method. This guarantees that it is impossible to create an instance of `MidpointSeries` with a "dirty" `Vector`. You release this new version of the program, wish good luck to Dave and his team, and leave for a well deserved lunch break.

As you return, you are surprised to find Vanessa, one of the data scientists, waiting at your desk. "The return series code still doesn't work", she says. The team was so excited to finally be given a working algorithm that they decided to skip lunch to play with it. Unfortunately, they discovered some inconsistencies with the results. You try to collect as much data as possible, and spend an hour looking at the invalid results that Vanessa is talking about. You noticed that they all involved trade executions for two specific symbols: FOO and BAR. A surprisingly small amount of trades is recorded for these symbols, and it is not unusual for several minutes to elapse between trade executions. You questioned Dave about these symbols. He explains that these are thinly traded tickers, and it is expected to see a lower trading volume for them. The problem is now clear to you. The midpoint series recorded for these symbols do not fulfill one of the prerequisite of your algorithm: at least one execution per minute. You refrain from reminding Dave that he assured you this situation was impossible and start working on a fix. The trader is always right!

You are not confident that you can rework the algorithm to make it more robust while preserving the current throughput. A better option would be to find a way to clean up the data to generate the missing data points. You seek advice from Vanessa. She explains that it would not disturb the trading algorithm to perform a linear extrapolation of the missing data points, based on the surrounding existing points. You write a short method to extrapolate a midpoint at a certain time using the previous and following points (respectively, a and b in the following snippet):

```
private def extrapolate(a: Midpoint,b: Midpoint, time: TimestampMinutes):
Midpoint = {
 val price = a.value +
   ((time.value - a.time.value) / (b.time.value - a.time.value)) *
     (b.value - a.value)
 Midpoint(time, price)
}
```

With this method, we can write a clean up method that follows the model of the previously mentioned `removeDuplicates` function to preprocess the data:

```
private def addMissingDataPoints(
  v: Vector[Midpoint]): Vector[Midpoint] = {
 @tailrec
 def loop(
```

```
                previous: Midpoint,
                rest: Vector[Midpoint],
                result: Vector[Midpoint]): Vector[Midpoint] = rest match {
                case current +: mPoints if previous.time.value == current.time.value - 1
      =>
                    // Nothing to extrapolate, the data points are consecutive
                    loop(current, mPoints, result :+ previous)

                case current +: mPoints if previous.time.value < current.time.value - 1
      =>
                    //Need to generate a data point
                    val newPoint = extrapolate(previous, current, previous.time.next)
                    loop(newPoint, rest, result :+ previous)

                case _ => result :+ previous
            }

        v match {
            case h +: rest => loop(h, rest, Vector.empty)
            case _ => Vector.empty
        }
    }
```

Our internal tail-recursive method handles the case where two points are already consecutive, and the case where a point is missing. In the latter case, we create a new point with our extrapolate method and insert it in the result Vector. Note that we use this new point to extrapolate consecutive missing points. We update our factory method to perform this additional clean up after removing possible duplicates:

```
def fromExecution(executions: Vector[Execution]): MidpointSeries = {
  new MidpointSeries(
    addMissingDataPoints(
      removeDuplicates(
        executions.map(Midpoint.fromExecution))))
}
```

We now have the assurance that our input data is clean and ready to be used by our return series algorithm.

Handling multiple return series

The team is impressed by the improvements that you implemented, and by how quickly you were able to fix the existing code. They mention a project they have had in mind for a while without knowing how to approach it. A couple of weeks ago, Vanessa designed a machine learning algorithm to evaluate trading strategies over several tickers, based on their return series. This algorithm requires that all the return series involved contain the same amount of data points. Your previous changes already took care of this requirement. However, another condition is that the return values must be normalized or scaled. A feature is a machine learning term for an individual measurable property. In our example, each return data point is a feature. Feature scaling is used to standardize the range of possible values to ensure that broad ranges of values do not distort a learning algorithm. Vanessa explains that scaling features will help her algorithm to deliver better results. Our program will handle a set of return series, compute a scaling vector, and calculate a new set of normalized return series.

Array

For this system, we consider switching from `Vector` to `Array`. `Array` is a mutable, indexed collection of values. It provides real constant complexity for random access, as opposed to `Vector`, which implements this operation in effectively constant time. However, contrary to `Vector`, `Array` is allocated once as a single and contiguous chunk of memory. Furthermore, it does not permit append and prepend operations. A Scala `Array` is implemented with a Java `Array`, which is memory optimized. A Scala `Array` is more user-friendly than the native Java `Array`. Most methods that are available on other Scala collections are made available when using `Array`. Implicit conversions are used to augment `Array` with `ArrayOps` and `WrappedArray`. `ArrayOps` is a simple wrapper for `Array` to temporarily enrich `Array` with all the operations found in indexed sequences. Methods called on `ArrayOps` will yield an `Array`. On the contrary, a conversion from `Array` to `WrappedArray` is permanent. Transformer methods called on `WrappedArray` yield another `WrappedArray`. We see this in the standard library documentation, as follows:

```
val arr = Array(1, 2, 3)
val arrReversed = arr.reverse    // arrReversed is an Array[Int]
val seqReversed: Seq[Int] = arr.reverse
// seqReversed is a WrappedArray
```

Having decided to use `Array` for our new module, we start working on the code to scale the features of each return series:

```
class ReturnSeriesFrame(val series: Array[Array[Return]]) {
  val scalingVector: Array[Double] = {
    val v = new Array[Double](series.length)
    for (i <- series.indices) {
      v(i) = series(i).max.value
    }
    v
```

```
    }
  }
```

A scaling vector is computed for a set of series. The first value of the vector is used to scale the first series, the second value for the second series, and so on. The scaling value is simply the greatest value in the series. We can now write the code to use the scaling vector and compute the normalized version of the frame:

```
object ReturnSeriesFrame {
  def scaleWithMap(frame: ReturnSeriesFrame): ReturnSeriesFrame = {
   new ReturnSeriesFrame(
      frame.series.zip(frame.scalingVector).map {
  case (series, scaling) => series.map(point => Return(point.value /
  scaling))
      })
  }
}
```

We zip each series with its scaling value, and create a new scaled return series. We can compare the presented version of the code using `Array` with another, almost identical, implementation using `Vector` (this code is omitted here for brevity, but it can be found in the source code attached to the book):

Benchmark	Series Size	Throughput in operations per second	Error as percentage of throughput
normalizeWithVector	60	101,116.50	± 0.85
normalizeWithArray	60	176,260.52	± 0.68
normalizeWithVector	1,440	4,077.74	± 0.71
normalizeWithArray	1,440	7,865.85	± 1.39
normalizeWithVector	28,800	282.90	± 1.06
normalizeWithArray	28,800	270.36	± 1.85

These results show that `Array` performs better than `Vector` for shorter series. As the size of the series increases, their respective performances are on-par. We can even see that the throughput is identical for a series containing 20 days of data (28,800 minutes). For larger sequences, the locality of `Vector` and its memory allocation model alleviate the difference with `Array`.

Our implementation is idiomatic: it uses higher-order functions and immutable structures. However, using transform functions, such as `zip` and `map`, creates new instances of `Array`. An alternative is to leverage the mutable nature of `Array` to limit the amount of garbage generated by our program.

Looping with the Spire cfor macro

Scala supports two loop constructs: the `for` loop and the `while` loop. The latter, in spite of its good performance characteristics, is usually avoided in functional programming. It requires the usage of mutable state and `var` to keep track of the looping condition. In this section, we will show you a technique to take advantage of `while` loop performance that prevents mutable references from leaking into application code.

Spire is a numeric library written for Scala that allows developers to write efficient numeric code. Spire leverages patterns, such as, type classes, macros, and specialization (remember specialization from `Chapter 3`, *Unleashing Scala Performance*). You can learn more about Spire at `https://github.com/non/spire`.

One of the macros made available by Spire is `cfor`. Its syntax is inspired from the more traditional for loop that is encountered in Java. In the following implementation of feature scaling, we use the `cfor` macro to iterate over our series and normalize the values:

```
def scaleWithSpire(frame: ReturnSeriesFrame): ReturnSeriesFrame = {
  import spire.syntax.cfor._

  val result = new Array[Array[Return]](frame.series.length)

  cfor(0)(_ < frame.series.length, _ + 1) { i =>
    val s = frame.series(i)
    val scaled = new Array[Return](s.length)
    cfor(0)(_ < s.length, _ + 1) { j =>
      val point = s(j)
      scaled(j) = Return(point.value / frame.scalingVector(i))
    }
    result(i) = scaled
  }

  new ReturnSeriesFrame(result)
}
```

This example highlights that `cfor` macros can be nested. The macro is essentially syntactic sugar that compiles to a Scala `while` loop. We can examine the following generated bytecode to prove this:

```
public highperfscala.dataanalysis.ArrayBasedReturnSeriesFrame
scaleWithSpire(highperfscala.dataanalysis.ArrayBasedReturnSeriesFrame);
    Code:
        0: aload_1
        1: invokevirtual #121              // Method
highperfscala/dataanalysis/ArrayBasedReturnSeriesFrame.series:()[[Lhighperf
scala/dataanalysis/Return;
        4: arraylength
        5: anewarray      #170              // class
"[Lhighperfscala/dataanalysis/Return;"
        8: astore_2
        9: iconst_0
       10: istore_3
       11: iload_3
    [... omitted for brevity]
       39: iload           6
    [... omitted for brevity]
       82: istore          6
       84: goto            39
    [... omitted for brevity]
       95: istore_3
       96: goto            11
       99: new             #16              // class
highperfscala/dataanalysis/ArrayBasedReturnSeriesFrame
      102: dup
      103: aload_2
      104: invokespecial #19               // Method
highperfscala/dataanalysis/ArrayBasedReturnSeriesFrame."<init>":([[Lhighper
fscala/dataanalysis/Return;)V
      107: areturn
```

We notice the two `goto` statements, instructions 96 and 84, which are used to loop back respectively to the beginning of the outer loop and the inner loop (which respectively begin with instructions 11 and 39). We can run a benchmark of this new implementation to confirm the performance gain:

Benchmark	Series size	Throughput (ops per second)	Error as percentage of throughput
normalizeWithArray	60	176,260.52	± 0.68
normalizeWithCfor	60	256,303.49	± 1.33
normalizeWithArray	1,440	7,865.85	± 1.39
normalizeWithCfor	1,440	11,446.47	± 0.89
normalizeWithArray	28,800	270.36	± 1.85
normalizeWithCfor	28,800	463.56	± 1.51

The macro, which is compiled to a while loop, is able to deliver better performance. Using the `cfor` construct, we are able to retain performance while avoiding the introduction of multiple vars. Although this approach sacrifices immutability, the scope of mutability is limited and less error-prone than an equivalent implementation using an imperative `while` or `for` loop.

Summary

In this chapter, we explored and experimented with various collection implementations. We discussed the underlying representation, complexity, and use cases of each data structure. We also introduced a third-party library, Spire, to improve the performance of our programs. Some of the implementations presented drifted away from typical functional programming practices, but we were able to restrict the use of mutable state to internal modules, while still exposing functional public APIs. We expect that you are eager to learn more, but in the next chapter, we will become lazy! In contrast to this chapter, which focused on eager collections, we turn our attention to lazy collections in the next chapter.

5
Lazy Collections and Event Sourcing

In the last chapter, we explored a number of Scala collections that readily perform evaluations eagerly. The Scala standard library provides two collections that operate lazily: views and streams. To motivate an exploration of these collections, we will tackle another performance dilemma at MVT revolving around performance reports that are generated for clients. In this chapter, we will cover the following topics:

- Views
- Stream processing with two real-world applications
- Event sourcing
- Markov chain generation

Improving the client report generation speed

Wanting to learn more about the customers of MVT, you decide to attend the weekly client status meeting. As you look around, you see that you are the only engineer here and everyone else is from the sales team. Johnny, the head of the MVT client management team, runs through a list of newly-signed on clients. Each time he reads off a name, a loud bell is rung. It seems like a strange custom to you, but the sales team is excitedly cheering each time the bell rings.

After the new client listing ends and the ringing in your ears stops, one of the sales team members asks Johnny, "When will the performance reports be generated faster? Clients are calling me everyday complaining about the inability to see their positions and profits and losses during the trading day. It's embarrassing that we do not have this kind of transparency, and we will lose business because of this." You realize that the report in question is a PDF that can be downloaded via the private web portal that is exposed by MVT to clients. Unless a client is sophisticated enough to set up his or her own reporting using MVT's performance API, then the client is dependent upon the portal to inspect recent trading performance.

Realizing that this is an opportunity to better understand the issue, you ask, "Hi, I'm from the engineering team. I thought I would sit in today to learn more about our clients. Can you share more about the reporting performance problem? I'd like to help address the concern." Through conversation with the sales team, you learn that the PDF report is a first step towards a real-time streaming web app. The PDF report allows MVT to quickly give trading performance insight to clients. Each time the client clicks **View Performance**, a report is generated that summarizes the performance trend by displaying whether or not the client has realized a profit or a loss in the last hour, day, and seven days. Particularly when the market is volatile, you learn that clients are more likely to generate reports. The sales team thinks this exacerbates the issue because reports generate even slower when everyone is trying to see recent trading performance. In some of the worst cases, the performance report takes about a dozen minutes to generate, which is totally unacceptable to clients that expect near real-time results.

Diving into the reporting code

Eager to dig into the problem, you find the repository that is responsible for working with reporting data. You explore the domain model to understand the concerns represented in this scope:

```scala
case class Ticker(value: String) extends AnyVal
case class Price(value: BigDecimal) extends AnyVal
case class OrderId(value: Long) extends AnyVal
case class CreatedTimestamp(value: Instant) extends AnyVal
case class ClientId(value: Long) extends AnyVal

sealed trait Order {
  def created: CreatedTimestamp
  def id: OrderId
  def ticker: Ticker
  def price: Price
  def clientId: ClientId
}
case class BuyOrder(created: CreatedTimestamp, id: OrderId, ticker: Ticker,
price:    Price, clientId: ClientId) extends Order

case class SellOrder(created: CreatedTimestamp, id: OrderId, ticker:
```

```
Ticker, price: Price,clientId: ClientId) extends Order

case class Execution(created: CreatedTimestamp, id: OrderId, price: Price)
```

In the reporting context, linking orders to executions is important to build the performance trend report because this association allows MVT to identify the profit or loss realized from the trade. `ClientId` is a concept that you have not worked with before when working on the order book or performing data analysis. The client ID is used to identify an MVT client's account. As trades are executed on behalf of clients, the client ID allows us to link an executed order to a client account.

Scanning the code base, you spot the representation of a performance trend report before it is converted into PDF format:

```
sealed trait LastHourPnL
case object LastHourPositive extends LastHourPnL
case object LastHourNegative extends LastHourPnL

sealed trait LastDayPnL
case object LastDayPositive extends LastDayPnL
case object LastDayNegative extends LastDayPnL

sealed trait LastSevenDayPnL
case object LastSevenDayPositive extends LastSevenDayPnL
case object LastSevenDayNegative extends LastSevenDayPnL

case class TradingPerformanceTrend(
  ticker: Ticker,
  lastHour: LastHourPnL,
  lastDay: LastDayPnL,
  lastSevenDay: LastSevenDayPnL)
```

The **profit and loss (PnL)** trend is represented by distinct ADTs for each supported time period: the last hour, last day, and last seven days. For each stock ticker, these three time periods are included in `TradingPerformanceTrend`. Across multiple tickers, you infer a client can identify whether or not MVT is generating a profit or a loss over time. Inspecting the signature of the `trend` method which is responsible for computing `TradingPerformanceTrend`, you confirm your thinking:

```
def trend(
  now: () => Instant,
  findOrders: (Interval, Ticker) => List[Order],
  findExecutions: (Interval, Ticker) => List[Execution],
  request: GenerateTradingPerformanceTrend):
List[TradingPerformanceTrend]
```

```
case class GenerateTradingPerformanceTrend(
  tickers: List[Ticker], clientId: ClientId)
```

Computing the performance trend requires a way to determine the current time in order to determine how far to look back to compute each time period's trend. The `findOrders` and `findExecutions` arguments are functions that query the reporting data store for orders and executions that were created within a time interval for a particular ticker. The final argument contains the client's ID and the tickers to report on. Each period's trend is computed by a generalized inner-method named `periodPnL`, which looks like the following:

```
def periodPnL(
  duration: Duration): Map[Ticker, PeriodPnL] = {
  val currentTime = now()
  val interval = new Interval(currentTime.minus(duration), currentTime)
  (for {
    ticker <- request.tickers
    orders = findOrders(interval, ticker)
    executions = findExecutions(interval, ticker)
    idToExecPrice = executions.groupBy(_.id).mapValues(es =>
      Price.average(es.map(_.price)))
    signedExecutionPrices = for {
      o <- orders
      if o.clientId == request.clientId
      price <- idToExecPrice.get(o.id).map(p => o match {
        case _: BuyOrder => Price(p.value * -1)
        case _: SellOrder => p
      }).toList
    } yield price
    trend = signedExecutionPrices.foldLeft(PnL.zero) {
      case (pnl, p) => PnL(pnl.value + p.value)
    } match {
      case p if p.value >= PnL.zero.value => PeriodPositive
      case _ => PeriodNegative
    }
  } yield ticker -> trend).toMap
}
```

The `periodPnL` method is an involved method that contains several logical steps. For each client-provided ticker, the associated orders and executions for the provided time period are retrieved. In order to correlate orders with executions, a map of `OrderId` to `Execution` is built by using `groupBy`. To simplify later calculations, the average execution price of each executed order is computed to reduce multiple executions for a single order to a single value.

With the `idToExecPrice` lookup table built, the next logical step is to filter out orders for other clients. Once only the client's orders remain, `idToExecution` is used to identify the orders that executed. The final two steps compute the performance trend by tabulating the client's absolute return (that is, profit and loss). The steps involve two additions to the domain model, as follows:

```
case class PnL(value: BigDecimal) extends AnyVal
object PnL {
  val zero: PnL = PnL(BigDecimal(0))
}

sealed trait PeriodPnL
case object PeriodPositive extends PeriodPnL
case object PeriodNegative extends PeriodPnL
```

The `PnL` value is a value class that is used to represent the client's dollar return. `PeriodPnL` is analogous to the previously introduced ADT that can be applied to any time period of data. This allows `PeriodPnL` to be reused for the last hour, last day, and last seven days trend computations.

When the trade represents a buy, the execution price is negated because the transaction represents cash being exchanged for stock. When the trade represents a sell, the execution price remains positive because the transaction represents exchanging stock for cash. After computing the performance trend for each ticker, the `List` of the `Ticker` and `PeriodPnL` tuples is converted to a `Map`.

Digesting this implementation, you can start to imagine why generating this PDF is time-consuming. There is no sign of caching results, which means that the trend report is recomputed each time a client makes a request. As the number of clients requesting reports increases, there is an increased wait time while reports are computed. Re-architecting the reporting infrastructure to cache reports is too large a near-term change. Instead, you try to identify incremental changes that can improve report generation performance.

Using views to speed up report generation time

When working on the order book, we learned that `List` eagerly evaluates results. This property means that, in `periodPnL`, the de-sugared for-comprehension `filter` and `map` operations performed on `orders` produce new lists. That is, each transformation produces a new collection. For customers with large order counts, it can be costly in terms of CPU time to iterate over an order set three times, in addition to incurring garbage collection costs due to repeated `List` creation. To ameliorate this concern, Scala provides a way to defer transforming elements until an element is needed by a downstream computation.

Conceptually, this is done by adding a view on top of the eagerly evaluated collection that allows transformations to be defined with deferred evaluation semantics. A lazily evaluated view of a collection can be constructed from any Scala collection by invoking `view`. For example, this snippet creates a view from a `List` of integers:

```
val listView: SeqView[Int, List[Int]] = List(1, 2, 3).view
```

From this snippet, we learn that Scala represents a view into a collection with a different `SeqView` type that is parameterized by two types: the collection element, and the collection type. Seeing a view in use makes it easier to understand its runtime differences with an eagerly evaluated collection. Consider the following snippet performing the same operations on a `List` and a view over a `List`:

```
println("List evaluation:")
val evens = List(0, 1, 2, 3, 4, 5).map(i => {
  println(s"Adding one to $i")
  i + 1
}).filter(i => {
  println(s"Filtering $i")
  i % 2 == 0
})

println("--- Printing first two even elements ---")
println(evens.take(2))

println("View evaluation:")
val evensView = List(0, 1, 2, 3, 4, 5).view.map(i => {
  println(s"Adding one to $i")
  i + 1
}).filter(i => {
  println(s"Filtering $i")
  i % 2 == 0
})

println("--- Printing first two even elements ---")
println(evensView.take(2).toList)
```

This snippet performs simple arithmetic and then filters to find the even elements. For the sake of deepening our understanding, the snippet breaks the functional paradigm by adding the `println` side effect. The output of the list evaluation is as expected:

```
List evaluation:
Adding one to 0
Adding one to 1
Adding one to 2
Adding one to 3
Adding one to 4
```

```
Adding one to 5
Filtering 1
Filtering 2
Filtering 3
Filtering 4
Filtering 5
Filtering 6
--- Printing first two even elements ---
List(2, 4)
```

With eager evaluation, each transformation is applied to each element before moving to the next transformation. Now, consider the following output from view evaluation:

```
View evaluation:
--- Printing first two even elements ---
Adding one to 0
Filtering 1
Adding one to 1
Filtering 2
Adding one to 2
Filtering 3
Adding one to 3
Filtering 4
List(2, 4)
```

As we discussed earlier, with lazy evaluation no transformations are applied until an element is needed. In this example, this means that the addition and filtering do not occur until the invocation of `toList`. The absence of output after "view evaluation" is evidence that zero transformations occurred. Curiously, we also see that only the first four of six elements are evaluated. When a view applies transformations, it applies all transformations to each element rather than applying each transformation to all elements. By applying all transformations in one step, the view is able to return the first two elements without evaluating the entire collection. Here, we see the potential performance gains from view usage due to lazy evaluation. Before applying the concept of views to the performance trend report, let's take a deeper look at view implementation.

Constructing a custom view

Views are able to defer evaluation by returning a data structure that composes the previous transformation state with the next transformation. The Scala implementation of views is admittedly complicated to digest because it provides a large number of capabilities while retaining support for all Scala collections. To build an intuition for how views are implemented, let's construct our own lazily evaluated view that works only for `List` and only supports `map` operations. To begin, we define the operations that are supported by our implementation of a `PseudoView` view:

```
sealed trait PseudoView[A] {
  def map[B](f: A => B): PseudoView[B]
  def toList: List[A]
}
```

The `PseudoView` is defined as a trait that supports lazy application of a transformation from A to B and also supports evaluating all transformations to return a `List`. Next, we define two view types of view to support the initial case when zero transformations have been applied and to support applying a transformation to a previously transformed view. The signatures are shown in the following snippet:

```
final class InitialView[A](xs: List[A]) extends PseudoView[A]
final class ComposedView[A, B](xs: List[A], fa: A => B) extends
PseudoView[B]
```

In both scenarios, the original `List` must be carried through to support eventually applying the transformations. In the `InitialView` base case, there are zero transformations, which is why there is no additional state. `ComposedView` supports chaining computations by carrying the state of the previous `fa` transformation.

Implementing `InitialView` is a straightforward delegation to `ComposedView`:

```
final class InitialView[A](xs: List[A]) extends PseudoView[A] {
  def map[B](f: A => B): PseudoView[B] = new ComposedView[A, B](xs, f)
  def toList: List[A] = xs
}
```

The `List` implementation shows how transformations are chained together using function composition:

```
final class ComposedView[A, B](xs: List[A], fa: A => B) extends
PseudoView[B] {
  def map[C](f: B => C): PseudoView[C] = new ComposedView(xs,
f.compose(fa))
  def toList: List[B] = xs.map(fa)
}
```

Let's construct a `PseudoView` companion object that provides view construction, as follows:

```
object PseudoView {
  def view[A, B](xs: List[A]): PseudoView[A] = new InitialView(xs)
}
```

We can now exercise `PseudoView` with a simple program to demonstrate that it defers evaluation:

```
println("PseudoView evaluation:")
val listPseudoView = PseudoView.view(List(0, 1, 2)).map(i => {
  println(s"Adding one to $i")
  i + 1
}).map(i => {
  println(s"Multiplying $i")
  i * 2
})

println("--- Converting PseudoView to List ---")
println(listPseudoView.toList)
```

Running this program, we see output equivalent to usage of Scala's view implementation:

```
PseudoView evaluation:
--- Converting PseudoView to List ---
Adding one to 0
Multiplying 1
Adding one to 1
Multiplying 2
Adding one to 2
Multiplying 3
List(2, 4, 6)
```

`PseudoView` helps build an intuition about how Scala implements views. From here, you can begin considering how to support other operations. For example, how can `filter` be implemented? The `filter` is interesting to consider because it constrains the original collection. As defined, `PseudoView` is ill-equipped to support the `filter` operations, which is one illustration of the complexity that is handled by Scala views. Scala views tackles this challenge by defining a trait named `Transformed`. The `Transformed` trait is the base trait for all view operations. A partial definition is shown, as follows:

```
trait Transformed[+B] extends GenTraversableView[B, Coll] {
  def foreach[U](f: B => U): Unit
  lazy val underlying = self.underlying
}
```

The `underlying` lazy value is how the originally wrapped collection is accessed. This is analogous to how `PseudoView` passed the `List` state into `ComposedView`. `Transformed` defines a side-effecting `foreach` operation to support collection operations in a lazy manner. Using `foreach` allows implementations of this trait to modify the underlying collection. This is how `filter` is implemented:

```
trait Filtered extends Transformed[A] {
  protected[this] val pred: A => Boolean
  def foreach[U](f: A => U) {
    for (x <- self)
      if (pred(x)) f(x)
  }
}
```

`Transformed` is used within the view API to maintain the state of necessary operations, while the external API supports interacting with `SeqView`. Following another pattern that is commonly found in Scala collections, `SeqView` inherits a number of operations by mixing in other traits. `SeqView` indirectly mixes in `TraversableViewLike`, which provides access to the `Transformed` operations.

Applying views to improve report generation performance

With our newly-developed intuition for views, we may view (no pun intended!) the construction of performance trend reports differently. Scala's implementation of views makes it trivial to switch from eagerly evaluated collections to a lazily evaluated version. If you recall, once the order ID to the average execution price lookup table is constructed, a series of transformations are applied to the orders that are retrieved for the duration and ticker. By converting `orders` to a view, there is an opportunity to avoid unnecessary transformations and improve the speed of the performance trend report.

While it is trivial to convert to a view, it is less trivial to identify under which conditions lazy evaluation out-performs eager evaluation. As a good performance engineer, you want to benchmark your proposed change, but you do not have access to historical order and execution data to build a benchmark. Instead, you write a microbenchmark that simulates the problem that you are modeling. The question that you are trying to answer is, "For what size collection and what number of operations does it make sense to use a view over a `List`?" There is a cost to constructing a view because it involves retaining information about the deferred transformation, which implies it will not always be the most performant solution. You come up with the following scenarios to help answer your question:

```
@Benchmark
def singleTransformList(state: ViewState): List[Int] =
  state.numbers.map(_ * 2)

@Benchmark
def singleTransformView(state: ViewState): Vector[Int] =
  state.numbers.view.map(_ * 2).toVector
```

```scala
@Benchmark
def twoTransformsList(state: ViewState): List[Int] =
  state.numbers.map(_ * 2).filter(_ % 3 == 0)

@Benchmark
def twoTransformsView(state: ViewState): Vector[Int] =
  state.numbers.view.map(_ * 2).filter(_ % 3 == 0).toVector

@Benchmark
def threeTransformsList(state: ViewState): List[Int] =
  state.numbers.map(_ * 2).map(_ + 7).filter(_ % 3 == 0)

@Benchmark
def threeTransformsView(state: ViewState): Vector[Int] =
  state.numbers.view.map(_ * 2).map(_ + 7).filter(_ % 3 == 0).toVector
```

For each collection type, a `List`, and a view over a `Vector`, you define three tests that exercise an increasing number of transformations. `Vector` is used instead of `List` because `toList` on a view is not specialized for `List`. As we have previously seen, `List` operations are written to take advantage of constant time and prepend performance. The `toList` performs linear time append operations, which gives the false impression that views deliver lower performance. Switching to `Vector` provides effectively constant time append operations. The state for this benchmark looks like the following:

```scala
@State(Scope.Benchmark)
class ViewState {

  @Param(Array("10", "1000", "1000000"))
  var collectionSize: Int = 0

  var numbers: List[Int] = Nil

  @Setup
  def setup(): Unit = {
    numbers = (for (i <- 1 to collectionSize) yield i).toList
  }
}
```

`ViewState` sweeps different collection sizes to help identify how sensitive view performance is to collection size. The benchmark is invoked via the following:

```
sbt 'project chapter5' 'jmh:run ViewBenchmarks -foe true'
```

This invocation produces the following results:

Benchmark	Collection size	Throughput (ops per second)	Error as percentage of throughput
singleTransformList	10	15,171,067.61	± 2.46
singleTransformView	10	3,175,242.06	± 1.37
singleTransformList	1,000	133,818.44	± 1.58
singleTransformView	1,000	52,688.80	± 1.11
singleTransformList	1,000,000	30.40	± 2.72
singleTransformView	1,000,000	86.54	± 1.17
twoTransformsList	10	5,008,830.88	± 1.12
twoTransformsView	10	4,564,726.04	± 1.05
twoTransformsList	1,000	44,252.83	± 1.08
twoTransformsView	1,000	80,674.76	± 1.12
twoTransformsList	1,000,000	22.85	± 3.78
twoTransformsView	1,000,000	77.59	± 1.46
threeTransformsList	10	3,360,399.58	± 1.11
threeTransformsView	10	3,438,977.91	± 1.27
threeTransformsList	1,000	36,226.87	± 1.65
threeTransformsView	1,000	58,981.24	± 1.80
threeTransformsList	1,000,000	10.33	± 3.58
threeTransformsView	1,000,000	49.01	± 1.36

The results give us an interesting insight into the cases where using a view yields better performance. For a small collection, such as 10 elements in our benchmark, a List performs better, regardless of the amount of operations, although this gap closes at 1,000,000 elements. When transforming a large collection, 1,000,000 elements in our benchmark, a view is more efficient with an increasing differential as the number of transformations increases. For example, with 1,000,000 elements and two transformations, views deliver approximately triple the throughput of List. In the case of a medium size collection, such as 1,000 elements in this example, this is not as clear-cut. When performing a single transformation, an eager `List` performs better, while a view delivers better throughput when applying more than one transformation.

As the volume of your data and the transformation count increase, it becomes more likely that a view offers better performance. Here, you see the tangible benefit of avoiding intermediate collections. A second axis of performance to consider is the nature of the transformation. Transformations that benefit from early termination (for example, `find`), benefit strongly from lazy evaluation. This benchmark illustrates that it is important to understand the size of your data and the transformations that you intend to perform.

View caveats

Views offer a simple way to improve performance with minimally invasive changes to your system. The ease of use is part of the allure of views, which may tempt you to use them more frequently than you otherwise would. As our benchmarking in the previous section shows, there is a nontrivial overhead to using views, which means defaulting to views is a suboptimal choice. Looking past the pure performance perspective, there are other reasons to tread carefully when using views.

SeqView extends Seq

As views mirror the collection API, it can be a challenge to identify when transformations are being applied lazily. For this reason, we recommend setting well-defined boundaries for view usage. When working on client reporting, we limited view usage to a single inner-function and used a `List` eager collection type as the return type. Minimizing the area of a system performing a lazy evaluation can reduce cognitive load when building a runtime execution mental model.

On a related note, we feel that it is important to be cautious about how a view is transformed into an eagerly evaluated collection type. We showed conversion by invoking `toList`, which makes the intent explicit. `SeqView` also provides a `force` method to force evaluation. As a general rule, we avoid using `force` because it typically returns `scala.collection.immutable.Seq`. `SeqView` retains the collection type as its second generic parameter, which allows `force` to return the original collection type when there is enough evidence. However, certain operations, such as `map`, cause the view to lose evidence of the original collection type. When this happens, `force` returns the more general `Seq` collection type. `Seq` is a trait that is a super-type to all sequences in the collection library, including views and another lazy data structure that we will discuss later, named `scala.collection.immutable.Stream`. This inheritance scheme allows the following three statements to compile:

```
val list: Seq[Int] = List(1, 2, 3)
val view: Seq[Int] = list.view
val stream: Seq[Int] = list.toStream
```

We believe this is undesirable because the Seq data type hides critical information about the underlying implementation. It represents both lazy and eagerly evaluated collections with the same type. Consider the following snippet example to understand why this is undesirable:

```
def shouldGenerateOrder(xs: Seq[Execution]): Boolean =
    xs.size >= 3
```

In this manufactured example, imagine that shouldGenerateOrder is invoked with a Vector, but then later the Vector is swapped out for SeqView. With Vector, identifying collection length is a constant time operation. With SeqView, you cannot reason with certainty about the runtime of the operation, except to say that it is definitely more expensive than Vector.size. Seq usage, and, therefore, the usage of force, should be avoided because it is difficult to reason about runtime behavior, and this can lead to unexpected side-effects.

In a typical software system, areas of responsibility are separated into discrete modules. Using the performance trend reporting example, you can imagine a separate module containing the translation from List[TradingPerformanceTrend] to a PDF report. You may be tempted to expose the view to other modules to extend the benefit of lazy transformations. If benchmarks justify making this type of change, then we encourage you to choose one of these options. Our preferred choice in this scenario is to use Stream, which is a lazily evaluated version of List. We explore Stream later in this chapter. Alternatively, if Stream cannot be used, be strict in your use of the SeqView datatype to clearly demarcate that the collection is lazily evaluated.

Views are not memoizers

One additional consideration when using views is to be cognizant of when transformations are repeatedly applied. For example consider this manufactured example that focuses on a use case where a view is used as a base for multiple computations:

```
> val xs = List(1,2,3,4,5).view.map(x => {  println(s"multiply $x"); x * 2
})
xs: scala.collection.SeqView[Int,Seq[_]] = SeqViewM(...)
> val evens = xs.filter(_ % 2 == 0).toList
multiply 1
multiply 2
multiply 3
```

```
multiply 4
multiply 5
evens: List[Int] = List(2, 4, 6, 8, 10)

> val odds = xs.filter(_ % 2 != 0).toList
multiply 1
multiply 2
multiply 3
multiply 4
multiply 5
odds: List[Int] = List()
```

In this example, xs is a view on a list of integers. A map transformation is lazily applied to multiply these integers by 2. The view is then used to create two List instances, one containing even elements, the other containing odd elements. We observe that the transformation is applied to the view twice, each time we turn the view into a list. This shows that the transformation is lazily applied, but the results of the computation are not cached. This is a characteristic of views to keep in mind, as expensive transformations applied several times can cause significant slowdowns. This is also the reason why side-effects should be avoided in transformations applied to views. If, for some reason, referential transparency is not upheld, the combination of side-effects and multiple evaluations due to view usage can lead to exceptionally difficult to maintain software.

This example is straightforward, and the misuse of views is easy to spot. However, even methods that are provided by the standard library can lead to undesirable results when used with views. Consider this snippet:

```
> val (evens, odds) = List(1,2,3,4,5).view.map(x => {  println(s"multiply
$x"); x * 2 }).partition(_ % 2 == 0)
evens: scala.collection.SeqView[Int,Seq[_]] = SeqViewMF(...)
odds: scala.collection.SeqView[Int,Seq[_]] = SeqViewMF(...)

> println(evens.toList, odds.toList)
multiply 1
multiply 2
multiply 3
multiply 4
multiply 5
multiply 1
multiply 2
multiply 3
multiply 4
multiply 5
(List(2, 4, 6, 8, 10),List())
```

This example achieves the same results as the previous sample, but we rely on the built-in `partition` method to split the original list into two distinct collections each operating on the original view. Again, we see the `map` transformation applied twice to the original view. This is due to the underlying implementation of `partition` in `TraversableViewLike`. The main takeaway is that views and lazy evaluation can help yield better performance, but they should be used carefully. It is a good idea to experiment and try your algorithm in the REPL to confirm that you are using views correctly.

In our running example on reporting on trading performance trends, we saw an easy-to-miss example of lazy evaluation when operating on a `Map`. Recall that there was a lookup table built using the following code:

```
executions.groupBy(_.id).mapValues(es =>
Price.average(es.map(_.price)))
```

The return type of `mapValues` is `Map[A, B]`, which does not suggest any difference in evaluation strategy. Let's run a simple example in the REPL:

```
> val m = Map("a" -> 1, "b" -> 2)
m: scala.collection.immutable.Map[String,Int] = Map(a -> 1, b -> 2)
> val m_prime = m.mapValues{ v => println(s"Mapping $v"); v * 2}
Mapping 1
Mapping 2
m_prime: scala.collection.immutable.Map[String,Int] = Map(a -> 2, b -> 4)
> m_prime.get("a")
Mapping 1
res0: Option[Int] = Some(2)
> m_prime.get("a")
Mapping 1
res1: Option[Int] = Some(2)
```

Notice how, each time we call `get` on `m_prime` to retrieve a value, we can observe the transformation being applied, even when using the same key. The `mapValues` is a lazily-evaluated transformation of each value in the map akin to a view operating on the keys of a map. The types that are involved do not provide any insight, and unless you inspect the implementation of `Map` or carefully read the documentation that is associated with `mapValues`, you will likely miss this important detail. Consider the caveats of views when working with `mapValues`.

Zipping up report generation

While investigating the implementation of `TradingPerformanceTrend`, we took a deep dive into views and found how they can improve performance. We now return to the implementation of `trend` to complete the generation of the `List[radingPerformanceTrend]`. The following snippet shows `trend` with the implementation of `periodPnL` hidden because we thoroughly reviewed it:

```
def trend(
  now: () => Instant,
  findOrders: (Duration, Ticker) => List[Order],
  findExecutions: (Duration, Ticker) => List[Execution],
    request: GenerateTradingPerformanceTrend):
List[TradingPerformanceTrend] = {
    def periodPnL(
      start: Instant => Instant): Map[Ticker, PeriodPnL] = { ... }
    val tickerToLastHour = periodPnL(now =>
      now.minus(Period.hours(1).getMillis)).mapValues {
      case PeriodPositive => LastHourPositive
      case PeriodNegative => LastHourNegative
    }
    val tickerToLastDay = periodPnL(now =>
      now.minus(Period.days(1).getMillis)).mapValues {
      case PeriodPositive => LastDayPositive
      case PeriodNegative => LastDayNegative
    }
    val tickerToLastSevenDays = periodPnL(now =>
      now.minus(Period.days(7).getMillis)).mapValues {
      case PeriodPositive => LastSevenDayPositive
      case PeriodNegative => LastSevenDayNegative
    }
    tickerToLastHour.zip(tickerToLastDay).zip(tickerToLastSevenDays).map({
      case (((t, lastHour), (_, lastDay)), (_, lastSevenDays)) =>
        TradingPerformanceTrend(t, lastHour, lastDay, lastSevenDays)
    }).toList
  }
```

This method focuses on marshaling the translation of PnL for a time period to the appropriate time period's performance trend. The final expression involving two invocations of `zip` makes the transformation from three maps with keys of `Ticker` and corresponding period PnL trend values to `List[TradingPerformanceTrend]` elegant. `zip` iterates over two collections to yield a tuple for each index of both collections. Here is a simple snippet to illustrate `zip` usage:

```
println(List(1, 3, 5, 7).zip(List(2, 4, 6)))
```

This yields the following:

```
List((1,2), (3,4), (5,6))
```

The result is that corresponding indexes are "zipped" together. For example, at index one, the first list's value is three and the second list's value is four, yielding the tuple, `(3, 4)`. The first list has four elements while the second list only has three elements; this is silently omitted from the resulting collection. This behavior is well-documented, but it might be unexpected at first glance. In our reporting use case, we are certain that each key (that is, each `Ticker`), appears in all three maps. In this use case, we are certain that all three maps are of equal length.

However, there is a subtle bug in our usage of `zip`. The `zip` uses a collection's iterator to iterate over elements, which implies that usage of `zip` is sensitive to ordering. Each of the three maps is constructed by invoking `toMap`, which indirectly delegates to a `scala.collection.immutable.HashMap` implementation of `Map`. Similar to `Set`, Scala provides several handwritten implementations of `Map` (for example, `Map2`) for small collection sizes before constructing a `HashMap`. By now, you may realize the flaw, `HashMap` does not guarantee ordering.

To fix this bug and retain usage of `zip`, we can leverage our earlier discovery of `SortedMap`, the trait backed by `TreeMap` with sorted keys. Swapping out `Map` for `SortedMap` and making appropriate changes to define an `Ordering` for `Ticker`, we now have a bug-free, elegant solution to generating trading performance trend reports. With a judicious usage of views, we found a way to deliver iterative performance improvements with minimally invasive changes. This will give the sales team something to ring the bell about! This gives us additional time to consider other approaches to generating reports.

Rethinking reporting architecture

After deploying a new version of the web portal that generates the performance report containing your view changes, you begin wondering what else can be done to improve report generation performance. It strikes you that, for a particular time interval, the report is immutable. The computed PnL trend for a particular hour never changes once computed. Although the report is immutable, it is needlessly being recomputed each time a client requests the report. Given this line of thinking, you wonder how difficult it is to generate a new report each hour as new execution data becomes available. On-the-fly, order and execution events can be transformed as they are created into the inputs that are required for the client performance trend report. With a pregenerated report, the web portal performance issues should completely disappear because the responsibility of report generation no longer belongs to the web portal.

This new report generation strategy leads us to explore a new design paradigm, called event sourcing. Event sourcing describes an architectural approach to designing systems that relies on processing events over time instead of relying on a model of the current state to answer different questions. The reporting system that we worked on performs significant work to identify the subset of orders that executed because current state rather than events is stored. Imagine that, instead of working with data, such as `Order` and `Execution`, we instead worked with events that represent things that happened in the system over time. One relevant event to report could be the `OrderExecuted` event that can be modeled, as follows:

```
case class OrderExecuted(created: CreatedTimestamp, orderId: OrderId,
price: Price)
```

This event describes something that happened instead of representing a snapshot of current state. To extend this example, imagine if `Order` also included an optional `Price` to denote execution price:

```
sealed trait Order {
  def created: CreatedTimestamp
  def id: OrderId
  def ticker: Ticker
  def price: Price
  def clientId: ClientId
  def executionPrice: Option[Price]
}
```

If this data model is mapped to a relational database, `executionPrice` would be a nullable database value that is overwritten when an execution occurs. When the domain model only reflects the current state, then immutability is lost. As a functional programmer, this statement should concern you because you understand the reasoning capabilities that immutability provides. Storing only the current state of data may also lead to excessively large objects that are difficult to program with. For example, how would you represent that an `Order` was canceled? With the current approach, the most expedient method is to add a Boolean flag named `isCanceled`. Over time, as your system's requirements become more complicated, the `Order` object will grow and you will track more characteristics about the current state. This means that loading a set of `Order` objects into memory from a database will grow more unwieldy due to growing memory requirements. This is a dilemma that you likely have experienced if you have extensive **Object Relational Mapping (ORM)** experience.

To avoid bloating `Order`, you may try to deconstruct the concept of an order to support multiple use cases. For example, if you are only interested in executed orders, the model may change the `executionPrice` datatype from `Option[Price]` to `Price`, and you may no longer require the canceled Boolean flag because, by definition, an executed order could not have been canceled.

Identifying multiple definitions or representations for what you once thought was a single concept is an important step toward addressing the shortcomings that we walked through. Extending this approach, we come back to the topic of event sourcing. We can replay a set of events to build `OrderExecuted`. Let's slightly modify the events emitted from the order book to look like the following:

```
sealed trait OrderBookEvent
case class BuyOrderSubmitted(created: CreatedTimestamp,
  id: OrderId, ticker: Ticker, price: Price, clientId: ClientId)
  extends OrderBookEvent
case class SellOrderSubmitted(created: CreatedTimestamp,
  id: OrderId, ticker: Ticker, price: Price clientId: ClientId)
  extends OrderBookEvent
case class OrderCanceled(created: CreatedTimestamp, id: OrderId)
  extends OrderBookEvent
case class OrderExecuted(created: CreatedTimestamp,
  id: OrderId, price: Price) extends OrderBookEvent
```

If all `OrderBookEvent`s were persisted (for example, to disk), it is then possible to write a program that reads all the events and constructs a set of `ExecutedOrders` by correlating `BuyOrderSubmitted` and `SellOrderSubmitted` events with `OrderExecuted` events. An advantage that we see with this approach is that, over time, we are able to ask new questions about what happened in our system and then easily answer them by reading the events. In contrast, if a model built on the current state did not include executions when it was first designed, it is impossible to retroactively answer the question, "Which orders executed last week?"

Our new idea is exciting, and it has the potential to yield great improvements. However, it comes with a set of challenges. The main difference with the previous section is that our new use case does not load the `Order` and `Execution` collections in memory from a data store. Instead, we are planning to process the incoming `OrderBookEvent` as it is generated by the order book. Conceptually, this approach still involves processing a sequence of data. However, with the previous approach, the entire data set existed prior to beginning any transformations. Processing events on-the-fly requires designing software that handles data that has not yet been generated. Clearly, neither eager collections nor views are a good tool for our new system. Luckily, the standard Scala library provides us with the right abstraction: `Stream`. Let's take a closer look at this new collection type to better understand how `Stream` can help us implement an event sourcing approach to the client performance reporting architecture.

An overview of Stream

A stream can be seen as a mix between a list and a view. Like a view, it is lazily evaluated and transformations are applied only when its elements are accessed or collected. Like a `List`, the elements of a `Stream` are only evaluated once. A `Stream` is sometimes described as an unrealized `List`, meaning that it is essentially a `List` that has not yet been fully evaluated, or realized.

Where a `List` can be constructed with the cons (`::`) operator, a `Stream` can be similarly constructed with its own operator:

```
> val days = "Monday" :: "Tuesday" :: "Wednesday" :: Nil
days: List[String] = List(Monday, Tuesday, Wednesday)

> val months = "January" #:: "February" #:: "March" #:: Stream.empty
months: scala.collection.immutable.Stream[String] = Stream(January, ?)
```

The syntax to create a `Stream` is close to the one to create a `List`. One difference is the returned value. Where a `List` is immediately evaluated, a `Stream` is not. Only the first element (`"January"`) is computed; the remaining values are still unknown (and denoted by a `?` character).

Let's observe what happens when we access part of the stream:

```
scala> println(months.take(2).toList)
List(January, February)
scala> months
res0: scala.collection.immutable.Stream[String] = Stream(January, February, ?)
```

We forced the evaluation of the first two elements of the `Stream` by turning it into a `List` (see the following sidebar). The first two months are printed. We then display the value of `months` to discover that the second element (`"February"`) is now computed.

In the preceding example, `toList` is the call that forces the evaluation of the `Stream`. `take(2)` is a lazily applied transformer that also returns an unevaluated `Stream`:

```
scala> months.take(2)
res0: scala.collection.immutable.Stream[String] = Stream(January, ?)
```

To highlight the evaluation characteristics of a Stream, we look at another example of creating a Stream:

```
def powerOf2: Stream[Int] = {
  def next(n: Int): Stream[Int] = {
    println(s"Adding $n")
    n #:: next(2 * n)
  }
  1 #:: next(1)
}
```

This short snippet defines a function that creates a Stream of powers of 2. It is an infinite Stream initialized with the first value 1 and the tail is defined as another Stream. We added a println statement to allow us to study the evaluation of the elements:

```
scala> val s = powerOf2
s: Stream[Int] = Stream(1, ?)

scala> s.take(8).toList
Adding 1
Adding 2
Adding 4
Adding 8
Adding 16
Adding 32
Adding 64
res0: List[Int] = List(1, 1, 2, 4, 8, 16, 32, 64)

scala> s.take(10).toList
Adding 128
Adding 256
res1: List[Int] = List(1, 1, 2, 4, 8, 16, 32, 64, 128, 256)
```

Note how the first eight elements are only evaluated when we perform the first conversion to a List. In the second call, only elements 9 and 10 are computed; the first eight are already realized and are part of the Stream.

Based on the previous example, you may wonder if a Stream is an immutable data structure. Its fully qualified name is scala.collection.immutable.Stream, so this should give you a good hint. It is true that accessing the Stream and realizing some of its elements causes a modification of the Stream. However, the data structure is still considered immutable. The values it contains never change once assigned; even before being evaluated, the values exist and have a definition in the Stream.

The previous example shows an interesting property of Stream: it is possible to create a virtually infinite Stream. The Stream that is created by powerOf2 is unbounded and it is always possible to create one more element thanks to our next method. Another useful technique is the creation of recursive streams. A recursive Stream refers to itself in its definition. Let's adapt our previous example. Instead of returning the complete sequence of powers of 2, we will allow the caller to set a starting value:

```
def powerOf2(n: Int): Stream[Int] = math.pow(2, n).toInt #:: powerOf2(n+1)
```

The math.pow is used to compute 2^n. Note that we calculate the first value and define the rest of the Stream as powerOf2(n+1), that is, the next power of 2:

```
scala> powerOf2(3).take(10).toList
res0: List[Int] = List(8, 16, 32, 64, 128, 256, 512, 1024, 2048, 4096)
```

The companion object of Stream provides several factory methods to instantiate a Stream. Let's look at a few of them:

- Stream.apply: This allows us to create a Stream for a finite sequence of values:

    ```
    scala> Stream(1,2,3,4)
    res0: scala.collection.immutable.Stream[Int] = Stream(1, ?)
    scala> Stream(List(1,2,3,4):_*)
    res1: scala.collection.immutable.Stream[Int] = Stream(1, ?)
    ```

- Stream.fill[A](n: Int)(a: => A): This produces a Stream containing the element a, n times:

    ```
    scala> Stream.fill(4)(10)
    res0: scala.collection.immutable.Stream[Int] = Stream(10, ?)
    scala> res0.toList
    res1: List[Int] = List(10, 10, 10, 10)
    ```

- Stream.from(start: Int): This creates an increasing sequence of integers beginning with start:

    ```
    scala> Stream.from(4)
    res0: scala.collection.immutable.Stream[Int] = Stream(4, ?)
    scala> res0.take(3).toList
    res1: List[Int] = List(4, 5, 6)
    ```

We invite you to look at the other methods that are available on the companion object. Note that a Stream can also be constructed from a List directly, as follows:

```
scala> List(1,2,3,4,5).toStream
res0: scala.collection.immutable.Stream[Int] = Stream(1, ?)
```

The previous code may be misleading. Turning a `List` into a `Stream` does not spare the price of evaluating the whole `List` in memory. Similarly, if we were to apply transformations (such as `map` or `filter`) to the `List` before the call to `toStream`, we would be performing these computations on the entire `List`.

Just like a `List`, you can pattern match on a `Stream`, as follows:

```scala
scala> val s = Stream(1,2,3,4)
s: scala.collection.immutable.Stream[Int] = Stream(1, ?)
scala> s match {
     | case _ #:: _ #:: i #:: _ => i
     | }
res0: Int = 3
```

This pattern matching extracts the third element from the `s` stream. Pattern matching on a stream forces the realization of the elements required to evaluate the match expression. In the preceding case, the first three items are calculated.

To pattern match on an empty stream, you can use the `Stream.Empty` object. It is a singleton instance to represent an empty `Stream`. It works similarly to `Nil` for `List`. Note that the object `Stream` contains an `empty` method returning this singleton; however, pattern matching requires a stable identifier, and it cannot use calls to a method as a valid `case`.

Transforming events

Returning to the reporting system, how can we apply the principles of event sourcing and leverage `Stream` to change how reports are generated? To compute `TradingPerformanceTrend` for a client, we need to compute PnL trend values for three time periods: each hour, each day, and each seven days. We can write a method with the following signature that gets us closer to identifying the PnL for each trend:

```scala
def processPnl(e: OrderBookEvent, s: TradeState): (TradeState,
Option[PnlEvent])
```

The signature of `processPnl` accepts an `OrderBookEvent` and state in the form of `TradeState` to produce a new `TradeState` and, optionally, a `PnlEvent`. Let's first inspect `PnlEvent` to understand the end result of this method before inspecting `TradeState`:

```scala
sealed trait PnlEvent
case class PnlIncreased(created: EventInstant, clientId: ClientId,
  ticker: Ticker, profit: Pnl) extends PnlEvent
```

```
case class PnlDecreased(created: EventInstant, clientId: ClientId,
  ticker: Ticker, loss: Pnl)extends PnlEvent

case class Pnl(value: BigDecimal) extends AnyVal {
  def isProfit: Boolean = value.signum >= 0
}
object Pnl {
  def fromExecution(buy: Price, sell: Price): Pnl =
    Pnl(sell.value - buy.value)

  val zero: Pnl = Pnl(BigDecimal(0))
}
```

We see that `PnlEvent` models an ADT that expresses when a client's PnL increased or decreased. Using the past tense to name the event (for example, increased) makes it clear that this is a fact or a record of something that has completed. We have not yet looked at how `TradeState` is defined or the implementation of `processPnl`, but we can already infer the behavior by studying the emitted events. We display the definition of `TradeState`, which is needed to correlate submitted orders with executions, as follows:

```
case class PendingOrder(ticker: Ticker, price: Price,
  clientId: ClientId)

  case class TradeState(
    pendingBuys: Map[OrderId, PendingOrder],
    pendingSells: Map[OrderId, PendingOrder]) {
    def cancelOrder(id: OrderId): TradeState = copy(
      pendingBuys = pendingBuys - id, pendingSells = pendingSells - id)
    def addPendingBuy(o: PendingOrder, id: OrderId): TradeState =
      copy(pendingBuys = pendingBuys + (id -> o))
    def addPendingSell(o: PendingOrder, id: OrderId): TradeState =
      copy(pendingSells = pendingSells + (id -> o))
  }
object TradeState {
 val empty: TradeState = TradeState(Map.empty, Map.empty)
}
```

Next, we inspect the implementation of `processPnl` to view how `PnlEvents` are created, as follows:

```
def processPnl(
  s: TradeState,
  e: OrderBookEvent): (TradeState, Option[PnlEvent]) = e match {
  case BuyOrderSubmitted(_, id, t, p, cId) =>
    s.addPendingBuy(PendingOrder(t, p, cId), id) -> None
  case SellOrderSubmitted(_, id, t, p, cId) =>
    s.addPendingSell(PendingOrder(t, p, cId), id) -> None
```

```
case OrderCanceled(_, id) => s.cancelOrder(id) -> None
case OrderExecuted(ts, id, price) =>
  val (p, o) = (s.pendingBuys.get(id), s.pendingSells.get(id)) match {
    case (Some(order), None) =>
      Pnl.fromBidExecution(order.price, price) -> order
    case (None, Some(order)) =>
      Pnl.fromOfferExecution(price, order.price) -> order
    case error => sys.error(
      s"Unsupported retrieval of ID = $id returned: $error")
  }
  s.cancelOrder(id) -> Some(
    if (p.isProfit) PnlIncreased(ts, o.clientId, o.ticker, p)
    else PnlDecreased(ts, o.clientId, o.ticker, p))
}
```

This implementation shows that the `PnlEvent` is pattern matched to determine the event type, and this is handled accordingly. When an order is submitted, `TradeState` is updated to reflect that there is a new pending order that will be either canceled or executed. When an order is canceled, the pending order is removed from `TradeState`. When an execution occurs, the pending order is removed and, additionally, a `PnlEvent` is emitted after computing the trade PnL. The trade PnL compares the execution price to the pending order's original price.

`PnlEvent` provides enough information to compute PnL trend performance for all three time periods (hour, day, and seven days) required by `TradingPerformanceTrend`. The transformation from `OrderBookEvent` to `PnlEvent` is side-effect-free, and the creation of a new event, instead of replacing current state, leads to an immutable model. In the light of these characteristics, `processPnl` is easily unit-testable and makes the intent explicit. By making the intent explicit, it is possible to communicate with less technical stakeholders about how the system works.

Using `PnlEvent` as an input to a method that follows the analogous `(State, InputEvent) => (State, Option[OutputEvent])` signature, we can now compute hourly PnL trend, as follows:

```
def processHourlyPnl(e: PnlEvent, s: HourlyState): (HourlyState,
Option[HourlyPnlTrendCalculated])
```

This signature shows that, by maintaining state in `HourlyState`, it is possible to emit the `HourlyPnlTrendCalculated` event. The emitted event is defined, as follows:

```
case class HourlyPnlTrendCalculated(
    start: HourInstant,
    clientId: ClientId,
    ticker: Ticker,
```

```
    pnl: LastHourPnL)
```

For a particular hour, client ID, and ticker, `HourlyPnlTrendCalculated` is a record of whether the last hour PnL is positive or negative. The `HourInstant` class is a value class with a companion object method that transforms an instant to the start of the hour:

```
case class HourInstant(value: Instant) extends AnyVal {
  def isSameHour(h: HourInstant): Boolean =
    h.value.toDateTime.getHourOfDay == value.toDateTime.getHourOfDay
}
object HourInstant {
  def create(i: EventInstant): HourInstant =
    HourInstant(i.value.toDateTime.withMillisOfSecond(0)
    .withSecondOfMinute(0).withMinuteOfHour(0).toInstant)
}
```

Let's have a look at how `HourlyState` is defined to better understand the state that is needed to yield `HourlyPnlTrendCalculated`:

```
case class HourlyState(
      keyToHourlyPnl: Map[(ClientId, Ticker), (HourInstant, Pnl)])
object HourlyState {
 val empty: HourlyState = HourlyState(Map.empty)
}
```

For a `ClientId` and a `Ticker`, the PnL for the current hour is stored in `HourlyState`. Accumulating the PnL allows `processHourlyPnl` to determine the PnL trend at the end of an hour. We now inspect the implementation of `processHourlyPnl` to see how `PnlEvent` is transformed into `HourlyPnlTrendCalculated`:

```
def processHourlyPnl(
 s: HourlyState,
 e: PnlEvent): (HourlyState, Option[HourlyPnlTrendCalculated]) = {
 def processChange(
   ts: EventInstant,
   clientId: ClientId,
   ticker: Ticker,
   pnl: Pnl): (HourlyState, Option[HourlyPnlTrendCalculated]) = {
   val (start, p) = s.keyToHourlyPnl.get((clientId, ticker)).fold(
     (HourInstant.create(ts), Pnl.zero))(identity)
   start.isSameHour(HourInstant.create(ts)) match {
     case true => (s.copy(keyToHourlyPnl = s.keyToHourlyPnl +
       ((clientId, ticker) ->(start, p + pnl))), None)
     case false => (s.copy(keyToHourlyPnl =
       s.keyToHourlyPnl + ((clientId, ticker) ->
         (HourInstant.create(ts), Pnl.zero + pnl))),
       Some(HourlyPnlTrendCalculated(start, clientId, ticker,
```

```
            p.isProfit match {
              case true => LastHourPositive
              case false => LastHourNegative
            })))
    }
  }

  e match {
    case PnlIncreased(ts, clientId, ticker, pnl) => processChange(
      ts, clientId, ticker, pnl)
    case PnlDecreased(ts, clientId, ticker, pnl) => processChange(
      ts, clientId, ticker, pnl)
  }
}
```

Handling an increased and decreased PnL follows the same flow. The inner-method named `processChange` handles the identical processing steps. The `processChange` determines whether or not to emit `HourlyPnlTrendCalculated` by comparing the `HourInstant` value that is added when an entry is first added to the state with the hour of the timestamp provided by the event. When the comparison shows the hour has changed, then the hourly PnL trend has been computed because the hour is completed. When the hour is unchanged, the provided PnL is added to the state's PnL to continue accumulating the hour's PnL.

An obvious shortcoming of this approach is that, when a client or a ticker does not have any executed orders, it will not be possible to determine that the hour is completed. For simplicity, we are not treating time as a first-class event. However, you can imagine how it is possible to model the passing of time as an event that is a second input to `processHourlyPnl`. For example, the event might be the following:

`case class HourElapsed(hour: HourInstant)`

To use this event, we could change the signature of `processHourlyPnl` to receive an event argument that is of the `Either[HourElapsed, PnlEvent]` type. Scheduling `HourElapsed` on a timer enables us to modify the implementation of `processHourlyPnl` to emit `HourlyPnlTrendCalculated` as soon as the hour elapses instead of when a trade occurs in the next hour. This simple example shows how you can model time as an explicit part of the domain when you consider your system from an event sourcing point of view.

It is straightforward to imagine writing analogous methods that emit events for the daily and seven day PnL trend events, and then a method that awaits all three PnL trend events to produce the `TradingPerformanceTrendGenerated` event. The final step is to write a side-effecting method that persists `TradingPerformanceTrend` so that it can be read by the web portal. At this point, we have a collection of methods that performs transformations on events, but they are not yet wired together cohesively. Next, we take a look at how to create a pipeline to transform events.

 Note that, in this case study, we do not actually calculate a PnL. Performing a real PnL calculation would involve more complicated algorithms and would force us to introduce more domain concepts. We opted for a simpler approach with a report that is closer to an exposure report. This allows us to focus on the code and the programming practices that we want to illustrate.

Building the event sourcing pipeline

We use the term pipeline to refer to an arranged set of transformations that may require multiple steps to yield a desired end result. This term brings to mind an image of a set of pipes spanning multiple directions with twists and turns along the way. Our goal is to write a program that receives `PnlEvents` traits and prints the `HourlyPnlTrendCalculated` events to a standard output. In a true production environment, you can imagine replacing printing to standard output with writing to a persistent data store. In either case, we are building a pipeline that performs a set of referentially transparent transformations and concludes with a side-effect.

The pipeline must accumulate the intermediate state of each transformation as new events are processed. In the functional programming paradigm, accumulation is often associated with a `foldLeft` operation. Let's look at a toy example that sums a list of integers to better understand accumulation:

```
val sum = Stream(1, 2, 3, 4, 5).foldLeft(0) { case (acc, i) => acc + i }
println(sum) // prints 15
```

Here, we see `foldLeft` applied to compute the sum of a list of integers by providing an initial sum value of zero and currying a function to add the current element to the accumulated sum. The `acc` value is an often used shorthand for 'accumulator'. In this example, the accumulator and the list elements share the same data type, integer. This is merely a coincidence and is not a requirement for `foldLeft` operations. This implies that the accumulator can be a different type than the collection element.

We can use `foldLeft` as the basis of our event sourcing pipeline to support processing a list of `OrderBookEvents` while accumulating intermediate state. From the implementation of the two processing methods, we saw the need to maintain `TradeState` and `HourlyState`. We define `PipelineState` to encapsulate the required state, as follows:

```
case class PipelineState(tradeState: TradeState, hourlyState: HourlyState)
object PipelineState {
  val empty: PipelineState = PipelineState(TradeState.empty,
HourlyState.empty)
}
```

`PipelineState` serves as the accumulator when folding over the `OrderBookEvent`, allowing us to store the intermediate state for both of the transformation methods. Now, we are ready to define the signature of our pipeline:

```
def pipeline(initial: PipelineState, f: HourlyPnlTrendCalculated => Unit,
xs: List[OrderBookEvent]): PipelineState
```

The `pipeline` accepts the initial state, a side-effecting function to be invoked when an `HourlyPnlTrendCalculated` event is generated, and a set of `OrderBookEvents` to source. The return value of the pipeline is the state of the pipeline once the events are processed. Let's look at how we can leverage `foldLeft` to implement `pipeline`:

```
def pipeline(
    initial: PipelineState,
    f: HourlyPnlTrendCalculated => Unit,
    xs: Stream[OrderBookEvent]): PipelineState = xs.foldLeft(initial) {
    case (PipelineState(ts, hs), e) =>
      val (tss, pnlEvent) = processPnl(ts, e)
      PipelineState(tss,
        pnlEvent.map(processHourlyPnl(hs, _)).fold(hs) {
          case (hss, Some(hourlyEvent)) =>
            f(hourlyEvent)
            hss
          case (hss, None) => hss
        })
    }
```

The implementation of `pipeline` is based on folding over the provided events using the provided `PipelineState` as a starting point for accumulation. The curried function provided to `foldLeft` is where the wiring of transformations takes place. Stitching together the two transformation methods and the side-effecting event handler requires handling several different scenarios. Let's walk through each of the possible cases to better understand how the pipeline works. The `processPnl` is invoked to produce a new `TradeState` and optionally yield a `PnlEvent`. If no `PnlEvent` is generated, then `processHourlyPnl` is not invoked and the previous `HourlyState` is returned.

If a `PnlEvent` is generated, then `processHourlyPnl` is evaluated to determine whether an `HourlyPnlTrendCalculated` is created. When `HourlyPnlTrendCalculated` is generated, then the side-effecting `HourlyPnlTrendCalculated` event handler is invoked and the new `HourlyState` is returned. If no `HourlyPnlTrendCalculated` is generated, then the existing `HourlyState` is returned.

We construct a simple example to prove that the pipeline works as intended, as follows:

```
val now = EventInstant(HourInstant.create(EventInstant(
    new Instant())).value)
  val Foo = Ticker("FOO")

  pipeline(PipelineState.empty, println, Stream(
    BuyOrderSubmitted(now, OrderId(1), Foo, Price(21.07), ClientId(1)),
OrderExecuted(EventInstant(now.value.plus(Duration.standardMinutes(30))),
      OrderId(1), Price(21.00)),
    BuyOrderSubmitted(EventInstant(now.value.plus(
      Duration.standardMinutes(35))),
      OrderId(2), Foo, Price(24.02), ClientId(1)),
OrderExecuted(EventInstant(now.value.plus(Duration.standardHours(1))),
      OrderId(2), Price(24.02))))
```

At the start of the hour, a buy order is submitted for the stock, FOO. Within the hour, the buy order is executed at a price lower than the buying price, indicating the trade was profitable. As we know, the current implementation relies on executions in the subsequent hour in order to produce `HourlyPnlTrendCalculated`. To create this event, a second buy order is submitted at the start of the second hour. Running this snippet produces a single `HourlyPnlTrendCalculated` event that is written to standard output:

```
HourlyPnlTrendCalculated(HourInstant(2016-02-15T20:00:00.000Z),ClientId(1),
Ticker(FOO),LastHourPositive)
```

Although the wiring together of transformations is somewhat involved, we managed to build a simple event sourcing pipeline using only the Scala standard library and our existing knowledge of Scala collections. This example demonstrated the power of `foldLeft` to help build an event sourcing pipeline. Using this implementation, we can write a fully-featured program that is able to write a pregenerated version of the performance report to a persistent data store that can be read by the web portal. This new design allows us to shift the burden of report generation outside the web portal's responsibilities, allowing the web portal to provide a responsive user experience. Another benefit of this new approach is how it puts a domain-oriented language at the center of the design. All our events use business terms and focus on modeling domain concepts, making it easier for developers and stakeholders to communicate with each other.

You might be wondering about a data structure that shares some characteristics of `Stream` that we did not yet mention: `Iterator`. As the name implies, `Iterator` provides facilities to iterate over a sequence of data. Its simplified definition boils down to the following:

```
trait Iterator[A] {
  def next: A
  def hasNext: Boolean
}
```

Like `Stream`, an `Iterator` is able to avoid loading an entire dataset into memory, which enables programs to be written with constant memory usage. Unlike `Stream`, an `Iterator` is mutable and intended for only a single iteration over a collection (it extends the `TraversableOnce` trait). It should be noted that, according to the standard library documentation, one should never use an iterator after calling a method on it. For example, calling `size` on an `Iterator` returns the size of the sequence, but it also consumes the entire sequence and renders the instance of `Iterator` useless. The only exceptions to this rule are `next` and `hasNext`. These properties lead to software that is difficult to reason with, which is the antithesis of what we strive for as functional programmers. For this reason, we omit an in-depth discussion about `Iterator`.

We encourage you to further explore event sourcing by reading the documentation of the Event Store database at `http://docs.geteventstore.com/introduction/event-sourcing-basics/`. Event Store is a database that is developed around the concept of event sourcing. Event Store was created by Greg Young, a notable writer on the topic of event sourcing. While enriching your understanding about event sourcing, reflect on when you believe it is appropriate to apply the event sourcing technique. For CRUD applications that have simple behavior, event sourcing may not be a worthwhile time investment. When you model more complex behaviors or consider scenarios involving strict performance and scaling requirements, the time investment for event sourcing may become justified. For example, like we saw with performance trend reporting, considering the performance challenges from the event sourcing paradigm exposed an entirely different way of approaching the design.

As you continue exploring the world of stream processing, you will discover that you wish to construct more complex transformations than our event sourcing pipeline example. To continue digging deeper into the the topic of stream processing, we suggest researching two relevant libraries: `akka streams` and `functional streams` (formerly, `scalaz-stream`). These libraries provide tools to build more sophisticated transformation pipelines using different abstractions than `Stream`. In combination with learning about Event Store, you will deepen your understanding of how event sourcing ties in with stream processing.

Streaming Markov chains

With the simple program at the end of the previous section, we demonstrated that we can wire together a pipeline of transformations operating on events. As a well-intentioned engineer, you wish to develop automated tests that prove the pipeline works as intended. One approach is to add a sample of historical production data into the repository to build tests. This is often a good choice, but you are concerned that the sample is not large enough to represent a broad number of scenarios. Another option is to write a generator of events that can create production-like data. This approach requires more up-front effort, but it yields a more dynamic way to exercise the pipeline.

A recent lunchtime conversation with Dave about Markov chains sparked the thought about testing the event sourcing pipeline with generated data. Dave described how a Markov chain is a statistical model of state transitions that only relies on the current state to determine the next state. Dave is representing the states of the stock market as a Markov chain, allowing him to build trading strategies based on whether or not he perceives the stock market to be in an upswing, downswing, or steady state. After reading through the Markov chain Wikipedia page, you envision writing an event generator based on a Markov chain.

Our end goal is to be able to generate an infinite number of `OrderBookEvents` that follows production-like patterns. For example, we know from previous experience that proportionally there are often more cancelations than executions, particularly during volatile markets. The event generator should be able to represent different probabilities of events occurring. As a Markov chain only depends on its current state to identify its next state, a `Stream` is a natural fit because we only need to inspect the current element to determine the next element. For our representation of a Markov chain, we need to identify the chance of transitioning from the current state to any of the other possible states. The following table illustrates one possible set of probabilities:

Current state	Chance of buy	Chance of sell	Chance of execution	Chance of cancel
`BuyOrderSubmitted`	10%	15%	40%	40%
`SellOrderSubmitted`	25%	10%	35%	25%
`OrderCanceled`	60%	50%	40%	10%
`OrderExecuted`	30%	30%	55%	30%

This table defines the likelihood of receiving an `OrderBookEvent` given the current `OrderBookEvent`. For example, given that a sell order was submitted, there is a 10% chance of seeing a second sell order next and a 35% chance that an execution occurs next. We can develop state transition probabilities according to the market conditions that we wish to simulate in the pipeline.

We can model the transitions using the following domain:

```
sealed trait Step
case object GenerateBuy extends Step
case object GenerateSell extends Step
case object GenerateCancel extends Step
case object GenerateExecution extends Step

case class Weight(value: Int) extends AnyVal
case class GeneratedWeight(value: Int) extends AnyVal
case class StepTransitionWeights(
  buy: Weight,
  sell: Weight,
  cancel: Weight,
  execution: Weight)
```

In this domain, `Step` is an ADT that models the possible states. For a given `Step`, we will associate `StepTransitionWeights` to define the probability of transitioning to different states based on provided weightings. `GeneratedWeight` is a value class that defines the weight generated for the current `Step`. We will use `GeneratedWeight` to drive the transition from one `Step` to the next `Step`.

Our next step, so-to-speak, is to make use of our domain to generate events according to probabilities that we define. To make use of `Step`, we define a representation of the Markov chain state that is required, as follows:

```
case class State(
  pendingOrders: Set[OrderId],
  step: Step)
```

The Markov chain requires knowledge of the current state, which is represented by `step`. Additionally, we put a twist on the Markov chain by maintaining the set of orders that are submitted that are neither canceled nor executed in `pendingOrders`. This additional state is needed for two reasons. First, generating cancel and execution events requires linking to a known order ID. Second, we constrain our representation of a Markov chain by requiring at least one pending order to exist before creating a cancel or an execution. If there are no pending orders, it is invalid to transition to a state that generates either `OrderCanceled` or `OrderExecuted`.

Using `State`, we can write a method with the following signature to manage transitions:

```
def nextState(
    weight: StepTransitionWeights => GeneratedWeight,
    stepToWeights: Map[Step, StepTransitionWeights],
    s: State): (State, OrderBookEvent)
```

Given a way to generate a weight from the current `StepTransitionWeights`, a mapping of `Step` to `StepTransitionWeights`, and the current `State`, we are able to produce a new `State` and an `OrderBookEvent`. For brevity, we omit the implementation of `nextState` because we want to focus most intently on stream processing. From the signature, we have enough insight to apply the method, but we encourage you to inspect the repository to fill in any blanks in your understanding.

The `nextState` method is the driver of state transitions in our Markov chain representation. We can now generate an infinite `Stream` of `OrderBookEvents` based on transition probabilities using the convenience `Stream` method, `iterate`. From the Scala documentation, `iterate` produces an infinite stream by repeatedly applying a function to the start value. Let's see how we can use `iterate`:

```
val stepToWeights = Map[Step, StepTransitionWeights](
    GenerateBuy -> StepTransitionWeights(
      Weight(10), Weight(25), Weight(40), Weight(40)),
    GenerateSell -> StepTransitionWeights(
      Weight(25), Weight(10), Weight(40), Weight(25)),
    GenerateCancel -> StepTransitionWeights(
      Weight(60), Weight(50), Weight(40), Weight(10)),
    GenerateExecution -> StepTransitionWeights(
      Weight(30), Weight(30), Weight(60), Weight(25)))

  val next = State.nextState(
    t => GeneratedWeight(Random.nextInt(t.weightSum.value) + 1),
    stepToWeights, _: State)

  println("State\tEvent")
  Stream.iterate(State.initialBuy) { case (s, e) => next(s) }
    .take(5)
    .foreach { case (s, e) => println(s"$s\t$e")  }
```

This snippet creates a Markov chain to generate various `OrderBookEvents` by providing a mapping of `Step` to `StepTransitionWeights` as the basis to invoke `State.nextState`. `State.nextState` is partially applied, leaving the current state unapplied. The `next` function has the `State => (State, OrderBookEvent)` signature. With the necessary scaffolding in place, `Stream.iterate` is used to generate an infinite sequence of multiple `OrderBookEvents` by invoking `next`. Similar to `foldLeft`, we provide an initial value to begin the `initialBuy` iteration, which is defined as follows:

```
val initialBuy: (State, OrderBookEvent) = {
    val e = randomBuySubmitted()
    State(Set(e.id), GenerateBuy) -> e
}
```

Running this snippet produces output that is similar to the following:

```
State = State(Set(OrderId(1612147067584751204)),GenerateBuy)
Event =
BuyOrderSubmitted(EventInstant(2016-02-22T23:52:40.662Z),OrderId(1612147067
584751204),Ticker(FOO),Price(32),ClientId(28))
State = State(Set(OrderId(1612147067584751204),
OrderId(7606120383704417020)),GenerateBuy)
Event =
BuyOrderSubmitted(EventInstant(2016-02-22T23:52:40.722Z),OrderId(7606120383
704417020),Ticker(XYZ),Price(18),ClientId(54))
State = State(Set(OrderId(1612147067584751204),
OrderId(7606120383704417020), OrderId(5522110701609898973)),GenerateBuy)
Event =
BuyOrderSubmitted(EventInstant(2016-02-22T23:52:40.723Z),OrderId(5522110701
609898973),Ticker(XYZ),Price(62),ClientId(28))
State = State(Set(OrderId(7606120383704417020),
OrderId(5522110701609898973)),GenerateExecution)
Event =
OrderExecuted(EventInstant(2016-02-22T23:52:40.725Z),OrderId(16121470675847
51204),Price(21))
State = State(Set(OrderId(7606120383704417020),
OrderId(5522110701609898973), OrderId(5898687547952369568)),GenerateSell)
Event =
SellOrderSubmitted(EventInstant(2016-02-22T23:52:40.725Z),OrderId(589868754
7952369568),Ticker(BAR),Price(76),ClientId(45))
```

Of course, each invocation differs depending upon the random values that are created for `GeneratedWeight`, which is used to probabilistically select the next transition. This snippet provides a base to compose larger-scale tests for the reporting infrastructure. Through this example, we see an interesting application of Markov chains to support generating representative events from various market conditions without requiring access to volumes of production data. We are now able to write tests to confirm whether or not the reporting infrastructure correctly computes PnL trends in different market conditions.

Stream caveats

For all their goodness, Stream should be used with caution. In this section, we mention a few of the main caveats of Stream, and how to avoid them.

Streams are memoizers

While views do not cache the result of a computation and, therefore, recalculate and realize each element each time it is accessed, Stream does save the final form of its elements. An element is only ever realized once, the first time it is accessed. While this is a great characteristic to avoid computing the same result several times, it can also lead to a large consumption of memory, to the point where your program may eventually run out of memory.

To avoid Stream memoization, it is good practice to avoid storing a Stream in a val. Using a val creates a permanent reference to the head of the Stream, ensuring that every element that is realized will be cached. If a Stream is defined as a def, it can be garbage collected as soon as it is no longer needed.

Memoization can happen when calling certain methods that are defined on Stream. For example, drop or dropWhile will evaluate and memoize all the intermediate elements to be dropped. The elements are memoized as the methods are defined on an instance of Stream (and Stream has a reference on its own head). We can implement our own drop function to avoid caching the intermediate elements in memory:

```
@tailrec
def drop[A](s: Stream[A], count: Int): Stream[A] = count match {
  case 0 => s
  case n if n > 0 => drop(s.tail, count - 1)
  case n if n < 0 => throw new Exception("cannot drop negative count")
}
```

We pattern match on the value of count to know whether we can return the given Stream or need to perform a recursive call on the tail. Our method is tail-recursive. This makes sure that we do not keep a reference to the head of the Stream, since a tail-recursive function recycles its reference each time that it loops. Our s reference will only point to the remaining part of the Stream, not the head.

Another example of a problematic method is `max`. Calling `max` will memoize all the elements of the `Stream` to determine which one is the greatest. Let's implement a safe version of `max`, as follows:

```
def max(s: => Stream[Int]): Option[Int] = {
  @tailrec
  def loop(ss: Stream[Int], current: Option[Int]): Option[Int] = ss match {
    case Stream.Empty => current
    case h #:: rest if current.exists(_ >= h) => loop(rest, current)
    case h #:: rest => loop(rest, Some(h))
  }
  loop(s, None)
}
```

This time, we used an internal tail recursive function to be able to expose a friendly API. We represent the current max value as an `Option[Int]` to handle the case where the method is called with an empty `Stream`. Note that `max` accepts `s` as a by-name parameter. This is important because, otherwise, we would be keeping a reference to the head of the `Stream` before calling the internal tail-recursive `loop` method. Another possible implementation is as follows:

```
def max(s: => Stream[Int]): Option[Int] = {
  @tailrec
  def loop(ss: Stream[Int], current: Int): Int = ss match {
    case Stream.Empty => current
    case h #:: hs if h > current => loop(hs, h)
    case h #:: hs if h <= current => loop(hs, current)
  }

  s match {
    case Stream.Empty => None
    case h #:: rest => Some(loop(rest, h))
  }
}
```

This implementation is arguably simpler. We check in the `max` function whether the `Stream` is empty or not; this allows us to either return right away (with `None`), or call `loop` with a valid default value (the first element in the `Stream`). The `loop` does not have to deal with `Option[Int]` anymore. However, this example does not achieve the goal of avoiding memoization. The pattern matching will cause `rest` to keep a reference on the entire tail of the original `Stream`, which will prevent garbage collection of the intermediate elements. A good practice is to only pattern match on a `Stream` inside a consuming, tail-recursive method.

Stream can be infinite

We saw during our overview that it is possible to define an infinite Stream. However, you need to be careful when working with an infinite Stream. Some methods may cause the evaluation of the entire Stream, leading to OutOfMemoryError. Some are obvious, such as toList, which will try to store the entire Stream into a List, causing the realization of all the elements. Others are more subtle. For example, Stream has a size method that is similar to the one defined on List. Calling size on an infinite Stream will cause the program to run out of memory. Similarly, max and sum will attempt to realize the entire sequence and crash your system. This behavior is particularly dangerous as Stream extends Seq, the base trait for sequences. Consider the following code:

```
def range(s: Seq[Int]): Int = s.max - s.min
```

This short method takes a Seq[Int] as single parameter, and returns its range, that is, the difference between the greatest and lowest elements. As Stream extends Seq the following call is valid:

```
val s: Stream[Int] = ???
range(s)
```

The compiler will happily and promptly generate the bytecode for this snippet. However, s could be defined as an infinite Stream:

```
val s: Stream[Int] = powerOf2(0)
range(s)
java.lang.OutOfMemoryError: GC overhead limit exceeded
  at .powerOf2(<console>:10)
  at $anonfun$powerOf2$1.apply(<console>:10)
  at $anonfun$powerOf2$1.apply(<console>:10)
  at scala.collection.immutable.Stream$Cons.tail(Stream.scala:1233)
  at scala.collection.immutable.Stream$Cons.tail(Stream.scala:1223)
  at scala.collection.immutable.Stream.reduceLeft(Stream.scala:627)
  at scala.collection.TraversableOnce$class.max(TraversableOnce.scala:229)
  at scala.collection.AbstractTraversable.max(Traversable.scala:104)
  at .range(<console>:10)
  ... 23 elided
```

The call to range never returns due to the implementation of max and min. This example illustrates a good practice that we mentioned earlier in this chapter.

Summary

Throughout this chapter, we explored two lazily evaluated collections that are provided by the standard Scala library: views and streams. We explored their characteristics and implementation details, as well as the limitations to bear in mind when using these abstractions. Leveraging your newly-acquired knowledge, you addressed a critical performance problem affecting MVT clients trying to view their performance trend.

In the *Stream* sections, we took the opportunity to tie the concept of stream processing to event sourcing. We briefly explored the event sourcing paradigm and introduced a simple event-driven transformation pipeline to improve the architecture of the reporting system and to define a stronger domain model. Lastly, we built a Markov chain event generator to exercise our new approach to generating reports.

By exploring both eager and lazy collections, you now possess a strong working knowledge of the collections that are provided by the Scala standard library. In the next chapter, we will continue our exploration of Scala concepts viewed through the functional paradigm by diving into concurrency.

6
Concurrency in Scala

In this chapter, we will switch our focus from collections to a different topic: concurrency. Being able to take advantage of all the CPU resources that your hardware provides is critical to writing performant software. Unfortunately, writing concurrent code is not an easy task because it is easy to write unsafe programs. If you come from Java, you may still have nightmares involving `synchronized` blocks and locks! The `java.util.concurrent` package provides numerous tools that make writing concurrent code simpler. However, designing stable and reliable concurrent applications can still be a daunting challenge. In this chapter, we will explore the tools that are provided by the Scala standard library to take advantage of concurrency. After a short presentation of the main abstraction, `Future`, we will study its behavior and usage pitfalls that we should avoid. We will end this chapter by exploring a possible alternative to `Future` named `Task`, which is provided by the Scalaz library. In this chapter, we will explore the following topics:

- Concurrency versus parallelism
- Future usage considerations
- Blocking calls and callbacks
- Scalaz Task

Parallelizing backtesting strategies

The data scientists are off and running with the data analysis tools that you built for them to research trading strategies. However, they have hit a wall because backtesting strategies is becoming too expensive. As they have built more sophisticated strategies that require more historical data, and employ more stateful algorithms, backtesting has taken longer. Once again, you are being called upon to help out at MVT by leveraging Scala and the functional paradigm to deliver performant software.

The data scientists have incrementally built out a backtesting tool that allows the team to determine a strategy's performance by replaying historical data. This works by providing a preset strategy to run, the ticker to test against, and the time interval of historical data to replay. The backtester loads market data and applies the strategy to generate trading decisions. Once the backtester finishes replaying historical data, it summarizes and displays strategy performance results. The backtester is heavily depended on to determine the efficacy of proposed trading strategies before putting them into production for live trading.

To begin familiarizing yourself with the backtester, you look into the code, as follows:

```
sealed trait Strategy
case class PnL(value: BigDecimal) extends AnyVal
case class BacktestPerformanceSummary(pnl: PnL)
case class Ticker(value: String) extends AnyVal

def backtest(
  strategy: Strategy,
  ticker: Ticker,
  testInterval: Interval): BacktestPerformanceSummary = ???
```

In the preceding snapshot from the data analysis repository, you see the primary method that drives backtesting. Given a `Strategy`, `Ticker`, and `Interval`, it can produce `BacktestPerformanceSummary`. Scanning the repository, you find a file named `CrazyIdeas.scala` that shows Dave as the only commit author. In here, you see example invocations of the backtester:

```
def lastMonths(months: Int): Interval =
  new Interval(new DateTime().minusMonths(months), new DateTime())
backtest(Dave1, Ticker("AAPL"), lastMonths(3))
backtest(Dave1, Ticker("GOOG"), lastMonths(3))
backtest(Dave2, Ticker("AAPL"), lastMonths(3))
backtest(Dave2, Ticker("GOOG"), lastMonths(3))
```

The usage of the backtester gives you a clue to a possible performance improvement. It looks like when Dave has a new idea, he wants to evaluate its performance on multiple symbols and compare it against other strategies. In its current form, backtests are performed sequentially. One way to improve the execution speed of the backtester is to parallelize the execution of all backtesting runs. If each invocation of the backtester is parallelized and if there are spare hardware resources, then backtesting multiple strategies and symbols will finish faster. To understand how to parallelize the backtester, we first need to dive into the topic of asynchronous programming and then see how Scala supports concurrency.

Before diving into the code, we need to enrich our vocabulary to discuss the properties of asynchronous programming. Concurrency and parallelism are often used interchangeably, but there is an important distinction between these two terms. Concurrency involves two (or more) tasks that are started and executed in overlapping time periods. Both tasks are in-progress (that is, they are running) at the same time, but only one task may be performing actual work at any instant in time. This is the case when you write concurrent code on a single-core machine. Only one task can progress at a time, but multiple tasks are ongoing concurrently. Parallelism exists only when both tasks are truly running at the same time. With a dual-core machine, you can execute two tasks at the same time. From this definition, we see that parallelism depends on the hardware that is available for use. This means that the property of concurrency can be added to a program, but parallelism is outside the control of the software. To better illustrate these concepts, consider the example of painting a room. If there is only one painter, the painter can paint the first coat on a wall, move on to the next wall, go back to the first wall for the second coat and then finish the second wall. The painter is painting both walls concurrently, but can only spend time on one wall at any given time. If two painters are on the job, they can each focus on one wall and paint them in parallel.

Exploring Future

The primary construct in Scala to drive concurrent programming is `Future`. Found in the `scala.concurrent` package, `Future` can be seen as a container for a value that may not yet exist. Let's look at a simple example to illustrate usage:

```
scala> import scala.concurrent.Future
import scala.concurrent.Future

scala> import scala.concurrent.ExecutionContext
import scala.concurrent.ExecutionContext

scala> val context: ExecutionContext =
scala.concurrent.ExecutionContext.global
context: scala.concurrent.ExecutionContext =
scala.concurrent.impl.ExecutionContextImpl@3fce8fd9

scala> def example(){
  println("Starting the example")
  Future{
    println("Starting the Future")
```

```
      Thread.sleep(1000)   // simulate computation
      println("Done with the computation")
   }(context)

   println("Ending example")
   }
```

The preceding example shows a short method, creating a `Future` value simulates an expensive computation and prints a couple of lines to make it easier for us to understand the flow of the application. When running `example`, we see the following output:

```
scala> example()
Starting the example
Ending example
Starting the future
// a pause
Done with the computation
```

We can see that `Future` was executed after the end of the `example` method. This is because when a `Future` is created, it starts its computation concurrently. You may be wondering, "What is this `context` object of the `ExecutionContext` type that is used when creating the `Future`?" We will explore `ExecutionContext` in-depth shortly, but for now, we treat it as the the object that is responsible for the execution of the `Future`. We import `scala.concurrent.ExecutionContext.global`, which is a default object that is created by the standard library to be able to execute the `Future`.

A `Future` object is a stateful object. It is either not yet complete when the computation is underway or completed once the computation finishes. Furthermore, a completed `Future` can be either a success when the computation was able to complete, or it can be a failure if an exception was thrown during the computation.

The `Future` API provides combinators to compose the `Future` instances and manipulate the result that they contain:

```
scala> import scala.concurrent.ExecutionContext.Implicits.global
import scala.concurrent.ExecutionContext.Implicits.global

scala> import scala.concurrent.Future
import scala.concurrent.Future

scala> Future(1).map(_ + 1).filter(_ % 2 == 0).foreach(println)

2
```

This snippet from the Scala console shows construction of a `Future` data type that wraps a constant integer value. We see that the integer contained in the `Future` data type is transformed using functions that are similar to the ones that we expect to find on `Option` and collection data types. These transforms are applied once the preceding `Future` completes, and return a new `Future`.

As promised, we now look into `ExecutionContext`. The `ExecutionContext` can be thought of as the machinery behind `Future` that provides runtime asynchrony. In the previous snippet, a `Future` was created to perform simple addition and modulo division without explicitly providing an `ExecutionContext` instance at the call site. Instead, only an import of the `global` object was provided. The snippet executes because `global` is an implicit value and the signature of `map` accepts an implicit `ExecutionContext`. Let's look at the following signature of `map` to deepen our understanding:

```
def map[S](f: T => S)(implicit executor: ExecutionContext): Future[S]
```

From the signature of `map`, we see that unlike the `map` transformation on `List`, the `Future` requires a curried, implicit `ExecutionContext` argument. To understand how an `ExecutionContext` provides runtime asynchrony, we need to first understand its operations:

```
trait ExecutionContext {
  def execute(runnable: Runnable): Unit
  def reportFailure(cause: Throwable): Unit
  def prepare(): ExecutionContext = this
}
```

The `execute` is a side-effecting method that operates on a `java.lang.Runnable`. For those familiar with concurrency in Java, you most likely recall that `Runnable` is the commonly-used interface to allow threads and other `java.util.concurrent` abstractions to execute code concurrently. Although we do not know how `Future` achieves runtime asynchrony yet, we do know there is a link between `Future` execution and creation of a `Runnable`.

The next question we will answer is, "How do I create an `ExecutionContext`?" By studying the companion object, we discover the following signatures:

```
def fromExecutorService(e: ExecutorService, reporter: Throwable => Unit):
ExecutionContextExecutorService
def fromExecutorService(e: ExecutorService):
ExecutionContextExecutorService
def fromExecutor(e: Executor, reporter: Throwable => Unit):
ExecutionContextExecutor
def fromExecutor(e: Executor): ExecutionContextExecutor
```

The standard library provides convenient ways to create an `ExecutionContext` from either a `java.util.concurrent.Executor` or `java.util.concurrent.ExecutorService`.

 If you are unfamiliar with the machinery that is provided by the `java.util.concurrent` package and you are looking for a deeper treatment than that provided by the API documentation, we encourage you to read *Java Concurrency in Practice* by Brian Goetz (`http://jcip.net/`). Although *Java Concurrency in Practice* was written around the release of JDK 6, it contains numerous principles that continue to apply today. Reading this book will provide you with a deep understanding of the JDK-provided concurrency primitives that are utilized by the Scala standard library.

The return type of the factory methods is a more specialized version of `ExecutionContext`. The standard library defines the following inheritance chain for `ExecutionContext`:

```
trait ExecutionContextExecutor extends ExecutionContext with
java.util.concurrent.Executor
trait ExecutionContextExecutorService extends ExecutionContextExecutor with
java.util.concurrent.ExecutorService
```

Also, in the `ExecutionContext` companion object, we find the implicit context used in our first example, as follows:

```
def global: ExecutionContextExecutor = Implicits.global
```

The documentation for the definition of `Implicits.global` indicates that this `ExecutionContext` is backed by a thread pool with a thread count that is equal to the available processor count. Our dive into `ExecutionContext` shows us how the simple `Future` example runs. We can illustrate how a `Future` applies its `ExecutionContext` to execute on multiple threads:

```
Future(1).map(i => {
  println(Thread.currentThread().getName)
  i + 1
}).filter(i => {
  println(Thread.currentThread().getName)
  i % 2 == 0
}).foreach(println)
```

We extend the original snippet to print the name of the thread performing each transformation. When run on a machine with multiple cores, this snippet yields variable output, depending on which threads pick up the transformations. Here is an example output:

```
ForkJoinPool-1-worker-3
ForkJoinPool-1-worker-5
2
```

This example shows that one `worker-3` thread performed the `map` transformation while another `worker-5` thread performed the `filter` transformation. There are two key insights to draw from our simple example about how `Future` affects control flow. First, `Future` is a data type for concurrency that enables us to break the control flow of a program into multiple logical threads of processing. Second, our example shows that `Future` begins execution immediately upon creation. This means that transformations are applied immediately in a different flow of the program. We can use these insights to improve the runtime performance of Dave's crazy ideas.

Future and crazy ideas

We apply `Future` to Dave's set of backtests to improve performance. We believe there is an opportunity for a performance improvement because Dave's laptop has four CPU cores. This means that by adding concurrency to our program, we will be able to benefit from runtime parallelism. Our first attempt utilizes a for-comprehension:

```
implicit val ec = scala.concurrent.ExecutionContext.Implicits.global
for {
    firstDaveAapl <- Future(backtest(Dave1, Ticker("AAPL"),
lastMonths(3)))
    firstDaveGoog <- Future(backtest(Dave1, Ticker("GOOG"),
lastMonths(3)))
    secondDaveAapl <- Future(backtest(Dave2, Ticker("AAPL"),
lastMonths(3)))
    secondDaveGoog <- Future(backtest(Dave2, Ticker("GOOG"),
lastMonths(3)))
  } yield (firstDaveAapl, firstDaveGoog, secondDaveAapl, secondDaveGoog)
```

Each backtest invocation is wrapped with the creation of a `Future` instance by calling `Future.apply`. This companion object method uses a by-name parameter to defer evaluation of the argument, which, in this case, is the invocation of `backtest`:

```
def apply[T](body: =>T)(executor: ExecutionContext): Future[T]
```

After running the new version of `CrazyIdeas.scala`, you are disappointed to see the runtime execution has not improved. You quickly double-check the number of CPUs on your Linux box, as follows:

```
$ cat /proc/cpuinfo  | grep processor | wc -l
8
```

Having confirmed there are eight cores available on your laptop, you wonder why the execution time matches the original serial execution time. The solution here is to consider how the for-comprehension is compiled. The for-comprehension is equivalent to the following simpler example:

```
Future(1).flatMap(f1 => Future(2).flatMap(f2 => Future(3).map(f3 => (f1,
f2, f3))))
```

In this desugared representation of the for-comprehension, we see that the second `Future` is created and evaluated within the `flatMap` transformation of the first `Future`. Any transformation applied to a `Future` (for example, `flatMap`) is only invoked once the value provided to the transform has been computed. This means that the `Future` in the preceding example and the for-comprehension are executed sequentially. To achieve the concurrency that we are looking for, we must instead modify `CrazyIdeas.scala` to look like the following:

```
val firstDaveAaplF = Future(backtest(Dave1, Ticker("AAPL"),
  lastMonths(3)))
val firstDaveGoogF = Future(backtest(Dave1, Ticker("GOOG"),
  lastMonths(3)))
val secondDaveAaplF = Future(backtest(Dave2, Ticker("AAPL"),
  lastMonths(3)))
val secondDaveGoogF = Future(backtest(Dave2, Ticker("GOOG"),
  lastMonths(3)))
for {
  firstDaveAapl <- firstDaveAaplF
  firstDaveGoog <- firstDaveGoogF
  secondDaveAapl <- secondDaveAaplF
  secondDaveGoog <- secondDaveGoogF
} yield (firstDaveAapl, firstDaveGoog, secondDaveAapl, secondDaveGoog)
```

In this snippet, four backtests are kicked off concurrently and the results are transformed into a `Future` of a `Tuple4` consisting of four `BacktestPerformanceSummary` values. Seeing is believing, and after showing Dave the faster runtime of his backtests, he is excited to iterate quickly on new backtest ideas. Dave never misses a chance to throw around a pun, exclaiming, "Using all my cores is making my laptop fans really whiz. Not sure I'm a fan of the noise, but I sure do like the performance!"

Future usage considerations

In the previous example, we illustrated the ease of use of the Future API by investigating how to introduce concurrency to the backtester. Like any powerful tool, your usage of Future must be disciplined to ensure correctness and performance. This section evaluates topics that commonly cause confusion and error when using the Future to add concurrency to your program. We will detail performing side-effects, blocking execution, handling failures, choosing an appropriate execution context, and performance considerations.

Performing side-effects

When programming with Future, it is important to remember that Future is inherently a side-effecting construct. Unless the success or failure factory methods are used to lift a value into a Future, work is scheduled to be executed on a different thread (part of the ExecutionContext that is used to create the Future). More importantly, once executed, a Future cannot be executed again. Consider the following snippet:

```scala
scala> import scala.concurrent.Future
import scala.concurrent.Future

scala> import scala.concurrent.ExecutionContext.Implicits.global
import scala.concurrent.ExecutionContext.Implicits.global

scala> val f = Future{ println("FOO"); 40 + 2}
FOO
f: scala.concurrent.Future[Int] =
scala.concurrent.impl.Promise$DefaultPromise@5575e0df

scala> f.value
res3: Option[scala.util.Try[Int]] = Some(Success(42))
```

The Future is computed and prints FOO as expected. We can then access the value wrapped in the Future. Note that when accessing the value, nothing is printing on the console. Once completed, the Future is merely a wrapper for a realized value. If you want to perform the computation again, you need to create a new instance of Future.

Note that the preceding example uses `Future.value` to extract the result of the computation. This is for the sake of simplicity. Production code should rarely, if ever, use this method. Its return type is defined as `Option[Try[A]]`. An `Option` is used to represent the case of a completed `Future` with a `Some`, and an unrealized `Future` with a `None`. Furthermore, remember that a realized `Future` can have two states: success or failure. This is the purpose of the inner `Try`. Like `Option.get`, it is almost never a good idea to use `Future.value`. To extract a value from a `Future`, refer to the additional techniques described next.

Blocking execution

When we added concurrency to the backtester, we wrote a for-comprehension returning `Future[(BacktestPerformanceSummary, BacktestPerformanceSummary, BacktestPerformanceSummary, BacktestPerformanceSummary)]`, which may leave you wondering how you access the value wrapped in the `Future`. Another way of asking the question is, "Given `Future[T]`, how do I return `T`?" The short answer is, "You don't!" Programming with many `Future` requires a shift in thinking away from synchronous execution towards asynchronous execution. When programming with an asynchronous model, the goal is to avoid working with `T` directly because it implies a synchronous contract.

In practice, there are situations where it is useful to have the `Future[T] => T` function. For example, consider the backtester snippet. If the code from the snippet is used to create a program by defining an `object` extending `App`, the program will terminate before backtesting completes. As the threads in the `ExecutionContext` global are daemon threads, the JVM terminates immediately after creating the `Future`. In this scenario, we need a synchronization mechanism to pause execution until the result is ready. By extending the `Awaitable` trait, `Future` is able to provide such facilities. The `Await` module exposes two methods that achieve this goal:

```
def ready[T](awaitable: Awaitable[T], atMost: Duration): awaitable.type
def result[T](awaitable: Awaitable[T], atMost: Duration): T
```

As `Future` extends `Awaitable`, a `Future` can be supplied as an argument to either method. The `ready` halts program flow until `T` is available and returns the completed `Future[T]`. In practice, `ready` is rarely used because it is conceptually strange to return a `Future[T]` from a synchronous call instead of `T`. You are more likely to commonly use `result`, which provides the desired transformation returning `T` given `Future[T]`. For example, `CrazyIdeas.scala` can be modified to look like the following:

```
    val summariesF = for {
      firstDaveAapl <- Future(backtest(Dave1, Ticker("AAPL"),
lastMonths(3)))
      firstDaveGoog <- Future(backtest(Dave1, Ticker("GOOG"),
lastMonths(3)))
      secondDaveAapl <- Future(backtest(Dave2, Ticker("AAPL"),
lastMonths(3)))
      secondDaveGoog <- Future(backtest(Dave2, Ticker("GOOG"),
lastMonths(3)))
    } yield (firstDaveAapl, firstDaveGoog, secondDaveAapl, secondDaveGoog)

    Await.result(summariesF, scala.concurrent.duration.Duration(1,
java.util.concurrent.TimeUnit.SECONDS))
```

In this snippet, we see the blocking, synchronous invocation of `Await.result` to return the `Tuple` of `Future[BacktestPerformanceSummary]`. This blocking call is parameterized with a timeout to defend against the scenario where the `Future` is not computed within a certain amount of time. Using a blocking call to retrieve the backtest results means that the JVM will only exit after the backtest completes or when the timeout expires. When the timeout expires and the backtest is incomplete, `result` and `ready` throw a `TimeoutException`.

Blocking execution of your program is potentially detrimental to your program's performance, and it should be used with caution. Using the methods on the `Await` companion object make blocking calls easy to recognize. As `ready` and `result` throw an exception when timing out, rather than returning a different data type, you must take extra caution to handle this scenario. You should treat any synchronous call involving asynchrony (that either does not provide a timeout or does not handle the timeout) as a bug.

Programming asynchronously requires a mindset shift to write a program that describes what to do when the value appears rather than writing programs that require a value to exist before acting on it. You should be suspicious of any use of `Await` that interrupts transformation of a to-be-computed value. A set of transformations should be composed by acting upon `Future[T]` instead of `T`. Usage of `Await` should be restricted to scenarios where a program has no other work to perform and requires the result of the transformation, as we saw with the backtester.

As the standard library models timeout with an exception instead of a different return type, it is hard to enforce that a timeout is always handled One way to improve safety is to write a utility method that returns `Option[T]` instead of `T` to account for the timeout scenario:

```
object SafeAwait {
  def result[T](
    awaitable: Awaitable[T],
    atMost: Duration): Option[T] =
    Try(Await.result(awaitable, atMost)) match {
      case Success(t) => Some(t)
      case Failure(_: TimeoutException) => None
      case Failure(e) => throw e
    }
}
```

With this new method, an entire error class is eliminated. As you encounter other unsafe transformations, consider defining methods that return a data type that encodes expected errors to avoid accidentally mishandling the transformation result. What other examples of unsafe transformations come to mind?

Handling failures

Working with `Future` requires disciplined handling of error scenarios to avoid writing a set of transformations that are difficult to reason about. When an exception is thrown inside a `Future` transformation, it bubbles up within the transformation's thread of computation and interrupts downstream transformations. Consider the following motivating example:

```
Future("not-an-integer").map(_.toInt).map(i => {
    println("Multiplying")
    i * 2
})
```

What do you expect to occur after the first `map` transformation? It is clear that the transformation will fail because the provided input cannot be cast to an integer. In this scenario, the `Future` is considered to be a failed `Future` and downstream transformations operating on the wrapped `Int` value, in this example, will not occur. In this simple example, it is obvious that the transformation cannot continue. Imagine a larger code base operating on data more complicated than a single integer with multiple failure scenarios across multiple namespaces and source files. In a real-world setting, it is more challenging to identify where an asynchronous computation broke down.

`Future` provides facilities for handling failures. It provides `recover` and `recoverWith` in order to continue downstream transformations. The signatures are as follows:

```
def recover[U >: T](pf: PartialFunction[Throwable, U])(implicit executor:
ExecutionContext): Future[U]
def recoverWith[U >: T](pf: PartialFunction[Throwable, Future[U]])(implicit
executor: ExecutionContext): Future[U]
```

The difference between these two recovery methods is that the partial function provided to `recover` returns `U`, while `recoverWith` returns `Future[U]`. In our previous example, we can use `recover` to supply a default value to continue a transformation, as follows:

```
Future("not-an-integer").map(_.toInt).recover {
  case _: NumberFormatException => -2
}.map(i => {
  println("Multiplying")
  i * 2
})
```

Running this snippet produces the following output:

```
Multiplying
Multiplication result = -4
```

This approach allows you to continue a pipeline of transformations when one transform fails, but it suffers from the same shortcoming as the methods on `Await`. The returned `Future[T]` data type does not reflect the possibility of failure. Using recovery methods is error-prone because it is impossible to know whether the error conditions have been handled without reading through the code.

The error handling that we investigated is appropriate to handle failures during a computation. It is likely that after a series of transformations complete, you will wish to perform special logic. Imagine you are building a web service that submits trading orders to exchanges. Order submission is successful if the order was submitted to the exchange; otherwise, it is considered a failed submission. As order submission involves communication with an external system, the exchange, you modeled this action with a `Future`. Here is what the method handling order submission looks like:

```
def submitOrder(
  ec: ExecutionContext,
  sendToExchange: ValidatedOrder => Future[OrderSubmitted],
  updatePositions: OrderSubmitted => Future[AccountPositions],
  o: RawOrder): Unit = {
  implicit val iec = ec

  (for {
```

```
      vo <- ValidatedOrder.fromRawOrder(o).fold(
        Future.failed[ValidatedOrder](new Exception(
        "Order failed validation")))(Future.successful)
      os <- sendToExchange(vo)
      ap <- updatePositions(os)
    } yield (os, ap)).onComplete {
      case Success((os, ap)) => // Marshal order submission info to caller
      case Failure(e) =>  // Marshal appropriate error response to caller
    }
  }
```

An `ExecutionContext`, a way to submit orders, and a way to update a customer's trading positions after the trade is submitted allow a customer provided `RawOrder` to be submitted to the exchange. In the first processing step, the `RawOrder` is converted into a `ValidatedOrder`, and then lifted into a `Future`. `Future.failure` and `Future.successful` are convenient ways to lift or to wrap a computed value into a `Future`. The value is lifted into a `Future` to allow the entire sequence of steps to be written as a single for-comprehension.

Following the completion of all processing steps, `onComplete` is invoked to asynchronously handle completion of request processing. You can imagine in this context that completing request processing implies creating a serialized version of a response and transmitting this to the caller. Previously, the only mechanism at our disposal to perform work once a value is computed is to block using `Await`. `onComplete` is an asynchronously invoked callback that registers a function to be invoked when the value is completed. As shown in the example, `onComplete` supports handling success and failure cases, which makes it a general-purpose tool to handle the outcome of a `Future` transformation. In addition to `onComplete`, `Future` provides `onFailure` specifically for failure cases and `onSuccess` and `foreach` specifically for success cases.

These callback methods expose a method signature that returns `Unit`. As a functional programmer, you should be leery of invoking these methods because they are side-effecting. The `onComplete` invocations should only happen at the absolute end of a computation when a side-effect can no longer be deferred. In the web service example, the side-effect is transmission of the response to the caller. Another common use case for using these side-effecting callbacks is to handle cross-cutting concerns, such as application metrics. Coming back to the web service, here is one way to increment an error counter when order submission to the exchange fails:

```
(for {
    vo <- ValidatedOrder.fromRawOrder(o).fold(
      Future.failed[ValidatedOrder](
      new Exception("Order failed validation")))(Future.successful)
    os <- {
```

```
        val f = sendToExchange(vo)
        f.onFailure({ case e => incrementExchangeErrorCount() })
        f
      }
    ap <- updatePositions(os)
  } yield (os, ap))
```

In this snippet, a side-effect is performed when submission to the exchange fails via the `onFailure` callback. In this isolated example, it is straightforward to track where the side-effect is happening. However, in a larger system it can be a challenge to identify when and where callbacks were registered. Additionally, from the `Future` API documentation, we learn that callback execution is unordered, which indicates that all callbacks must be treated independently. This is why you must be disciplined about when and where you apply these side-effects.

An alternative approach to error handling is to use a data type that can encode errors. We have seen this approach applied with `Await` when `Option` was the returned data type. `Option` makes it clear that the computation might fail while remaining convenient to use because its transformations (for example, `map`) operate on the wrapped value. Unfortunately, `Option` does not allow us to encode the error. In this case, it is helpful to use another tool from the Scalaz library called disjunction. Disjunction is conceptually similar to `Either`, which can be used to represent one of two possible types. Disjunction is different from `Either` because its operations are right-biased. Let's take a look at a simple example to illustrate this idea:

```
scalaz.\/.right[Throwable, Int](1).map(_ * 2)
```

The `\/` is the shorthand symbol used by Scalaz to represent a disjunction. In this example, a right disjunction is created by wrapping the one integer literal. This disjunction either has the `Throwable` value or the `Int` value, and it is analogous to `Either[Throwable, Int]`. In contrast to `Either`, the `map` transformation operates on the right side of the disjunction. In this example, `map` accepts an `Int` value as input because the right side of the disjunction is an `Int` value. As disjunction is right-biased, it is a natural fit to represent failure and success values. Using the infix notation, it is common to define error handling with `Future` as `Future[Throwable \/ T]`. In place of `Throwable`, one can define an ADT of possible error types to make error handling explicit. This approach is favorable because it enforces handling of failure cases without relying on the author to invoke a recovery method. If you are interested to learn more about how to use disjunction as a tool for error handling, review Eugene Yokota's excellent Scalaz tutorial at `http://eed3si9n.com/learning-sc alaz/Either.html`.

Hampering performance through executor submissions

As `Future` provides an expressive and easy-to-use API, it is common to perform numerous transforms to complete a computation in a large-scale system. Reflecting on the order submission web service mentioned in the previous section, you can imagine multiple application layers operating on a `Future`. A production-ready web service typically composes together multiple layers to service a single request. An example request flow may contain the following stages: request deserialization, authorization, application service invocation, database lookups and/or third-party service callouts, and response translation to a JSON format. If each of these stages in the workflow is modeled with a `Future`, then it is common to have five or more transformations to handle a single request.

Decomposing your software system into small areas of responsibility in a way that is similar to the preceding example is a good engineering practice to support testing in isolation and improving maintainability. However, this approach to software design comes with a performance cost when working with `Future`. As we have seen through our example usage, nearly all transforms on a `Future` require submitting work to an `Executor`. In our example workflow, most stages in the transformation are small. In this scenario, the overhead of submitting work to the executor dominates the execution time of the computation. If the order submission web service services numerous customers with stringent throughput and latency requirements, then it is possible that engineering practices focusing on testability and maintainability will result in poorly performing software.

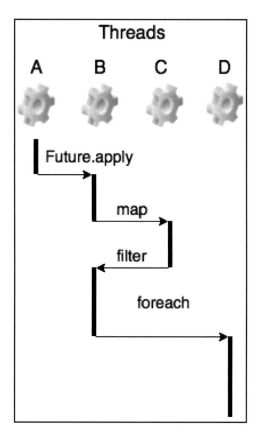

If you consider the preceding diagram, you can see a thread pool with four threads being used to apply transforms to a Future. Each transform is submitted to the pool and there is a chance that a different thread is picked for the computation. This diagram visualizes how multiple small transforms may hamper performance due to the overhead of Executor submissions.

Just how large is the overhead of Executor submissions? This is the motivating question to write a benchmark to quantify the overhead of submitting work to an Executor. The benchmark focuses on adding 1 to an integer N-times in two ways. One approach is to perform the addition operation within a single Future, while the second approach is to perform each addition operation with a new Future transformation. The latter approach is a proxy for the stages of order submission request processing that uses multiple Future transformations in a larger software system. Performing integer addition is the proxy operation because it is an extremely cheap computation, which means that the execution time will be dominated by Executor submissions. The benchmarks look like the following:

```
@Benchmark
def manyTransforms(state: TransformFutureState): Int = {
  import scala.concurrent.ExecutionContext.Implicits._
  val init = Future(0)
  val res = (1 until state.operations).foldLeft(init)
    ((f, _) => f.map(_ + 1))
  Await.result(res, Duration("5 minutes"))
}

@Benchmark
def oneTransform(state: TransformFutureState): Int = {
  import scala.concurrent.ExecutionContext.Implicits._
  val res = Future {
    (1 until state.operations).foldLeft(0)((acc, _) => acc + 1)
  }
  Await.result(res, Duration("5 minutes"))
}
```

TransformFutureState allows the number of operations to be parameterized.
manyTransforms represents each addition operation using a map transformation that
involves submitting work to an Executor. oneTransform performs all addition operations
using a single Executor submission via Future.apply. In this controlled
test, Await.result is used as a blocking mechanism to await the completion of the
computation. The results of running this test on a two-core machine with five
transformations and ten transformations can be seen in the following table:

Benchmark	Map count	Throughput (ops per second)	Error as percentage of throughput
manyTransforms	5	463,614.88	± 1.10
oneTransform	5	412,675.70	± 0.81
manyTransforms	10	118,743.55	± 2.34
oneTransform	10	316,175.79	± 1.79

While both scenarios yield comparable results with five transformations, we can see a clear
difference with ten transforms being applied. This benchmark makes it clear that Executor
submissions can dominate performance. Although the cost can be high, our advice to you is
to model your system without considering this cost up-front. In our experience, it is easier
to rework a well-modeled system for performance improvements than it is to extend or to
rework a poorly-modeled but performant system. For this reason, we advise against going
to great lengths to group Executor submissions when attempting to put together the initial
version of a complex system.

Once you have a good design in place, the first step is to benchmark and to profile in order to identify whether `Executor` submissions are the bottleneck. In the event that you discover that your style of `Future` usage is causing performance bottlenecks, there are several courses of action you should consider.

The lowest cost development option is to replace unnecessarily costly `Future` creation with the use of `Future.success` or `Future.failure`. The order submission web service took advantage of these factory methods to lift values into a `Future`. As the value is already computed, these factory methods avoid submitting any tasks to the `Executor` that are referenced by the provided `ExecutionContext`. Replacing usages of `Future.apply` with either `Future.successful` or `Future.failure` when the value is already computed can yield cost savings.

A more expensive alternative in terms of development effort is to rework your implementation to group together `Future` transformations in a way similar to `manyTransforms`. This tactic involves reviewing each application layer to determine whether transforms within a single layer can be combined. If possible, we recommend that you avoid merging transformations across application layers (for example, between request deserialization or authorization and application service processing) because this weakens your model and increases maintenance cost.

If neither of these options produces acceptable performance, then it may be worthwhile to discuss with the product owners the option of addressing the performance issue with hardware. As your system's design has not been compromised and it reflects solid engineering practices, then it likely can be horizontally scaled or clustered. Depending on the state tracked by your system, this option might be possible without additional development work. Perhaps product owners value a system that can be easily maintained and extended more than performance. If this is the case, adding scale to your system may be a viable way forward.

Provided that you are unable to buy your way out of the performance challenge, then there are three additional possibilities. One option is to investigate an alternative to `Future`, named `Task`. This construct, which is provided by the Scalaz library, allows computations to be performed with fewer `Executor` submissions. This option involves significant development because the `Future` data type will need to be replaced throughout the application with `Task`. We will explore `Task` at the end of this chapter and investigate the performance benefits that it can provide.

Independent of using `Task`, it can be useful to review your application's model to critically question whether or not there is unnecessary work being done on the critical path. As we saw with MVT's reporting infrastructure and the introduction of stream processing, it is sometimes possible to rethink a design to improve performance. Like the introduction of `Task`, reconsidering your system's architecture is a large-scale change. The last resort option is to merge application layers in order to support grouping `Future` transformations. We advise against exercising this option, unless all other suggestions have failed. This option results in a code base that is more difficult to reason about because concerns are no longer separated. In the short-run, you may reap performance benefits, but in our experience, these benefits are outweighed in the long-run by the cost of maintaining and extending such a system.

Handling blocking calls and callbacks

As described in the first part of this chapter, the `Future` API provides an elegant way to write concurrent programs. As it is considered a bad practice to block on a `Future`, it is not unusual to see `Future` being widely used across an entire code base. However, it is unlikely that your system is only composed of your own code. Most real-world applications leverage existing libraries and third-party software to avoid re-implementing existing solutions to some common problems (such as data encoding and decoding, communication over HTTP, database drivers, and so on). Unfortunately, not all libraries use the future API, and it may become a challenge to gracefully integrate them into your system. In this section, we will examine some common pitfalls that you may encounter and mention possible workarounds.

ExecutionContext and blocking calls

While working on the backtester, you noticed that one module of the code is used to load some historical buy orders from a relational database. Since you started rewriting the application to take advantage of `Future`, the module API is fully asynchronous:

```
def findBuyOrders(
  client: ClientId,
  ticker: Ticker)(implicit ec: ExecutionContext): Future[List[Order]] = ???
```

However, after profiling the application, you noticed that this part of the code performs quite poorly. You attempted to increase the database connection count, first doubling it, then tripling it, both without success. Attempting to understand the cause of the problem, you look at all the locations where the method is called, and you noticed the following pattern:

```
import scala.concurrent.ExecutionContext.Implicits.global
findBuyOrders(clientId, tickerFoo)
```

All the callers are importing the global `ExecutionContext` to be implicitly used by the method. The default thread pool is backed by a `ForkJoinPool`, and it is sized based on the available cores on the machine. As such, it is CPU-bound and designed to handle nonblocking, CPU intensive operations. This is a good choice for applications that do not perform blocking calls. However, if your application runs blocking calls asynchronously (that is, in a `Future` execution), relying on the default `ExecutionContext` will most likely quickly degrade performance.

Asynchronous versus nonblocking

Before going further, we want to clarify some of the terms used in this section. Nonblocking can be a confusing term in the context of concurrency. When using `Future`, we perform asynchronous operations, meaning that we start a computation so it can proceed with the flow of the program. The computation is executed in the background and will eventually yield a result. This behavior is sometimes called nonblocking, meaning that the API call returns immediately. However, blocking and nonblocking most often refer to I/O operations and how they are performed, especially how the thread that is performing the operation is used. For example, writing a sequence of bytes to a local file can be a blocking operation because the thread calling `write` will have to wait (block) until the I/O operation is completed. When using nonblocking constructs, such as the ones provided in the `java.nio` package, it is possible to perform I/O operations that will be executed without blocking a thread.

It is possible to implement an API with a combination of the following behaviors:

API characteristics	Returns	Blocks a thread?
Synchronous/blocking	At the end of the computation	Yes, the calling thread executes the operation
Asynchronous/blocking	Immediately	Yes, this blocks a thread from a dedicated pool
Asynchronous/nonblocking	Immediately	No, the thread is freed-up while the blocking operation is performed

Using a dedicated ExecutionContext to block calls

Clearly, our problem is that we are using the `ExecutionContext` global to perform blocking calls. We are querying a relational database, and most JDBC drivers are implemented to perform blocking calls. The pooled threads call the driver and block while waiting for the query and the response to travel over the network, making them unusable by other computations. An option is to create a dedicated `ExecutionContext` to execute the `Future`, including blocking operations. This `ExecutionContext` is sized with more threads in the anticipation that they will be blocked when performing their computation:

```
val context = ExecutionContext.fromExecutorService(
  Executors.newFixedThreadPool(20)
)
findBuyOrders(clientId, tickerFoo)(context)
```

The first benefit is that we have more threads available, meaning that we can initiate more queries concurrently. The second benefit is that the other asynchronous computations performed in our system are done on a separate pool (for example, the global context), and they will avoid starvation since no threads are blocked.

We write a short benchmark to evaluate the performance of our new system. In this example, we use a mock implementation of `findBuyOrders` to simulate querying the database:

```
def findBuyOrders(
  client: ClientId,
  ticker: Ticker)(ec: ExecutionContext): Future[List[Order]] = Future {
  Thread.sleep(100)
  Order.staticList.filter(o => o.clientId == client
    && o.ticker == ticker)
} (ec)
```

We pass the `ExecutionContext` as a parameter. Our benchmark compares the throughput of an application relying on the default `ExecutionContext` and one using an `ExecutionContext`, which is dedicated to blocking operations; the latter is initializedwith twenty times more threads. The results are as follows:

Benchmark	Operation count	Throughput (ops per second)	Error as percentage of throughput
`withDefaultContext`	10	3.21	± 0.65
`withDedicatedContext`	10	9.34	± 1.00
`withDefaultContext`	1,000	0.04	± 2.56
`withDedicatedContext`	1,000	0.73	± 0.41

The results confirm our intuition. The dedicated pool is bigger than the default context in anticipation of threads being blocked waiting for a blocking operation to finish. Having more threads available, it is able to start more blocking operations concurrently, thus achieving a better throughput. Creating a dedicated `ExecutionContext` is a good way to isolate blocking operations and make sure that they do not slow down CPU-bound computations. When designing your dedicated thread pool, make sure that you understand how the underlying resources (for example, connections, file handles, and so on) are used. For example, when dealing with a relational database, we know that one connection can only be used to perform one query at a time. A good rule of thumb is to create a thread pool with as many threads as the amount of connections that you want to open with your database server. If the number of connections is less than the thread count, some threads may be waiting for a connection and remain unused. If you have more connections than threads, the opposite situation may occur and some connections may remain unused.

A good strategy is to rely on the type system and the compiler to ensure that you are not mixing up different `ExecutionContext` instances. Unless the type is differentiated, you may accidentally use a CPU-bound context when performing blocking operations. You can create your own `DatabaseOperationsExecutionContext` type wrapping an `ExecutionContext`, and accept this type when creating your database access module. Another idea is to use tagged types that are provided by Scalaz. Refer to Chapter 3, *Unleashing Scala Performance,* for a refresher on tagged types. Consider the following example:

```
object DatabaseAccess {

  sealed trait BlockingExecutionContextTag

  type BlockingExecutionContext = ExecutionContext @@
BlockingExecutionContextTag

  object BlockingExecutionContext {
    def fromContext(ec: ExecutionContext): BlockingExecutionContext =
      Tag[ExecutionContext, BlockingExecutionContextTag](ec)

    def withSize(size: Int): BlockingExecutionContext =
fromContext(ExecutionContext.fromExecutor(Executors.newFixedThreadPool(size
)))
  }
}

class DatabaseAccess(ec: BlockingExecutionContext) {
  // Implementation elided
}
```

Using a tagged types for our `ExecutionContext` gives us additional safety. It is easy to make a mistake in the `main` method while wiring up your application, and inadvertently use the wrong `ExecutionContext` when creating yourmodules.

Using the blocking construct

The standard library provides a `blocking` construct that can be used to signal blocking operations executed inside a `Future`. We can modify our previous example to leverage `blocking` instead of a dedicated `ExecutionContext`:

```
import scala.concurrent.ExecutionContext.Implicits.global
def findBuyOrders(
 client: ClientId,
 ticket: Ticker): Future[List[Order]] = Future {
   scala.concurrent.blocking{
     Thread.sleep(100)
     Order.staticList.filter(o => o.clientId == client && o.ticker ==
ticker)
   }
 }
```

Note that in the preceding implementation, we use the default `ExecutionContext` to execute the `Future`. The `blocking` construct is used to notify the `ExecutionContext` that a computation is blocking. This allows the `ExecutionContext` to adapt its execution strategy. For example, the default global `ExecutionContext` will temporarily increase the number of threads in the pool when it performs a computation wrapped with `blocking`. A dedicated thread is created in the pool to execute the blocking computation, making sure that the rest of the pool remains available for CPU-bound computations.

You should use `blocking` cautiously. The `blocking` construct is merely used to notify `ExecutionContext` that the wrapped operation is blocking. It is the responsibility of the `ExecutionContext` to implement a specific behavior or ignore the notification. The only implementation that actually takes it into account and implements special behavior is the default `ExecutionContext` global.

Translating callbacks with Promise

While `Future` is the main construct of the `scala.concurrent` API, another useful abstraction is `Promise`. `Promise` is another way to create and complete a `Future`. The `Future` is a read-only container for a result that will eventually be computed. `Promise` is a handle that allows you to explicitly set the value contained in a `Future`. A `Promise` is always associated with only one `Future`, and this `Future` is specific to the `Promise`. It is possible to complete the `Future` of a `Promise` with a successful result, or an exception (which will fail the `Future`).

Let's look at a short example to understand how `Promise` works:

```
scala> val p = Promise[Int]   // this promise will provide an Int
p: scala.concurrent.Promise[Int] =
scala.concurrent.impl.Promise$DefaultPromise@d343a81

scala> p.future.value
res3: Option[scala.util.Try[Int]] = None
// The future associated to this Promise is not yet completed

scala> p.success(42)
res4: p.type = scala.concurrent.impl.Promise$DefaultPromise@d343a81

scala> p.future.value
res5: Option[scala.util.Try[Int]] = Some(Success(42))
```

A `Promise` can only be used once to complete its associated `Future`, either with a success or a failure. Attempting to complete an already realized `Promise` will throw an exception, unless you use `trySuccess`, `tryFailure`, or `tryComplete`. These three methods will attempt to complete the `Future` that is linked to the `Promise` and return `true` if the `Future` was completed or `false` if it was already previously completed.

At this point, you may be wondering in what circumstances you would really take advantage of `Promise`. Especially considering the previous example, would it be simpler to return the internal `Future` instead of relying on a `Promise`? Keep in mind that the preceding snippet is meant to demonstrate a simple workflow that illustrates the `Promise` API. However, we understand your question. In practice, we see two common use cases for `Promise`.

From callbacks to a Future-based API

The first use case is to turn a callback-based API into a `Future`-based API. Imagine having to integrate with a third-party product, such as the proprietary database that MVT obtained recently by purchasing usage licenses. This is a great product that is used to store historical quotes per timestamp and ticker. It comes with a library to be used by a client application. Unfortunately, this library, while fully asynchronous and nonblocking, is callback-oriented, as follows:

```
object DatabaseClient {
  def findQuote(instant: Instant, ticker: Ticker,
    f: (Quote) => Unit): Unit = ???

  def findAllQuotes(from: Instant, to: Instant, ticker: Ticker,
    f: (List[Quote]) => Unit, h: Exception => Unit): Unit = ???
}
```

There is no doubt that the client works fine; after all, MVT paid a lot of money for it! However, it will not be easy to integrate it with your own application. Your program relies heavily on Future. This is where Promise can help us, as follows:

```scala
object DatabaseAdapter {

  def findQuote(instant: Instant, ticker: Ticker): Future[Quote] = {
    val result = Promise[Quote]

    DatabaseClient.findQuote(instant, ticker, {
      q: Quote =>
        result.success(q)
    })

    result.future
  }

  def findAllQuotes(from: Instant, to: Instant, ticker: Ticker):
  Future[List[Quote]] = {
    Val result = Promise[List[Quote]]
    DatabaseClient.findQuote(from, to, ticker, {
      quotes: List[Quote] => result.success(quotes)
    }, {
      ex: Exception => result.failure(ex)
    }
  }

    result.future
}
```

Thanks to the Promise abstraction, we are able to return a Future. We simply use success and failure in the respective callbacks to call the proprietary client. This use case often arises in production when you have to integrate with a Java library. Even though Java 8 introduced a significant improvement to the Java concurrent package, most Java libraries still rely on callbacks to implement asynchronous behavior. Using Promise, you can fully leverage the existing Java ecosystem in your program without giving up on Scala support for concurrent programming.

Combining Future with Promise

Promise can also be used to combine instances of Future. For example, let's add a timeout capability to Future:

```scala
def run[A](f: => Future[A], timeout: Duration): Future[A] = {
  val res = Promise[A]
```

```
    Future {
      Thread.sleep(timeout.getMillis)
        res.tryFailure(new Exception("Timed out")
    }

    f onComplete {
    case r => res.tryCompleteWith(f)
    }

    res.future
  }
```

Our method takes a by-name `Future` (that is, a `Future` that has not started its execution yet) as well as the timeout value to apply. In the method, we use a `Promise` as a container for the result. We start an internal `Future` that will block for the timeout duration before failing the `Promise` with an `Exception`. We also start the main `Future` and register a callback to complete the `Promise` with the result of the computation. The first of the two `Futures` that terminates will effectively complete the `Promise` with its result. Note that in this example, we use `tryFailure` and `tryCompleteWith`. It is likely that both `Futures` will eventually terminate and try to complete the `Promise`. We are only interested in the result of the first one that completes, but we also want to avoid throwing an `Exception` when attempting to complete an already realized `Promise`.

The preceding example is a naive implementation of a timeout. It is mostly a prototype used to demonstrate how `Promise` can be leveraged to enriched `Future` and implement complex behavior. A more realistic implementation would probably involve a `ScheduledExecutorService`. A `ScheduledExecutorService` allows you to schedule the execution of a computation after a certain delay. It allows us to schedule the call to `tryFailure` without blocking a thread with a call to `Thread.sleep`. We made the choice to keep this example simple and not introduce a new type, but we encourage you to research this implementation of `ScheduledExecutorService`.

In practice, you may occasionally have to write your own custom combinators for `Future`. `Promise` is a useful abstraction in your toolbox if you need to do this. However, `Future` and its companion object already provide a number of built-in combinators and methods that you should try to leverage as much as possible.

Tasked with more backtest performance improvements

Discovering `Future` and adopting an asynchronous mindset helped you better utilize your computing resources to test multiple strategies and tickers faster. You improved performance by treating the backtest as a black box. Without changing the implementation of the backtest, there were straightforward performance wins. Identifying logical sequences of transformations as candidates for concurrency is a good strategy to apply when considering how to speed up your software.

Let's extend this idea to a smaller logical unit of processing within the backtester. A backtest exercises a strategy for a ticker across a time period. After speaking with Dave, you discover that MVT does not maintain positions overnight. At the end of each trading day, MVT trading systems mitigate risk by ensuring that all stock positions are liquidated. This is done to defend against volatile overnight price moves after the market closes, which the company is unable to react to by trading. As positions are not held overnight, each trading day can be simulated independently of the previous trading day. Returning to our asynchronous mindset, this insight implies that trading day simulations can be performed concurrently.

Before jumping into the implementation using `Future`, we will share an alternative abstraction, named `Task`, which is provided by the Scalaz library. `Task` provides compelling usage reasons for our proposed backtest modifications. We introduce `Task` next, provided that you are up to the task!

Introducing Scalaz Task

Scalaz`Task` provides a different approach to achieve concurrency. Although `Task` can be used in a way that mimics `Future`, there are important conceptual differences between these two abstractions. `Task` allows fine-grained control over asynchronous execution, which provides performance benefits. `Task` maintains referential transparency as well, which provides stronger reasoning abilities. Referential transparency is a property of expressions that are side-effect free. To better understand this principle, consider the following simple `sum` method:

```
def sum(x: Int, y: Int): Int = x + y
```

Imagine that we are performing two summations:

```
sum(sum(2, 3), 4)
```

As `sum` is side-effect free, we can replace `sum(2, 3)` with its result, as follows:

```
sum(5, 4)
```

This expression will always evaluate to 9, which satisfies referential transparency. Now imagine a twist in the implementation of `sum`:

```
class SumService(updateDatabase: () => Unit) {
  def sum(x: Int, y: Int): Int = {
    updateDatabase()
    x + y
  }
}
```

Now, `sum` includes a side-effect of writing to a database that breaks referential transparency. We can no longer perform the replacement of `sum(2, 3)` with the value 9 because then the database will not be updated. Referential transparency is a concept at the heart of the functional programming paradigm because it provides strong reasoning guarantees. The Haskell wiki provides additional commentary and examples worth reviewing at `https://wiki.haskell.org/Referential_transparency`.

Let's take a look at common `Task` API usage to better understand how `Task` works.

Creating and executing Task

The methods provided by the`Task` companion object are the main entry points to the API, and the best ways to create an instance of `Task`. The `Task.apply` is the first method to inspect. It takes a computation returning an instance of A (that is, a by-name parameter of the A type) and an implicit `ExecutorService` to run the computation. Contrary to `Future`, which uses `ExecutionContext` as an abstraction for a thread pool, `Task` uses the `ExecutorService`, which is defined in the Java standard library:

```
scala> val t = Task {
     |    println("Starting task")
     |    40 + 2
     | }
t: scalaz.concurrent.Task[Int] = scalaz.concurrent.Task@300555a9
```

The first thing that you may have noticed is that, even though we instantiated a new `Task`, nothing is printed on the screen. This is an important difference when comparing `Task` and `Future`; while `Future` is eagerly evaluated, a `Task` is not computed until you explicitly ask for it:

```
scala> t.unsafePerformSync
```

```
Starting task
res0: Int = 42
```

The preceding example calls the `unsafePerformSync` instance method to execute the task. We can see the `println` as well as the returned result 42. Note that `unsafePerformSync` is an unsafe call. If the computation throws an exception, the exception is re-thrown by `unsafePerformSync`. To avoid this side-effect, calling `unsafePerformSyncAttempt` is preferred. The `unsafePerformSyncAttempt` instance catches the exception and has a return type of `Throwable \/ A`, which allows you to cleanly handle the failure case. Note that when creating the task `t`, we did not provide an `ExecutorService`. By default, `apply` creates a `Task` to be run on `DefaultExecutorService`, a fixed thread pool for which the size is based on the count of available processors on the machine using a default parameter. The `DefaultExecutorService` is analogous to the global `ExecutionContext` that we explored with `Future`. It is CPU-bound and sized based on the available cores on the machine. We can also supply a different `ExecutorService` at creation time:

```
scala> val es = Executors.newFixedThreadPool(4)
es: java.util.concurrent.ExecutorService =
java.util.concurrent.ThreadPoolExecutor@4c50cd8c[Running, pool size = 0,
active threads = 0, queued tasks = 0, completed tasks = 0]

scala> val t = Task {
 println("Starting task on thread " + Thread.currentThread.getName)
 40 + 2
}(es)
t: scalaz.concurrent.Task[Int] = scalaz.concurrent.Task@497db010

scala> println("Calling run from " + Thread.currentThread.getName)
Calling run from run-main-1

scala> t.unsafePerformSync
Starting task on thread pool-8-thread-2
res2: Int = 42
```

The output shows that the `Task` is executed on the supplied `ExecutorService`, not on the main thread.

Speaking of `Task` execution, let's perform a little experiment. We will create an instance of `Task` and call `unsafePerformSync` twice in a row:

```
scala> val t = Task {
     |    println("Starting task")
     |    40 + 2
     | }
t: scalaz.concurrent.Task[Int] = scalaz.concurrent.Task@300555a9
```

```
scala> t.unsafePerformSync
Starting task
res0: Int = 42

scala> t.unsafePerformSync
Starting task
res1: Int = 42
```

We observe that `Starting task` prints after each call to `unsafePerformSync`. This indicates that the full computation is executed each time we call `unsafePerformSync`. That is another difference with `Future`. While a `Future` memorizes its result after the computation, a `Task` performs its computation each time we call `unsafePerformSync`. In other words, `Task` is referentially transparent and, therefore, closer to the functional programming paradigm than `Future`.

Asynchronous behavior

Like `Future`, it is possible (and even recommended) to use `Task` in an asynchronous way. An instance of `Task` can be executed asynchronously by calling `unsafePerformAsync`. This method takes a callback of type `(Throwable \/ A) => Unit` that is called at the end of the computation. Observe the following snippet:

```
def createAndRunTask(): Unit = {
 val t = Task {
   println("Computing the answer...")
   Thread.sleep(2000)
   40 + 2
 }

 t.unsafePerformAsync {
   case \/-(answer) => println("The answer is " + answer)
   case -\/(ex) => println("Failed to compute the answer: " + ex)
 }

 println("Waiting for the answer")
}
```

We create our`Task`, and add a `Thread.sleep` to simulate an expensive computation. We call `unsafePerformAsync` and use a simple callback to print the answer (or an exception, if the computation fails). We call `createAndRunTask` and observe the following output:

```
scala> TaskExample.createAndRunTask()
Waiting for the answer

scala> Computing the answer...
```

```
The answer is 42
```

We can see that our last statement, "Waiting for the answer" was printed first. This is because `unsafePerformAsync` returns immediately. We can see the statement from our computation, as well as the answer printed in our callback. This method is a rough equivalent to `onComplete`, which is defined on Scala's `Future`.

Another useful method provided by the companion object of `Task` is `async`. Remember how we previously used `Promise` to turn a callback-based API into an API returning an instance of `Future`? It is possible to achieve the same goal with `Task`; that is, we can turn a callback-based API into a more monadic API returning a `Task`, as follows:

```
object CallbackAPI {
  def doCoolThings[A](a: => A, f: (Throwable \/ A) => Unit): Unit = ???
}

def doCoolThingsToTask[A](a: => A): Task[A] =
 Task.async { f =>
   CallbackAPI.doCoolThings[A](a, res => f(res))
 }
```

Evaluating this method in the REPL yields the following:

```
> val t = doCoolThingsToTask(40+2)
> t.map(res => res / 2).unsafePerformSync
res2: Int = 21
```

Our `doCoolThingsToTask` method uses `Task.async` to create a `Task` instance from a callback-based API that is defined in `CallbackAPI`. The `Task.async` can even be used to turn a Scala `Future` into a Scalaz `Task`:

```
def futureToTask[A](future: Future[A])(implicit ec: ExecutionContext):
Task[A] =
 Task.async { f =>
   future.onComplete {
     case Success(res) => f(\/-(res))
     case Failure(ex) => f(-\/(ex))
   }
 }
```

Note that we have to supply an `ExecutionContext` to be able to call `onComplete` on `Future`. This is due to `Future` eager evaluation. Almost all methods that are defined on `Future` will submit a computation to a thread pool immediately.

It is also possible to convert a `Task` to a `Future`:

```
def taskToFuture[A](t: Task[A]): Future[A] = {
  val p = Promise[A]()
  t.unsafePerformAsync {
    case \/-(a) => p.success(a)
    case -\/(ex) => p.failure(ex)
  }
  p.future
}
```

The execution model

Understanding the `Task` execution model requires understanding the Scalaz `Future` execution model because `Task` composes a Scalaz `Future` and adds error handling. This is visible from the definition of `Task`:

```
class Task[+A](val get: Future[Throwable \/ A])
```

In this definition, `Future` is the not the Scala standard library version, but instead this is an alternative version that is provided by Scalaz. The Scalaz `Future` decouples defining transformations from execution strategy, providing us with fine-grained control over `Executor` submissions. Scalaz `Future` accomplishes this by defining itself as a trampolining computation. Trampolining is a technique that describes a computation as a discrete series of chunks that are run using constant space. To dive into the details of how a trampoline works, we recommend reading Runar Bjarnason's paper, *Stackless Scala With Free Monads,* available at `http://blog.higher-order.com/assets/trampolines.pdf`.

`Task` builds on Scalaz `Future` by providing error handling with the Scalaz `\/` disjunction. `Task` is the description of a computation. Transformations add to the description of the computation that will eventually be executed by a thread pool. To begin evaluation, a `Task` must be explicitly started. This behavior is interesting because when a `Task` is finally executed, we can limit computation execution to a single thread. This improves thread reuse and reduces context switching.

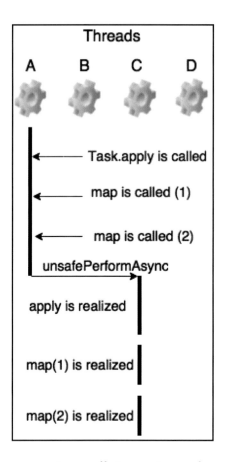

In the preceding diagram, we see various calls to `apply` and `map`. These calls are merely modifying the definition of the task to be performed. It is only when we call `unsafePerformAsync` that the computation is realized in a different thread. Note that all the transforms are applied by the same thread.

We can exercise `Future` and `Task` performance in a short microbenchmark comparing their throughput based on the transform (for example, `map` and `flatMap`), and the count of transformations applied. A snippet of the benchmark can be found, as follows:

```
@Benchmark
def mapWithFuture(state: TaskFutureState): Int = {
  implicit val ec = state.context
  val init = Future(0)
  val res = (1 until state.operations).foldLeft(init)
    ((f, _) => f.map(_ + 1))
  Await.result(res, Duration("5 minutes"))
```

```
}

@Benchmark
def mapWithTask(state: TaskFutureState): Int = {
  val init = Task(0)(state.es)
  val res = (1 until state.operations).foldLeft(init)
    ((t, _) => t.map(_ + 1))
  res.unsafePerformSync
}
```

Both scenarios run similar computations. We create an initial instance of `Future` or `Task` containing 0, and we apply several consecutive `map` operations to add 1 to the accumulator. Two other scenarios performed the same computation but with `flatMap` instead. The results for `flatMap` are displayed in the following table:

Benchmark	Operation count	Throughput (ops per second)	Error as percentage of throughput
flatMapWithFuture	5	41,602.33	± 0.69
flatMapWithTask	5	59,478.50	± 2.14
flatMapWithFuture	10	31,738.80	± 0.52
flatMapWithTask	10	43,811.15	± 0.47
flatMapWithFuture	100	4,390.11	± 1.91
flatMapWithTask	100	13,415.30	± 0.60

The results for `map` operations can be found in the following table:

Benchmark	Operation count	Throughput (ops per second)	Error as percentage of throughput
mapWithFuture	5	45,710.02	± 1.30
mapWithTask	5	93,666.73	± 0.57
mapWithFuture	10	44,860.44	± 1.80
mapWithTask	10	91,932.14	± 0.88
mapWithFuture	100	19,974.24	± 0.55
mapWithTask	100	46,288.17	± 0.46

This benchmark highlights the performance gain due to the different execution model of `Task`. Even for a small number of transforms, the throughput is better with a deferred evaluation.

Modeling trading day simulations with Task

Equipped with our understanding of `Task`, we now have the knowledge necessary to add concurrency to the execution of a single backtest run. You may recall that we discovered from Dave that MVT closes its positions at the end of each trading day. This insight allows us to model each trading day independently. Let's familiarize ourselves with the current implementation by beginning with the model, as follows:

```scala
case class PnL(value: BigDecimal) extends AnyVal
object PnL {
  def merge(x: PnL, y: PnL): PnL = PnL(x.value + y.value)
  val zero: PnL = PnL(0)
}
case class BacktestPerformanceSummary(pnl: PnL)
case class DecisionDelayMillis(value: Long) extends AnyVal
```

The profit-and-loss is the output of each simulated trading day. `PnL` provides a convenient method to add together two `PnL` instances, which can be used to sum the simulation `PnL` across multiple trading days. Once all the trading days are simulated, a `BacktestPerformanceSummary` is created to capture the simulation profit-and-loss. For our work on the backtester, we will use a `Thread.sleep` to simulate computationally expensive work in place of an actual decisioning strategy. The length of the sleep is parameterized by `DecisionDelayMillis`.

We show a simplified version of the backtester that shows how `DecisionDelayMillis` is used to simulate a trading day, as follows:

```scala
def originalBacktest(
  testDays: List[MonthDay],
  decisionDelay: DecisionDelayMillis): BacktestPerformanceSummary =
  {
  val pnls = for {
    d <- testDays
    _ = Thread.sleep(decisionDelay.value)
  } yield PnL(10)
  BacktestPerformanceSummary(pnls.reduceOption(PnL.merge).getOrElse(
    PnL.zero))
}
```

The original backtest displays how a list of days is simulated in a synchronous fashion. For reproducibility, we substitute a constant profit-and-loss of $10 in place of a dynamic value. This backtest ignores the application of a ticker and a strategy to focus on the core of our dilemma: How can we use `Task` to add concurrency to a backtest?

From our examples, we saw that `Task` introduces concurrency through submission of multiple `Tasks` to an `ExecutorService` and by performing the side-effect of running a `Task` with `unsafePerformAsync` to avoid a blocking wait for the result. As a first step, let's implement a version of the backtest that uses `Task` without introducing concurrency:

```
def backtestWithoutConcurrency(
  testDays: List[MonthDay],
  decisionDelay: DecisionDelayMillis): Task[BacktestPerformanceSummary] =
  {
  val ts = for (d <- testDays) yield Task.delay {
    Thread.sleep(decisionDelay.value)
    PnL(10)
  }
  Task.gatherUnordered(ts).map(pnls => BacktestPerformanceSummary(
    pnls.reduceOption(PnL.merge).getOrElse(PnL.zero)))
}
```

This implementation changes the return type to `Task[BacktestPerformanceSummary]`. Since the `Task` is not run, referential transparency is maintained within this method. Each trading day is simulated using `Task.delay`. `delay` is a lazy variant of `Task.now` that defers evaluation of the provided value. Let's look at the following signature to confirm:

```
def delay[A](a: => A): Task[A]
```

If we had instead used `Task.now` in place of `Task.delay`, the sleep (that is, the simulation) would have taken effect before running `Task`. We also see the use of another new capability, `Task.gatherUnordered`. `gatherUnordered` is useful when you wish to make the following transformation:

```
List[Task[A]] => Task[List[A]]
```

Although `List` is used here, this relationship exists for any `Seq`. `gatherUnordered` provides a way to take a collection of `Task` and instead operate on a single `Task` that wraps a collection of the underlying type. Let's look at the following signature to make our understanding more concrete:

```
def gatherUnordered[A](tasks: Seq[Task[A]], exceptionCancels: Boolean =
false): Task[List[A]]
```

This signature closely matches the previous function that we defined with the addition of an optional Boolean parameter. When `exceptionCancels` is set to `true`, any pending `Task` will not be evaluated. `gatherUnordered` allows us to merge together the results of each trading day's profit-and-loss and return a single `Task` wrapping `BacktestPerformanceSummary`. The Scala `Future` companion object provides an analogous method, named `sequence`, that performs the same operation on a sequence of `Futures`.

This is a functioning implementation of the backtest, but it does not add concurrency to the simulation of historical trading days. For our next iteration, we take advantage of a new part of the `Task` API, `Task.fork`. Let's see how it is used, and then we will explain how it works:

```
def backtestWithAllForked(
  testDays: List[MonthDay],
  decisionDelay: DecisionDelayMillis): Task[BacktestPerformanceSummary] =
  {
  val ts = for (d <- testDays) yield Task.fork {
    Thread.sleep(decisionDelay.value)
    Task.now(PnL(10))
  }
  Task.gatherUnordered(ts).map(pnls => BacktestPerformanceSummary(
    pnls.reduceOption(PnL.merge).getOrElse(PnL.zero)))
}
```

This implementation gathers trading day `PnL` in the same way as before, but instead this uses a combination of `Task.fork` and `Task.now` to simulate the trading day. Let's look at the signature of `Task.fork` to understand how runtime behavior changes:

```
def fork[A](a: => Task[A])(implicit pool: ExecutorService =
Strategy.DefaultExecutorService): Task[A]
```

`fork` accepts a `Task` as a by-name parameter and an implicit `ExecutorService` that defaults to the CPU-bound executor. The signature shows that `fork` submits the provided `Task` to `pool` in order to fork the computation into a different thread. `fork` is an explicit way to control concurrency with `Task`. Conceptually, `fork` is analogous to any `Future` transformation (for example, `map`) that involves submission to an executor. As `fork` lazily evaluates its argument, `Task.now` can be used to lift the trading day's profit-and-loss into a `Task`. With this implementation, the `Task` that represents each trading day is submitted to an executor. If we assume 30 trading days are being backtested and the computer used has two cores, then this implementation allows each core to simulate 15 trading days instead of a single core simulating 30 days.

As we saw in earlier benchmarks, submitting a high volume of small computations to an executor is expensive. As we have explicit control over concurrency with `Task` using `fork`, we can improve our performance by optimizing the frequency of executor submissions. In our third attempt, we take advantage of knowing the number of trading days to be simulated to control executor submissions. The implementation now looks like the following:

```
def backtestWithBatchedForking(
  testDays: List[MonthDay],
```

```
  decisionDelay: DecisionDelayMillis): Task[BacktestPerformanceSummary] =
  {
  val ts = for (d <- testDays) yield Task.delay {
    Thread.sleep(decisionDelay.value)
    PnL(10)
  }
  Task.gatherUnordered(ts.sliding(30, 30).toList.map(xs =>
    Task.fork(Task.gatherUnordered(xs)))).map(pnls =>
    BacktestPerformanceSummary(
      pnls.flatten.reduceOption(PnL.merge).getOrElse(PnL.zero)))
}
```

This implementation returns to representing the simulation of each trading day without any concurrency using `Task.delay`. In contrast to the previous implementations, the list of trading day simulation `Tasks` is divided into chunks of 30 using `sliding`. Each chunk of 30 `Tasks` is wrapped with an invocation of `Task.fork` to execute concurrently. This approach allows us to balance the benefits of concurrency with the overhead of executor submissions.

Of these three implementations, which is most performant? The answer is not straightforward because it depends on the number of simulation trading days and the computational cost of simulating a trading day. To better understand the tradeoffs, we write a microbenchmark that tests each of the three backtest implementations. We show the state required to run the benchmark, as follows:

```
@State(Scope.Benchmark)
class BenchmarkState {
  @Param(Array("1", "10"))
  var decisionDelayMillis: Long = 0
  @Param(Array("1", "12", "24" ))
  var backtestIntervalMonths: Int = 0

  var decisionDelay: DecisionDelayMillis = DecisionDelayMillis(-1)
  var backtestDays: List[MonthDay] = Nil

  @Setup
  def setup(): Unit = {
    decisionDelay = DecisionDelayMillis(decisionDelayMillis)
    backtestDays = daysWithin(trailingMonths(backtestIntervalMonths))
  }
}
```

This benchmark allows us to sweep different backtest interval and decision delay combinations. Using a `daysWithin` method, which is omitted from the snippet, a count representing the number of months is converted into the list of simulation trading days. We display the implementation of only one benchmark because the other two are identical, as follows:

```
@Benchmark
def withBatchedForking(state: BenchmarkState): BacktestPerformanceSummary =
  Backtest.backtestWithBatchedForking(state.backtestDays,
    state.decisionDelay)
      .unsafePerformSync
```

To accurately time how long it takes to complete the `Task` computation, we start the computation with the blocking `unsafePerformSync` method. This is a rare example where it is acceptable to make a blocking call without a timeout. In this controlled test, we are confident that all invocations will return. For this test, we sweep the the month count, leaving the decision delay fixed at 1 ms. Running this benchmark on a machine with four cores produces the following results:

Benchmark	Months	Decision delay milliseconds	Throughput (ops per second)	Error as percentage of throughput
withoutConcurrency	1	1	25.96	± 0.46
withAllForked	1	1	104.89	± 0.36
withBatchedForking	1	1	27.71	± 0.70
withoutConcurrency	12	1	1.96	± 0.41
withAllForked	12	1	7.25	± 0.22
withBatchedForking	12	1	8.60	± 0.49
withoutConcurrency	24	1	0.76	± 2.09
withAllForked	24	1	1.98	± 1.46
WithBatchedForking	24	1	4.32	± 0.88

The results make the tradeoff between the overhead and the benefits of batching clearer. Batching is a clear win as the number of months increase with a short 1 ms computational delay. Consider the scenario of backtesting 24 months with a 1 ms decision delay. Assuming 30-day months, there are 720 trading days to simulate. Split into batches of 30, there are 24 invocations of `fork` instead of 720. The overhead for splitting the `Task` into batches, and gathering each batch's results, is overshadowed by the order of magnitude of fewer executor submissions. Our explicit control over forking yielded a doubling of throughput in this scenario.

As the number of months decreases, the overhead of creating `Task` batches becomes a dominating factor. In a 12-month backtest, there are 360 trading days, yielding 12 batches. Here, batching yields about a 20% throughput improvement over forking all `Task`. Cutting the number of trading days in half from the 24-month test reduced the performance advantage by more than half. In the worst-case scenario, when there is one month to simulate, the batching strategy fails to take to advantage of all the cores on the machine. In this scenario, one batch is created, leaving CPU resources underutilized.

Wrapping up the backtester

As we have seen, there are a number of variables at play here. Accounting for computational costs, the number of available cores, the expected number of `Task` executor submissions, and batching overhead can be challenging. To extend our work, we can investigate a more dynamic batching strategy that takes better advantage of CPU resources with smaller backtest intervals. Using this benchmark, we got a taste for the additional tools that `Task` provides, and how explicit control of executor submissions can affect throughput.

The insights that we gleaned by working on the backtester can be applied to larger-scale software systems as well. We focused on analyzing results with a short 1 ms decision delay. As the cost of executing each `Task` increases (for example, 10 ms decision delay), diminishing marginal performance improvements are gained from batching. This is because the cost of executor submissions becomes overshadowed by the cost of the computation. While 1 ms appears to be a small amount of time, there are a potentially surprising number of computations that can be completed in this time frame. Consider that a throughput of 1,000 operations per second translates to 1 operation per millisecond. Reflecting on benchmarks that we have performed in our earlier efforts and through your own work, you can find numerous examples where we worked with operations that have a throughput higher than 1 operation per millisecond. The takeaway from this thought experiment is a large number of use cases fit within the definition of a short computation (that is, 1 ms), which means that there are a significant number of opportunities to optimize concurrency through the judicious use of `fork`.

 The backtester is a prime candidate for batching because the amount of work, namely the number of days to simulate, is known at the start of processing. In a stream processing environment, the amount of work is unknown. For example, consider the order book receiving events on-the-fly. How can you implement batching in a streaming environment?

We hope that backtester provided an illustrative example to give you a feeling for `Task`. There are additional tools that are provided by `Task` that we did not explore. We invite you to read the documentation for `Task` in the Scalaz library. In the book entitled, *Functional Programming in Scala*, written by two Scalaz contributors, Rúnar Bjarnason and Paul Chiusano, there is an excellent chapter describing the implementation of a simplified version of Scalaz `Task`. This is a great resource to understand the design of the API.

Summary

In this chapter, we discovered how to harness the power of asynchronous programming with the Scala standard library using `Future` and `Promise`. We improved MVT backtesting performance by introducing concurrency to improve runtime performance and discovered how `Promise` can be used to extend `Future`. Along the way, we investigated the shortcomings of `Future` along with the techniques to mitigate these shortcomings. We also explored an alternative to `Future` with Scalaz `Task`, which provides compelling performance benefits while retaining referential transparency. Using what you have learned in this chapter, you can take full advantage of multicore hardware using Scala to scale your software systems and deliver higher throughput. In our final chapter, Chapter 7, *Architecting for Performance*, we explore a set of advanced functional programming techniques and concepts to enrich your functional programming toolbox.

7
Architecting for Performance

We have come a long way in our exploration of Scala and various techniques to write performant code. In this final chapter, we look at more open-ended topics. The final topics are largely applicable beyond Scala and the JVM. We dive into various tools and practices to improve the architecture and the design of an application. In this chapter, we explore the following topics:

- Conflict-free replicated data types (CRDTs)
- Throughput and latency impact of queueing
- The Free monad

Distributed automated traders

Thanks to our hard work, MVT is thriving. The sales department is signing contracts like there is no tomorrow, and the sales bell is ringing from sunrise to sunset. The order book is able to handle more orders, and as a result of the increase in traffic, another product offered by MVT is incurring performance issues: the automated trading system. The automated trader receives orders from the order book and applies various trading strategies in real time to automatically place orders on behalf of the customers. As the order book is processing an order of magnitude of more trade orders, the automated trading system is unable to keep up, and, therefore, cannot efficiently apply its strategies. Several big customers recently lost a lot of money due to bad decisions made by the algorithm and the high latency of execution. The engineering team needs to solve this performance issue. Alice, your technical lead, has tasked you with finding a solution and preventing the company from losing newly-acquired customers.

In the previous chapter, we studied and took advantage of concurrency. We learned how to design code to leverage the power of multicore hardware. The automated trader is already optimized to run concurrent code and utilize all the CPU resources on the machine. The truth is, there is only so much one machine can handle, even with several cores. To scale the system and keep up with the traffic coming from the order book, we will have to start implementing a distributed system.

A glimpse into distributed architectures

Distributed computing is a rich topic, and we cannot pretend to address it entirely in a single chapter. This short section gives a brief and incomplete description of distributed computing. We will try to give you an overview of the paradigm and point to some of the main benefits and challenges of distributed systems.

The idea behind distributed computing is to design a system involving several components, which runs on different machines and communicates with each other (for example, over a network) to achieve a task or provide a service. A distributed system can involve components of different natures, each component providing a specific service and participating in the realization of the task. For example, a web server can be deployed to receive HTTP requests. To service a request, the web server may communicate over the network to query an authentication service to validate credentials and a database server in order to store and retrieve data and complete the request. Together, the web server, the authentication service, and the database form a distributed system.

A distributed system can also involve several instances of the same component. These instances form a cluster of nodes, and they can be used to divide the work among them. This topology allows a system to scale out and support a higher load by adding more instances to the cluster. As an example, if a web server is able to handle 20,000 requests per second, it may be possible to run a cluster of three identical servers to handle 60,000 requests per second (assuming that your architecture allows your application to scale linearly). Distributed clusters also help achieve high availability. If one of the nodes crashes, the others are still up and able to fulfill requests while the crashed instance is restarted or recovers. As there is no single-point of failure, there is no interruption of service.

For all their benefits, distributed systems come with their drawbacks and challenges. The communication between components is subject to failure and network disruptions. The application needs to implement a retry mechanism and error handling, and then deal with lost messages. Another challenge is managing shared state. For example, if all the nodes use a single database server to save and retrieve information, the database has to implement some form of a locking mechanism to ensure that concurrent modifications do not collide. It is also possible that once the cluster node count grows sufficiently large, the database will not be able to serve them all efficiently and will become a bottleneck.

Now that you have been briefly introduced to distributed systems, we will go back to MVT. The team has decided to turn the automated trader into a distributed application to be able to scale the platform. You have been tasked with the design of the system. Time to go to the whiteboard.

The first attempt at a distributed automated trader

Your first strategy is simple. You plan to deploy several instances of the automated trader to form a cluster of nodes. These nodes can share the work and handle each part of the incoming orders. A load balancer in front of the cluster can distribute the load evenly among the nodes. This new architecture helps scale out the automated trader. However, you are facing a common problem with distributed systems: the nodes have to share a common state to operate. To understand this requirement, we explore one of the features of the automated trader. To be able to use MVT's automated trading system, customers have to open an account with MVT and provision it with enough money to cover their trades. This is used as a safety net by MVT to execute orders on behalf of its clients without running the risk of a customer being unable to honor their transactions. To ensure that the automated strategies do not overspend, the automated trader keeps track of the current balance of each customer and checks the balance of a customer before placing an automated order on their behalf.

Your plan consists of deploying several instances of the automated trading system. Each instance receives a portion of the orders processed by the order book, runs a strategy and places matching order on behalf of a customer. Now that the system consists of several identical instances running in parallel, each instance can place orders on behalf of the same customer. To be able to perform the balance validation, they all need to be aware of the current balance of all customers. Customer balances become a shared state that has to be synchronized in the cluster. To solve this problem, you envision a balance monitor server deployed as an independent component and holding the state of each customer's balance. When a trade order is received by a node of the automated trading cluster, the node interrogates the balance monitor server to verify that a customer's account has enough funds to place an automated trade. Similarly, when a trade is executed, a node instructs the balance monitor server to update the balance of the customer.

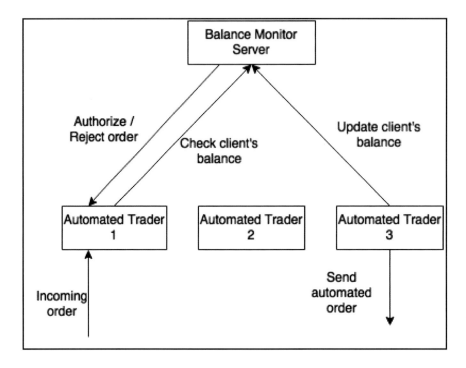

The preceding diagram describes various interactions between the components of your architecture. **Automated Trader 1** receives an incoming trade and queries the balance monitor server to check whether the client has enough funds to perform a trade. The balance monitor server either authorizes or rejects the order. At the same time, **Automated Trader 3** sends an order that was previously approved by the balance monitor server and updates the client's balance.

You probably spotted a flaw in this design. It is possible to run into a race condition where two different instances of the automated trader may validate the balance of the same customer, receive an authorization from the **Balance Monitor Server**, place both trades in parallel and go over the limit of the client's account. This is comparable to a race condition that you can encounter with a concurrent system running on a single machine. In practice, the risk is low and is accepted by companies that are similar to MVT. The limit used to cut-off a client is usually set lower than the actual balance to account for this risk. Designing a platform to handle this case would increase the latency of the system because we would have to introduce more drastic synchronization across the nodes. This is a good example of business and technical domains working together to optimize the solution.

At the end of this design session, you take a short walk to clear your mind while drinking a bottle of carbonated water. As you return to the whiteboard, the crude reality hits you. Like a flat bottle of carbonated water, your idea has fizzled out. You realize that all these arrows linking rectangles are in reality messages that are traveling over the network. Currently, while a single automated trader relies on its internal state to execute strategies and place orders, this new design requires the automated trader to query an external system over the network and wait for the answer. This query happens on the critical path. This is another common issue with distributed systems: components with focused roles need to communicate with each other to accomplish their tasks. This communication comes at a cost. It involves serialization, I/O operations, and transfer over a network. You share your reflections with Alice, who confirms that this is a problem. The automated trader has to keep the internal latency as low as possible for its decisions to be relevant. After a short discussion, you agree that it would endanger performance for the automated trader to perform a remote call on the critical path. You are now left with the task of implementing a distributed system with components sharing a common state without communicating with each other on the critical path. This is where we can start talking about CRDTs.

Introducing CRDTs

CRDT stands for **Conflict-free Replicated Data Types**. CRDTs were formally defined by Marc Shapiro and Nuno Preguiça in their paper, *Designing a commutative replicated data type* (refer to `https://hal.inria.fr/inria-00177693/document`). A CRDT is a data structure that is specifically designed to ensure eventual consistency across multiple components without the need for synchronization. Eventual consistency is a well-known concept in distributed system, which is not exclusive to CRDTs. This model guarantees that eventually, if a piece of data is no longer modified, all nodes in a cluster will end up with the same value for this piece of data. Nodes send each other update notifications to keep their state synchronized. The difference with strong consistency is that at a given time, some nodes may see a slightly outdated state until they receive the update notice:

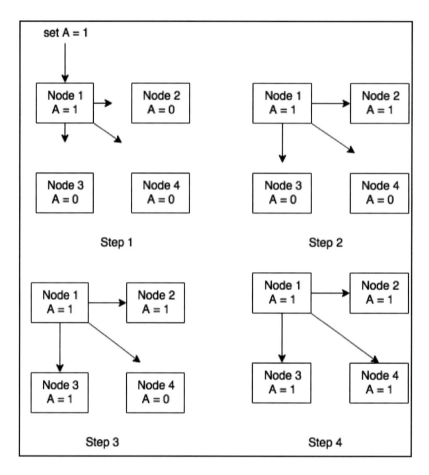

The preceding diagram shows an example of eventual consistency. All the nodes of the cluster hold the same piece of data (A = 0). Node 1 receives an update to set the value of A to 1. After updating its internal state, it broadcasts the update to the rest of the cluster. The messages reach their targets at different instants, which means that until we reach step 4, A has a different value depending on the node. If a client queries node 4 for the value of A at step 3, they receive an older value as the change has not yet been reflected in node 4.

A problem that may arise with eventual consistency is the resolution of conflicts. Imagine a simple example where nodes in a cluster share the state of an array of integers. The following table describes a sequence of events involving updating the state of this array:

Instant	Event	State change
T0	Initialization of the cluster	Nodes 1 and 2 hold the same value for the array of integers: [1,2,3]
T1	Node 1 receives a request to update the value at index 1 from 2 to 4	Node 1 updates its internal state to [1,4,3] and sends an update message to node 2
T2	Node 2 receives a request to update the value at index 1 from 2 to 5	Node 2 updates its internal state to [1,5,3] and sends an update message to node 1
T3	Node 1 receives the update from node 2	Node 1 needs to decide whether it should ignore or take into account the update message

Our cluster now needs to resolve the conflict. Should node 1 update its state when receiving the update from node 2? If node 2 does the same, we end up with two nodes holding a different state. What about the other nodes? Some may receive the broadcast from node 2 before the one from node 1 and vice versa.

Various strategies exist to deal with this problem. Some protocols use timestamps or vector clocks to determine which update was performed later in time and should take precedence. Others simply assume that the last writer wins. This is not a simple problem and CRDTs are designed to completely avoid conflicts altogether. Actually, CRDTs are defined to make conflicts mathematically impossible. To be defined as a CRDT, a data structure has to support only commutative updates. That is, regardless of the ordering in which the update operations are applied, the end state must always be the same. This is the secret of eventual consistency without merge conflict. When a system uses CRDTs, all the nodes can send each other update messages without a need for strict synchronization. The messages can be received in any order, and all the local states will converge to the same value eventually.

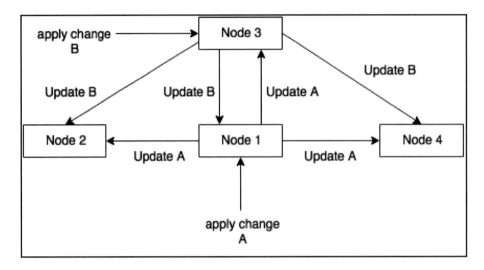

In the preceding diagram, we see that node 3 and node 1 receive two different changes. They send this update information to all the other nodes. Note that we are not concerned with the order in which the updates are received by the other nodes. As the updates are commutative, their order has no impact on the final state that will be computed by each node. They are guaranteed to hold the same piece of data once all of them have received all the update broadcasts.

There exist two types of CRDT:

- Operation-based
- State-based

They are equivalent in that it is always possible to define a state-based CRDT for each operation-based CRDT and vice-versa. However, their implementations differ and provide different guarantees in terms of error-recovery and performance. We define each type and consider its characteristics. As an example, we implement each version of the simplest CRDT: an increase-only counter.

The state-based increase-only counter

With this model, when a CRDT receives an operation to perform from a client, it updates its state accordingly and sends an update message to all the other CRDTs in the cluster. This update message contains the full state of the CRDT. When the other CRDTs receive this message, they perform a merge of their state with the received new state. This merge operation has to guarantee that the end state will always be the same. It has to be commutative, associative, and idempotent. Let's look at a possible implementation of this data type:

```scala
case class CounterUpdate(i: Int)
case class GCounterState(uid: Int, counter: Int)

class StateBasedGCounter(
 uid: Int, count: Int, otherCounters: Map[Int, Int]) {

 def value: Int = count + otherCounters.values.sum

 def update(
   change: CounterUpdate): (StateBasedGCounter, GCounterState) =
   (new StateBasedGCounter(uid, count + change.i, otherCounters),
    GCounterState(uid, count))

 def merge(other: GCounterState): StateBasedGCounter = {
   val newValue = other.counter max otherCounters.getOrElse(other.uid,0)
   new StateBasedGCounter(uid, count, otherCounters.+(other.uid ->
newValue) )
 }
}
```

The `update` method can be used by clients to increase the value of the counter. This returns a new state-based counter containing an updated count, and it generates a `CounterState` object that can be sent to all the other CRDTs in the cluster. The `merge` is used to handle these `CounterState` messages and merge the new state of the other counters with the local state. A counter has a unique ID in the cluster. The internal state is composed of the local state (that is, `count`) and the states of all the other counters in the cluster. We keep these counters in a map that we update in the `merge` method when receiving state information from a different counter. Merging is a simple operation. We compare the incoming value with the one that we have in the map and keep the greatest one. This is to ensure that if we receive two update messages in the wrong order, we do not override the latest state (that is, the greatest number) with an older update message that was delayed.

The operation-based increase-only counter

Operation-based CRDTs are similar to state-based CRDTs with the difference that update messages only contain a description of the operation that was just performed. These CRDTs do not send their full-state in an update message, but they are merely a copy of the operation that they just performed to update their own state. This ensures that all the other CRDTs in the cluster perform the same operation and maintain their state in sync. The updates can be received in a different order by each node of the cluster. To guarantee that the end state is the same for all the nodes, the updates have to be commutative. You can see an example of this data structure, as follows:

```
class OperationBasedCounter(count: Int) {

  def value: Int = count

  def update(change: CounterUpdate): (OperationBasedCounter, CounterUpdate)
  =
    new OperationBasedCounter(count + change.i) -> change

  def merge(operation: CounterUpdate): OperationBasedCounter =
    update(operation)._1
}
```

This implementation is shorter than the state-based example. The update method still returns an updated instance of the counter, and the CounterUpdate object that was applied. For an operation-based counter, it is enough to broadcast the operation that was applied. This update is received by the merge method of the other instances to apply the same operation to their own internal state. Note that update and merge are equivalent, merge is even implemented in terms of update. In this model, there is no need for a unique ID per counter.

Operation-based CRDTs use potentially smaller messages because they only send each discrete operation as opposed to their full internal state. In our example, the state-based update contains two integers, as opposed to only one for the operation-based update. Smaller messages can help reduce bandwidth usage and improve the throughput of your system. However, they are sensitive to communication failures. If an update message is lost during the transmission and does not reach a node, this node will be out of sync with the rest of the cluster with no way of recovering. If you decide to use operation-based CRDTs, you have to be able to trust your communication protocol and be confident that all update messages reach their destination and are properly processed. State-based CRDTs do not suffer from this issue because they always send their entire state in an update message. If a message is lost and does not reach a node, this node will only be out of sync until it receives the next update message. It is possible to make this model even more robust by implementing a periodic broadcast of the node's state, even when no updates are performed. This would force all nodes to regularly send their current state and ensure that the cluster is always eventually consistent.

CRDTs and automated traders

Based on the requirements of our system, it seems that CRDTs are a good fit for our implementation. Each node can keep the current state of each customer's balance in memory as a counter, update it when placing orders, and broadcast update messages to the rest of the system. This broadcast can be done outside the critical path, and we do not have to worry about handling conflicts, as this is what CRDTs are designed for. Eventually, all nodes will have in memory the same value for each balance, and they will be able to locally check for trade authorization. The balance monitor server can be removed entirely.

To implement the state of the balance as a CRDT, we need a more sophisticated counter than the one we previously explored. The balance cannot be represented as an increase-only counter because, occasionally, orders are canceled and the system must credit the customer's account. The counter has to be able to handle both increment and decrement operations. Luckily, such a counter exists. Let's look at a simple implementation of a state-based counter:

```
case class PNCounterState(incState: GCounterState, decState: GCounterState)

class StateBasedPNCounter private(
  incCounter: StateBasedGCounter,
  decCounter: StateBasedGCounter) {

  def value = incCounter.value - decCounter.value

  def update(change: CounterUpdate): (StateBasedPNCounter, PNCounterState) =
  {
    val (newIncCounter, newDecCounter, stateUpdate) =
      change match {
        case CounterUpdate(c) if c >= 0 =>
          val (iC, iState) = incCounter.update(change)
          val dState = GCounterState(decCounter.uid, decCounter.value)
          (iC, decCounter, PNCounterState(iState, dState))
        case CounterUpdate(c) if c < 0 =>
          val (dC, dState) = decCounter.update(change)
          val iState = GCounterState(incCounter.uid, incCounter.value)
          (incCounter, dC, PNCounterState(iState, dState))
      }

    (new StateBasedPNCounter(newIncCounter, newDecCounter), stateUpdate)
  }

  def merge(other: PNCounterState): StateBasedPNCounter =
    new StateBasedPNCounter(
      incCounter.merge(other.incState),
      decCounter.merge(other.decState)
```

```
    )
  }
```

The PN counter leverages our previous implementation of an increase-only counter to provide the decrement capability. To be able to represent a counter as a state-based CRDT, we need to keep track of the state of both increment and decrement operations. This is necessary to guarantee that we do not lose information if our update messages are received in the wrong order by other nodes.

 Remember that the increase-only counter guarantees conflict resolution by assuming that the highest value of the counter is necessarily the most up-to-date. This invariant does not hold true for the PN counter.

This implementation shows you another interesting property of CRDTs: simple and basic structures can be composed to create more complex and feature-rich CRDTs. Should we proceed to demonstrate the implementation of an operation-based counter? As it turns out and we are sure you spotted this earlier, our previous increase-only counter already supports decrement operations. Applying a positive or a negative delta is handled by the operation-based counter.

When the balance is not enough

You have finished the implementation of the proof-of-concept and call Alice to get some feedback. She spends a few minutes studying your new design and your code. "Looks good to me. Do not forget to synchronize the account blacklist as well." What is she talking about? "Checking the account balance is only one of the criteria to allow or block an automated trade. Other attributes of the client need to be taken into consideration. Today, the automated trader runs a trust algorithm in the background, and it calculates a score for each customer. If the score falls below a certain threshold, the account is blacklisted until the end of the trading day, and all automated orders are denied. I like your design, but you need to incorporate this blacklist into the new system." Faced with this new challenge, you think that the best solution would be to implement the blacklist as a CRDT as well, provided that it fits your current design.

A new CRDT – the grow-only set

One CRDT is designed to handle our new use case. The grow-only set data type implements a set that only supports the addition of new elements without duplicates. We can implement the blacklist as a grow-only set. Each node can run its own trust algorithm and can decide whether a client should be blacklisted and denied automated trading for the rest of the day. At the end of the day, the system can clear the set. We display a possible implementation of a state-based grow-only set, as follows:

```
case class AddElement[A](a: A)
case class GSetState[A](set: Set[A])

class StateBasedGSet[A](val value: Set[A]) {

  def contains(a: A): Boolean = value.contains(a)

  def update(a: AddElement[A]): (StateBasedGSet[A], GSetState[A]) = {
    val newSet = new StateBasedGSet(value + a.a)
    (newSet, GSetState(newSet.value))
  }

  def merge(other: GSetState[A]): StateBasedGSet[A] = {
    new StateBasedGSet(value ++ other.set)
  }

}
```

Our implementation supports adding an element by calling the `update` method. It returns a new instance of `StateBasedGSet` with an updated set, as well as a `GSetState` instance to be broadcast to the other nodes. This update contains the entire state of the counter, that is, the internal set. An operation-based implementation is trivial and left as an exercise for the reader (a possible solution is provided in the code repository). Similar to the increment-decrement counter explored earlier, it is possible to create a set that supports both adding and removing an element. There is one caveat though: as adding and removing an element are not commutative operations, one must take precedence on the other. In practice, a 2P-set can be created to support adding and removing items, but once removed, an element cannot be added again. The remove operation takes precedence and guarantees that the operations are commutative and can be handled without conflicts. A possible implementation is to combine two grow-only sets, one for adding elements, and the other to remove them. Again, we see the power of simple CRDTs that can be combined to create more powerful data types.

Free trading strategy performance improvements

You stare at your agile burn down chart and discover that you completed all your story points before the sprint ends tomorrow. You are excited to have delivered this week's features early, but you are left wondering whether or not you will have yet another discussion with the scrum master about estimation. Instead of spending mental energy on estimating, you instead return your attention to an issue that Dave raised. At a recent lunch together, Dave talked about how the company's trading strategies lose money when trading decisions are made based on stale information. Even several milliseconds can make the difference between extremely profitable trades and losses. His words piqued your interest to see if you can improve the performance of MVT's trading strategies.

MVT's trading strategies are downstream consumers of the order book. The trading strategies listen for changes in the best bid and offer (BBO) in order to determine when to submit buy or sell orders. At lunch, Dave explained that tracking the BBO has historically proven to give the most signals for MVT's trading strategies. The best bid refers to the bid with the highest price, and the best offer refers to the offer with the lowest price. When either side of the BBO changes due to a cancellation, execution, or new limit order, then a BBO update event is transmitted to downstream trading strategies. The model representing this event is BboUpdated, and it looks like the following:

```
case class Bid(value: BigDecimal) extends AnyVal
case class Offer(value: BigDecimal) extends AnyVal
case class Ticker(value: String) extends AnyVal
case class BboUpdated(ticker: Ticker, bid: Bid, offer: Offer)
```

MVT deploys each trading strategy within its own JVM to ensure that failures do not affect other running strategies. When deployed, each trading strategy maintains BBO subscriptions for the set of tickers it trades.

Having spent a significant amount of time working on the order book, you hope to find opportunities to apply your functional programming knowledge to yield better performance. During your lunch with Dave, you discovered that "better performance" has a slightly different meaning for trading strategy development than it does for other systems. You asked Dave, "If you could choose between an improvement in latency or throughput, which would you choose?" Dave sarcastically replied, "Why do I have to choose? I want both!" Afterwards, he went on to say, "Latency! Almost every time a trading strategy makes a decision using old BBO updates, we lose money. In fact, if we could, I would rather throw away old BBO updates. We only trade high-volume tickers, so we are pretty much guaranteed to see another BBO update immediately." As you start looking into the code base, you wonder whether you can utilize Dave's thinking to improve trading strategy performance.

Benchmarking the trading strategy

Recalling the lessons that you learned when working on the order book, your first step is to benchmark. You select one of MVT's production trading strategies and adapt the benchmark that you wrote to exercise the order book, `FinalLatencyBenchmark`, to send the `BboUpdated` events to the trading strategy. Originally, the benchmark focused on displaying the 99th percentile latency and higher. As you know that latency is the most important factor in your performance investigation, you modify the benchmark to also emit the median and 75th percentile latencies. This will give you a more holistic view into the latency of trading strategy performance.

Looking at the production metrics system, you see a time series trading volume chart for the system that you want to benchmark. It shows that it is a low-volume day, only about 4,000 BBO updated events per second. You dig through historical metrics to find the highest volume day in the last few weeks. The market has been volatile again, so a recent high-volume day is likely a good proxy for a high throughput rate to benchmark. About two weeks ago, there was a trading day with a sustained peak of 12,000 BBO updated events per second. You plan to begin benchmarking at the lower end of the spectrum with 4,000 events per second, ramping up to 12,000 events per second to see how performance changes.

The testing methodology is to measure latency for an equivalent number of events across throughput rates while ensuring a thorough test at each throughput level. To accomplish this goal, you multiply the higher throughput, 12,000 events per second, by 30 trials for a sum total of 360,000 events. At 4,000 events per second, running the benchmark for 90 trials produces the equivalent of 360,000 events. Running the benchmarks in a test environment replicating production gives the results displayed in the following table. The table abbreviates events per second as EPS:

Percentile	4,000 EPS	12,000 EPS
50th (median)	0.0 ms	1,063.0 ms
75th	0.0 ms	1,527.0 ms
99th	10.0 ms	2,063.0 ms
99.9th	22.0 ms	2,079.0 ms
100th (maximum)	36.0 ms	2,079.0 ms

These results illustrate a startling contrast in performance. At 4,000 events per second, the trading strategy appears to perform well. 99% of events are responded to within 10 ms, and we observe that up to the 75th percentile, the strategy is responding with miniscule delay. This suggests that on low-volume days, this trading strategy is able to decide on information quickly, which should bode well for profitability. Unfortunately, at 12,000 events per second, the performance is unacceptable. Having not yet looked at the code, you wonder whether you can spot any sudden changes in performance by sweeping several more throughputs. You try a binary search between 4,000 and 12,000 events per second and get the following results:

Percentile	9,000 EPS	10,000 EPS	11,000 EPS	11,500 EPS
50th (median)	0.0 ms	4.0 ms	41.0 ms	487.0ms
75th	5.0 ms	9.0 ms	66.0 ms	715.0 ms
99th	32.0 ms	47.0 ms	126.0 ms	871.0 ms
99.9th	58.0 ms	58.0 ms	135.0 ms	895.0 ms
100th (maximum)	67.0ms	62.0 ms	138.0 ms	895.0 ms

You chose 9,000 events per second as a starting point because it divided evenly into the total event count, 360,000. At this level of throughput, the strategy's profile is qualitatively closer to the 4,000 events per second profile. As results looked reasonable at this level, you increased the throughput approximately halfway between 9,000 and 12,000 events per second to the next level that divides evenly into 360,000. At 10,000 events per second, we once again observe a profile that remains similar to the 4,000 events per second profile. There is a discernible increase in the median and 75th percentile latencies, suggesting the strategy's performance is beginning to degrade. Next, you increase the throughput to the midpoint, 11,000 events per second. As you cannot run 32.72 trials, you instead round up to 33 trials for a total of 363,000 events. These results are qualitatively worse than the 4,000 events per second results by approximately an order of magnitude at each measured percentile. Admittedly, these are weak performance results, but does this profile closely resemble the profile at 12,000 events per second?

You are now a bit alarmed because 11,000 events per second is approximately 90% of the throughput at 12,000 events per second. Yet, the results do not display close to 90% similarity. If the trading strategy decreased linearly you would expect to see latencies approximating 90% of the latencies that were observed at 12,000 events per second. Unsatisfied with this performance profile, you try one more throughput, 11,500 events per second. At this throughput level, you run the benchmark for 31 trials, totaling 356,500 events. Increasing the throughput by approximately 5% resulted in an observed median latency that is roughly 11 times greater and an observed 99th percentile latency that is nearly six times greater. These results make it clear that the strategy's runtime performance degrades exponentially. To better reason about the results, you quickly throw together the following bar graph:

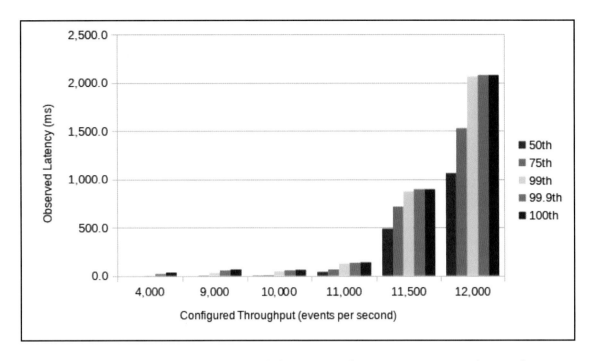

This bar graph visualizes the exponential decay in performance. Interestingly, we observe that all measured latency percentiles follow consistent patterns of decay, further substantiating the hypothesis that the strategy has exhausted its capacity to process requests. Before jumping into improving the trading strategy performance, you ponder, "How can I bound the exponential increases in latency?"

Instead of seeing consistent decay across all measured latency percentiles, imagine that the median and 75th percentiles remained qualitatively constant across all configured throughput levels. Does this profile suggest the same types of performance impediment as the scenario that we are working through? Take a moment to consider what could cause such a distribution to arise.

The danger of unbounded queues

Benchmarking revealed a universal truth about performance tuning: unbounded queues kill performance. Here, we use the term queue to broadly mean a waiting line, instead of specifically focusing on the queue data structure. For example, this benchmark queues events to be transmitted at specific points in time in a `List`. In a production environment, this queue exists at multiple levels. The sender of the `BboUpdated` events likely queues events at the application-level, and subsequently, the network protocol (for example, TCP) may employ its own sets of queues to manage transmission to the consumer. When events are processed at a rate slower than they are produced, the system becomes unstable because the backlog of work always increases. Given infinite memory and zero response time guarantees, it is possible for an application to continue processing an ever-growing queue of items. However, in practice, when a system cannot stabilize itself by increasing its consumption rate to match or exceed the production rate, the system eventually spirals out of control. A system's hardware resources are finite, and as a consumer falls behind, it will require increasing amounts of memory to cope with the growing backlog. Taken to an extreme, increasing memory requirements causes more frequent garbage collections, which in turn, further slow down consumption. This is a cyclical problem that will eventually exhaust memory resources, causing a system to crash.

By inspecting the trading system code, you will discover that there is a queue for message processing within the trading system. This application-level queue is a `LinkedBlockingQueue` that separates the network I/O thread from the application thread. In the benchmark, the thread driving the benchmark adds events directly to the queue, simulating the behavior of a production network thread receiving events from the outside world. It is a common practice to group together logical parts of an application into separate thread pools in order to gain efficiencies by parallelizing processing work.

 When we previously explored concurrency with `Future` and `Task`, we indirectly worked with queues. The `ExecutorService` that receives submissions from `Future` and `Task` manages its workload by enqueuing tasks into a `BlockingQueue`. The factory methods that are provided in `Executors` do not allow the caller to provide a queue. If you explore the implementation of these factory methods you discover the kind and the size of `BlockingQueue` created.

Adding a buffer between the network layer and the application layer typically bodes well for performance. A queue can enable an application to tolerate momentary consumption slowdowns and bursts of messages from a producer. However, as we have seen in our benchmarking, buffers are a double-edged sword. The default constructor for `LinkedBlockingQueue` is effectively unbounded, setting a limit that is equal to the maximum supported integer value. By buffering messages indefinitely when the rate of production is consistently higher than the consumption rate, the trading system's performance degrades to an unusable state.

Applying back pressure

What would happen if we instead chose to bound the queue that is receiving events to a smaller limit? When the production rate exceeds the consumption rate and the queue reaches capacity, one option is for the system to block until a spot is available in the queue. Blocking forces event production to halt, which describes a strategy for applying back pressure. In this context, pressure refers to the queue of events to be processed. The pressure manifests itself with increasing resource usage (for example, memory). By adopting a policy of blocking further production, the system is applying pressure back to the producer. Any queues that exist between the application-level consumer and the producer will also eventually reach capacity, forcing the producer to change its production rate in order to continue transmitting events.

To implement this back pressure policy, all queues must be bounded to a size that avoids excessive resource usage, and production into queues must block when full. This is straightforward to implement with implementations of the JDK-provided `BlockingQueue` interface. For example, the following snippet displays this strategy with `LinkedBlockingQueue`:

```
val queue = new LinkedBlockingQueue[Message](1000)
queue.put(m)
```

In this snippet, we see construction of a `LinkedBlockingQueue` with a capacity limit of 1,000 messages. Based on knowledge of the production environment, you feel comfortable retaining up to 1,000 messages in-memory without exhausting memory resources. The second line in the snippet demonstrates a blocking operation to enqueue an element via `put`.

When applying back pressure, the choice in queue size is critical. To illustrate why, let's assume that we measured the maximum trading system processing latency to be 0.5 ms once a message is consumed from the event queue. At maximum, the total processing latency for an event is equal to 0.5 ms plus the time spent waiting to be processed. Consider the scenario where the queue has a size of 1,000 and 999 events are queued when a new event arrives. In the worst case scenario, the new event waits 499.5 ms for the 999 other events that are already enqueued to be processed, plus 0.5 ms to be processed. Configuring a queue size of 1,000 yielded a maximum latency of 500 ms, showing that maximum latency is directly proportional to queue size.

A more disciplined approach to sizing queues involves considering environment resources and understanding the maximum latency that is tolerated by the business. From informal discussions with Dave, we learned that even several milliseconds can make or break a trading strategy's profitability. Until we have a moment to check in with him, let's assume that 10 ms is the maximum delay the strategy can tolerate without risking significant trading losses. Using this information, we can calculate a queue size that ensures that the 10 ms latency limit is respected. In the previous example, we performed the following worst-case scenario arithmetic:

```
maximum total processing latency = queue size * maximum processing time
```

We can rearrange this formula to solve for queue size, as follows:

```
queue size = maximum total processing latency / maximum processing time
```

From this arithmetic, we substitute in known values to compute queue size, as follows:

```
queue size = 10ms / 0.5ms = 20
```

The arithmetic suggests that we bound the queue size for twenty elements to ensure that in the worst case scenario an event can be enqueued and processed within 10 ms. To explore back pressure deeper, we encourage you to read the following blog post by Martin Thompson at `http://mechanical-sympathy.blogspot.com/2012/05/apply-back-p ressure-when-overloaded.html`. Martin is an authority on high-performance software development, and this particular blog post was an invaluable learning source for back pressure.

Applying load-control policies

Back pressure is a strategy that works well when the message producer respects consumers that operate at different rates and does not penalize slow consumers. Particularly when dealing with third-party systems, there are situations where applying back pressure to force the producer to slow down will not be well received. In these scenarios, we need to consider additional strategies that improve the capacity of our systems without requiring algorithmic improvements to our business logic.

The authors have worked in the **real-time bidding** (**RTB**) space where a bidding system participates in auctions to bid on opportunities to display advertisements. In this industry, there is low tolerance for bidding systems that are unable to cope with the configured auction rate. Failure to respond to a high percentage of auctions with a bidding decision (either bid or no-bid) in a timely manner results in the bidding system being penalty-boxed. While in the penalty box, the bidding systems received a reduced auction rate. Bidding systems that remain in the penalty box for extended periods of time may be disallowed from participating in any auctions until their performance improves.

Let's revisit a scenario that we considered when describing back pressure to motivate our discussion. The precondition to apply back pressure is reaching the capacity of a queue. When a queue is filled, our first strategy blocks further additions until there is room available. Another option that we can investigate is to discard the event because the system is saturated. Discarding the event requires extra domain knowledge to understand the semantics of what it means to abruptly terminate processing. In the trading system domain, the trading strategy is only required to send back a response when a bid or an offer is made. The trading strategy is not required to send back a response when it does not decide to make either a bid or an offer. For the trading system domain, discarding an event simply means halting processing. In other domains, such as RTB, discarding an event implies halting processing and responding with a message indicating that there will not be a bid placed in this auction.

Additionally, it is relevant that that each event is a snapshot of the best bid and offer. In contrast to the snapshot, imagine if instead of `BboUpdated`, the trading strategy received discrete events for changes in the best bid and offer. This is analogous to the state-based versus operation-based CRDT operations that we explored. Discarding an event would mean having partial information until a subsequent event is received. In this scenario, it is important to work with domain experts and product owners to determine if and for how long operating with partial information is acceptable.

Introducing load-control policies is another shift in thinking when working on high performance systems. Like the introduction of back pressure, this is another opportunity to reconsider assumptions that are made along the way to improve performance. Our lunchtime discussion with Dave provided great insight into a load-control policy that we can apply. Dave stated that he believes latent `BboUpdated` events cause more harm than good for trading strategy profitability. There are two assumptions we can challenge:

- All events must be processed
- An event being processed must complete processing

We can challenge these assumptions because Dave also indicated that MVT trades only high-volume tickers. If a BBO update is discarded, Dave is confident that a new BBO update is sure to follow quickly. Let's take a deeper look at how these policies can be defined.

Rejecting work

Rejecting work is not about rejecting sprint tasks, sorry! When we discuss work in this context, the term refers to processing effort. In the case of the benchmarked trading system, the work in hand is processing a new `BboUpdated` event. Although we have not dived into the code yet, we do know from previous benchmarking work that there is a queue used to accept the `BboUpdated` events from the network for application-level processing. This queue is the entry point into the application, and it represents the first application-level opportunity to reject the event due to capacity constraints.

From our earlier domain investigation, we learned that to reject a request, it can simply be dropped on the floor without response. A trading strategy is only required to respond when it wishes to trade. This means that the policy of rejecting work can be implemented by dropping the request on the floor when the queue is at capacity.

By inspecting the trading system source code, we see that the architecture is quite barebones. At start-up, a `LinkedBlockingQueue` is created to buffer the `BboUpdated` events, and a consumer thread is started to consume from the queue. The following snippet shows this logic:

```
val queue = new LinkedBlockingQueue[(MessageSentTimestamp, BboUpdated)](20)
  val eventThread = new Thread(new Runnable {
    def run(): Unit = while (true) {
      Option(queue.poll(5, TimeUnit.SECONDS)) match {
        case Some((ts, e)) => // process event
        case None => // no event found
      }
    }
  })
  eventThread.setDaemon(true)
  eventThread.start()
```

As per our earlier work, we see that the work queue is sized with twenty elements to ensure a maximum processing latency of 10 ms. After the queue is instantiated, the consumer thread is created and started. The processing logic is omitted from this snippet, but we observe that the sole purpose of this thread is to consume events as they become available. The logic to add work to the queue is trivial. This snippet assumes a `MessageSentTimestamp` and a `BboUpdated` event are in lexical scope with the names, `ts` and `e`, respectively:

```
queue.put((ts, e))
```

Our exploration of back pressure application indicated that `put` is a blocking call. As our intent is now to discard work, `put` is no longer a viable strategy. Instead, we can make use of `offer`. As per the API documentation, `offer` returns a `boolean` value, indicating whether or not the element was added to the queue. When the queue is full, it returns false. These are exactly the semantics that we wish to enforce. We can modify this snippet accordingly:

```
queue.offer((ts, e)) match {
  case true => // event enqueued
```

```
    case false => // event discarded
}
```

 The pattern matching in the preceding snippet provides a good entry point to introduce application metrics for introspection and transparency. For example, it is likely an interesting business metric to track how many events a trading system discards over time. This information may also be useful to the data science team for offline analysis in order to determine interesting patterns between discarded events and profitability. Whenever you encounter state changes, it is worth considering whether a metric should be recorded or whether an event should be emitted. Take a moment to consider state changes in your application. Are you making state changes available for introspection to nontechnical team members?

Performing a benchmark with 12,000 events per second and 30 trials, totaling 360,000 events processed, yields the following result:

Metric	12,000 EPS with queue size = 20
50th (median) latency	0.0 ms
75th latency	0.0 ms
99th latency	3.0 ms
99.9^{th} latency	11.0 ms
100th (maximum) latency	45.0 ms
Mean latency	0.1 ms
Events processed as percentage of total events	31.49%

This table introduces two rows to record the observed mean latency and the percentage of events processed out of the 360,000 that are provided. This row is important because the system now rejects events, which is an example of trading throughput for latency improvements. The latency profile looks great in comparison to the first benchmarking attempt at 12,000 events per second. The maximum latency is four times larger than our desired maximum latency. This suggests that our performance model is optimistic. The higher maximum latency can be attributed to an unlucky garbage collection pause in combination with wrongly estimating the actual processing latency. Even so, the maximum latency is two orders of magnitude lower than the maximum latency that was observed during the first benchmarking trial. We also observe that 99.9% of requests have a latency less than or equal to 11 ms, which is within 10% of our stated maximum latency goal.

While the latency profile looks excellent, the same cannot be said about the throughput. Due to our new load-control policy, only approximately 30% of the provided events were processed. When an event is processed, it is processed quickly, but unfortunately events are discarded two-thirds of the time. Another takeaway from performance tuning with load-control policies is that you will likely require multiple iterations to properly tune a policy for the right balance between trading throughput for latency and vice-versa. Reviewing the results of the benchmark, you note the mean observed latency is 0.1 ms. As a next step, you choose to calibrate the queue size according to the mean latency. By tuning according to the mean latency, you are implying that you are willing to introduce latency in exchange for improved throughput. Performing the arithmetic reveals the new queue size:

```
queue size = maximum total processing latency / maximum processing time =
10ms / 0.1ms = 100
```

After re-running the benchmark with the new queue size, you observe the following results:

Metric	12,000 EPS with queue size = 100
50th (median) latency	3.0 ms
75th latency	5.0 ms
99th latency	19.0 ms
99.9^{th} latency	43.0 ms
100th (maximum) latency	163.0 ms
Mean latency	3.9 ms
Events processed as percentage of total events	92.69%

As expected, the latency profile lost ground when compared to the trial with a queue size of 20. Except for the maximum latency, each percentile experienced at least a doubling in latency. The good news from this experiment is that the tail latencies did not experience exponential growth. The throughput picture is dramatically changed as well. We observe more than a doubling in throughput, yielding nearly 93% of all events processed. The mean latency is 39 times larger than the previously recorded 0.1 ms mean latency. For comparative purposes, the mean reflects the significant increase in median and 75th percentile latencies.

As a final test, out of curiosity, you try doubling the throughput rate while retaining a queue size of 100 elements. Will the trading system crash and burn, will it process all the requests, or will it do something different? Running the benchmark produces the following results:

Metric	24,000 EPS with queue size = 100
50th (median) latency	7.0 ms
75th latency	8.0 ms
99th latency	23.0 ms
99.9th latency	55.0 ms
100th (maximum) latency	72.0 ms
Mean latency	8.4 ms
Events processed as percentage of total events	44.58%

The good news is that the trading system did not crash and burn. It withstood receiving double the throughput that previously caused second delays with a latency profile qualitatively similar to the same trial at 12,000 events per second. This suggests that the work rejection policy has made the trading system significantly more robust to high volumes of incoming events.

The tradeoff for improved durability and acceptable processing latencies at higher volumes is lower throughput. These experiments revealed the value of bounding queue sizes, which we learned about when studying how to apply back pressure along with the value of rejecting work. After implementing the load-control policy and only tuning queue size, we are able to produce dramatically different results. There is definitely room for further analysis and tuning. Further analysis should involve product owners to weigh the throughput versus latency tradeoffs. It is important to remember that although the load control policy's implementation relies on knowledge of highly technical topics, the benefit should be measured in terms of business value.

Interrupting expensive processing

A second idea that we can explore is to halt processing before it completes. This is a powerful technique to ensure processing cycles are not spent on work that is already stale. Consider a request that is taken from the queue and undergoes partial processing before being interrupted by a garbage collection cycle. If the garbage collection cycle takes more than a couple of milliseconds, the event is now stale and will likely harm trading strategy profitability. Worse, all subsequent events in the queue are also now more likely to be stale as well.

To address this shortcoming, we can apply a technique that is analogous to rejecting work by imposing latency limits throughout processing. By carrying a timestamp that indicates when processing was started, it is possible to evaluate a computation's latency at discrete points in time. Let's consider a manufactured example to illustrate the idea. Consider the following processing pipeline, which runs arbitrary business logic for an event after journaling the event and updating metrics:

```
def pipeline(ts: MessageSentTimestamp, e: Event): Unit = {
    val enriched = enrichEvent(e)
    journalEvent(enriched)
    performPreTradeBalanceChecks(enriched)
    runBusinessLogic(enriched)
  }
}
```

To avoid processing latent events, we may write logic similar to the following:

```
def pipeline(ts: MessageSentTimestamp, e: Event): Unit = {
    if (!hasEventProcessingExpiryExpired(ts)) {
      val enriched = enrichEvent(e)
      if (!hasEventProcessingExpiryExpired(ts)) journalEvent(enriched)
      if (!hasEventProcessingExpiryExpired(ts))
performPreTradeBalanceChecks(enriched)
      if (!hasEventProcessingExpiryExpired(ts)) runBusinessLogic(enriched)
    }
  }
}
```

In this snippet, a `hasEventProcessingExpiryExpired` method is introduced to branch processing, which is based on time. The implementation of this method is omitted, but you can imagine that system time is queried and compared to a known and allowed processing duration (for example, 5 ms). While this approach accomplishes our goal of interrupting latent event processing, the code is now cluttered with multiple concerns. Even in this trivial example, it becomes more challenging to follow the sequence of processing steps.

The pain point with this code is that the business logic is intertwined with the cross-cutting concern of interrupting latent processing. One way to improve the readability of this code is to separate the description of what is being accomplished from how this description is executed. There is a construct in functional programming, known as the free monad that can help us do exactly this. Let's take a deeper look at the free monad to see how we can use it to improve the trading strategy's performance.

Free monads

Monads and their mathematical underpinnings in the subject of category theory are dense subjects deserving a dedicated exploration. As your sprint ends tomorrow and you want to deliver improved trading strategy performance, we instead provide a practitioner's perspective on free monads to show how you can use them to address a real-world problem. To demonstrate the power of applying free monads to our problem, we start by showing the end result and work backwards to develop an intuition about how free monads work. To begin, let's consider the sequence of processing steps that are required for a trading strategy to process a BboUpdated event once picked up from the work queue:

```
val enriched = enrichEvent(bboEvent)
journalEvent(enriched)
performPreTradeBalanceChecks(enriched)
val decision = strategy.makeTradingDecision(enriched)
decision.foreach(sendTradingDecision)
```

There are three steps that happen before the trading strategy makes a trading decision. If the trading decision is to submit a bid or an offer, the decision is sent to the exchange. strategy is an implementation of the TradingStrategy trait, which looks like the following:

```
trait TradingStrategy {
   def makeTradingDecision(e: BboUpdated): Option[Either[Bid, Offer]]
}
```

Next, let's look at how we can translate this processing sequence into the free monad and also add in early termination logic.

Describing a program

To build our new version of the trading strategy pipeline, we use the Scalaz-provided free monad implementation, scalaz.Free. The end result of our efforts to use the free monad in conjunction with a domain-specific language (DSL) for simpler construction looks like the following:

```
val pipeline = for {
    enriched <- StartWith(enrichEvent) within (8 millis) orElse (e =>
      enrichmentFailure(e.ticker))
    _ <- Step(journalEvent(enriched)) within (9 millis) orElse
      tradeAuthorizationFailure
    _ <- Step(performPreTradeBalanceChecks(enriched)) within (10 millis)
      orElse metricRecordingFailure
    decision <- MakeTradingDecision(enriched)
  } yield decision
```

Recall that our first attempt at implementing short-circuiting logic involved a series of if-statements. Instead of if-statements, the free monad-based snippet shows that the processing pipeline can now be defined as a for-comprehension. This approach removes the branching statements, making it simpler to understand what is happening. Without seeing how the DSL is made, you likely can already infer what this pipeline will do. For example, you likely inferred that if `journalEvent` takes more than 10 ms to execute, then the processing is halted and neither `performPreTradeBalanceChecks` nor `MakeTradingDecision` will be invoked.

The construction of the pipeline is only one half of the story. Underlying the implementation of this for-comprehension is the free monad. Creating a free monad involves two parts:

- Building a description of a program
- Writing an interpreter to execute the description

The for-comprehension represents our description of a program. It is a description of how to process the `BboUpdated` events that also defines execution delay constraints. To execute this description, we must build an interpreter.

Building an interpreter

Our interpreter looks like the following:

```
def runWithFoldInterpreter(
  recordProcessingLatency: ProcessingLatencyMs => Unit,
  strategy: TradingStrategy,
  ts: MessageSentTimestamp,
  e: BboUpdated): Unit = {
  val (_, decision) = pipeline.free.foldRun(
    PipelineState(ts, strategy, e)) {
    case (state, StartProcessing(whenActive, whenExpired, limitMs)) =>
      state -> (hasProcessingTimeExpired(state.ts, limitMs) match {
        case true => whenExpired(e)
        case false => whenActive(e)
      })
    case (state, Timed(whenActive, whenExpired, limitMs)) =>
      state -> (hasProcessingTimeExpired(state.ts, limitMs) match {
        case true => whenExpired()
        case false => whenActive()
      })
    case (state, TradingDecision(runStrategy)) =>
      state -> runStrategy(state.strategy)
  }
```

```
      decision.fold(logFailure, {
        case Some(order) =>
          sendTradingDecision(order)
          recordProcessingLatency(ProcessingLatencyMs(
            System.currentTimeMillis() - ts.value))
        case None =>
          recordProcessingLatency(ProcessingLatencyMs(
            System.currentTimeMillis() - ts.value))
      })
    }
```

The `foldRun` method is a method that is provided by `Free` to execute the description of the program that we wrote. Analogous to the signature of `foldLeft`, `foldRun` accepts a value representing an initial state, a curried function that accepts the current state, and the next processing step from our processing pipeline. The next processing step is represented as an ADT named `Thunk` with the following members:

```
sealed trait Thunk[A]
case class Timed[A](
  whenActive: () => A,
  whenExpired: () => A,
  limit: LimitMs) extends Thunk[A]
case class StartProcessing[A](
  whenActive: BboUpdated => A,
  whenExpired: BboUpdated => A,
  limit: LimitMs) extends Thunk[A]
case class TradingDecision[A](
  makeDecision: TradingStrategy => A) extends Thunk[A]
```

The `Thunk` algebra defines the possible operations that can be transcribed into the free monad. The pipeline that we previously showed is constructed by composing together combinations of the `Thunk` members. This pipeline hides the construction behind the DSL to eliminate verbosity and to improve readability. The following table maps each processing step to its associated `Thunk`:

Step DSL	Thunk
StartWith	StartProcessing
Step	Timed
MakeTradingDecision	TradingDecision

Returning to the curried `foldRun` function, we see that the interpreter pattern matches to determine which `Thunk` is the next processing step. These pattern match statements are how the interpreter applies the behavior that is described by our program's description. `StartProcessing` and `Timed` use system time to determine which method to execute, based on the provided millisecond expiry (`LimitMs`). `StartProcessing` and `TradingDecision` require states from the outside world to support execution. For `StartProcessing`, the `BboUpdated` event from the work queue must be supplied, and for `TradingDecision`, a `Strategy` must be provided to yield a trading decision.

The return value of `foldRun` is a tuple of the accumulated state, which is discarded in the snippet, and the return value of interpreting the free monad. The return value of executing the sequence of `Thunks` that is defined by `pipeline` is `\/[BboProcessingFailure, Option[Either[Bid, Offer]]]`. The return value is a disjunction to account for failure scenarios, which can occur as part of the business logic or because the processing expiry expired. These failures are represented with an ADT of type `BboProcessingFailure`. The right side of the disjunction matches the return type of `TradingStrategy`, indicating that completing all steps in `pipeline` yields a trading decision. The final step is to fold over the trading decision to record processing latency when the pipeline was completed (that is, a `\/-` was returned) and to conditionally send the order to the exchange.

At this juncture, the intuition that you should have developed is that we have separated the description of what we would like to have happen from how it happens. The free monad allows us to do this by first creating a description of our program, and then secondly, building an interpreter to execute the instructions that are provided by the description. As a concrete example, our program description in `pipeline` is not bogged down with providing a strategy for how to implement early termination. Instead, it only describes that certain steps in the processing sequence are subject to time constraints. The interpreter provided to `foldRun` enforces this constraint using system time. Having built a functioning version of the trading strategy pipeline, let's benchmark again to see what effect our changes had.

Benchmarking the new trading strategy pipeline

Running the benchmark at 12,000 and 24,000 events per second using the new trading strategy pipeline yields the following results. The results columns show two values per row. The value before the slash is the result from running with the new implementation that provides early termination. The value after the slash is the copied over result from running without the early termination for comparative purposes:

Metric	12,000 EPS with queue size = 100	24,000 EPS with queue size = 100
50th (median) latency	1.0 ms / 3.0 ms	6.0 ms / 7.0 ms
75th latency	3.0 ms / 5.0 ms	7.0 ms / 8.0 ms

99th latency	7.0 ms / 19.0 ms	8.0 ms / 23.0 ms
99.9th latency	10.0 ms / 44.0 ms	16.0 ms / 55.0 ms
100th (maximum) latency	197.0 ms / 163.0 ms	26.0 ms / 72.0 ms
Mean latency	2.0 ms / 3.9 ms	6.0 ms / 8.4 ms
Events processed as percentage of total events	90.43% / 92.69%	36.62% / 44.58%

From a latency perspective, early termination appears to be a clear win. Excluding maximum latency, early termination yielded lower latencies at each percentile. For example, at 12,000 events per second, half of all requests are processed in one-third of the time, a mere millisecond, as compared to the median when processing is not interrupted. At 12,000 events per second, the observed maximum latency increases, which is likely indicative of garbage collection pauses after the early termination checks. There are two possible improvements to make to our implementation:

- Check the processing duration after invoking `performPreTradeBalanceChecks` before the `TradingStrategy` is executed
- Check the processing duration after the trading decision is created

In both scenarios, processing could be interrupted if the latency exceeds a threshold. It is straightforward to see that these two steps of the processing require attention to reduce the maximum latency because of the clear separation of concerns provided by our free monad implementation. Consider how much more challenging it would be to reason about execution with the pipeline and early termination logic intertwined.

From a throughput perspective, we see a reduction in throughput in both trials. The throughput drop arises from the latent events that are discarded. Here, we again see the tradeoff between throughput and latency. We sacrificed throughput for a better latency profile. Arguably, it is a worthy tradeoff because the higher throughput included stale events, which are more likely to yield trading losses.

A Task interpreter

Our efforts so far have yielded a significantly improved latency profile while sacrificing throughput. What if we could have the best of both worlds? An improved latency profile with higher throughput would be ideal but seems to be out of reach. One strategy for improved throughput is to introduce concurrency. Perhaps, we can make the trading strategy execution concurrent to take advantage of hardware with multiple cores. Before diving in, you ping Gary, your colleague who helped you discover the lineage of the order book implementations. You double-check with Gary to confirm that MVT strategies are thread-safe. He responds with a thumbs up emoji, which gives us the green light to parallelize execution of trading strategies.

In our exploration of the free monad thus far, we have seen the relationship between the program description and the interpreter. The program description, which is represented with the Thunk ADT, is agnostic to the interpreter. This statement represents the essence of the free monad and is best stated by Adam Warski in his excellent free monad blog post at h ttps://softwaremill.com/free-monads/. The semantics of the term "free" in free monad is that the monad is free to be interpreted in any way. We will see this idea in practice by demonstrating that we can transform our existing interpreter to a Task interpreter. To do this, we must map Thunk to Task. Scalaz provides a trait to express this mapping, called NaturalTransformation, with a type alias of ~>. The following snippet shows how to map from Thunk to Task via a NaturalTransformation:

```
private def thunkToTask(ps: PipelineState): Thunk ~> Task =
  new (Thunk ~> Task) {
  def apply[B](t: Thunk[B]): Task[B] = t match {
    case StartProcessing(whenActive, whenExpired,
      limitMs) => Task.suspend(
      hasProcessingTimeExpired(ps.ts, limitMs) match {
        case true => Task.now(whenExpired(ps.event))
        case false => Task.now(whenActive(ps.event))
      })
    case Timed(whenActive, whenExpired, limitMs) => Task.suspend(
      hasProcessingTimeExpired(ps.ts, limitMs) match {
        case true => Task.now(whenExpired())
        case false => Task.now(whenActive())
      })
    case TradingDecision(runStrategy) =>
      Task.fork(Task.now(runStrategy(ps.strategy)))
  }
}
```

The trait defines one method to be implemented that is provided a Thunk and returns a Task. As with our previous interpreter within foldRun, the interpreter requires the same state to provide the BboUpdated event, MessageSentTimestamp, and TradingStrategy. We use pattern matching to handle the mapping of each ADT member. Note the usage of Task.suspend, which has the following signature:

```
def suspend[A](a: => Task[A]): Task[A]
```

In contrast to `Task.now`, `suspend` defers evaluation of the argument. This is necessary because the interpreter has the side-effect of checking the system clock when invoking `hasProcessingTimeExpired`. Using `suspend` defers the call to the system clock until the `Task` is run instead of executing at `Task` construction time.

A second interesting implementation note is the usage of `Task.fork` when translating `TradingDecision`. Here is the introduction of concurrency to the trading strategy pipeline. With our transformation complete, the remaining step is to run the interpreter. Fortunately, `Free` provides a method analogous to `foldRun` that accepts a `NaturalTransformation` named `foldMap`. The following snippet shows how the existing `Thunk` pipeline can be executed using `Task`:

```
pipeline.free.foldMap(thunkToTask(PipelineState(ts, strategy, event)))
    .unsafePerformAsync {
      case -\/(ex) => logException(ex)
      case \/-(\/-(decision)) =>
        decision.foreach(sendTradingDecision)
        recordProcessingLatency(ProcessingLatencyMs(
          System.currentTimeMillis() - ts.value))
      case \/-(-\/(failure)) => logFailure(failure)
    }
```

Invoking `foldMap` applies the transformation, yielding a `Task`. The `Task` is executed asynchronously via `unsafePerformAsync`. Let's run a benchmark at 24,000 events per second with our new implementation and compare the results against the `foldRun` interpreter:

Metric	24,000 EPS with queue size = 100
50th (median) latency	0.0 ms / 6.0 ms
75th latency	0.0 ms / 7.0 ms
99th latency	4.0 ms / 8.0 ms
99.9th latency	13.0 ms / 16.0 ms
100th (maximum) latency	178.0 ms / 26.0 ms
Mean latency	0.13 ms / 6.0 ms
Events processed as percentage of total events	96.60 % / 36.62%

Running the `Task` interpreter on a computer with four cores yields a substantive difference in latency and performance. From a throughput perspective, nearly all events can be processed, in contrast to the 36% processing rate previously. The throughput improvement is indicative of the extra capacity gained by use of `Task.fork`, which is providing runtime parallelism. We also observe a significant reduction in lower percentile latencies, which can also be attributed to the use of `Task.fork` on a multicore machine. Interestingly, the higher percentile latencies remain quite similar. As we previously noted, this is because we are still not defending against latent events at the end of the processing pipeline. The takeaway from this benchmark is that judicious usage of `Task` yields double the throughput with an improved latency profile. This is an exciting result to have achieved by treating the trading strategy as a black box and only changing how the system interacts with the trading strategy.

Exploring free monads further

Our exploration into free monads has deliberately avoided a deep dive into monads and instead focused on showing you the practical results from using this approach. With free monads, we have shown you that we can separate the description of a program from its execution. This allowed us to cleanly introduce logic to interrupt the processing of latent events. We also added concurrency to the processing pipeline without affecting its construction by writing a `Task` interpreter. The core business logic remains pure while retaining excellent runtime characteristics. Here, we see the salient point about the free monad. The description of our program is a value and the interpreter is responsible for handling side-effects.

At this point, you can see the benefits of applying this technique, but you are still in the dark about the underlying mechanisms. A full treatment of monads is beyond the scope of our exploration. By studying the source code that is associated with these examples and exploring other learning sources, you will gain a deeper understanding of how to apply this technique in your own systems. We recommend reading Adam Warski's aforementioned blog post in-depth and reviewing the presentation linked from another free monad example built by Ken Scrambler that is available at `https://github.com/kenbot/free`. To get a deeper understanding of monads, we encourage you to read, *Functional Programming in Scala* by Paul Chiusano and Rúnar Bjarnason.

Summary

In this chapter, we focused on high-performance system design in a more language-agnostic context. We introduced distributed architectures and explained how they can help scale a platform. We presented some of the challenges that such a paradigm involves, and we focused on solving the problem of shared state inside a cluster. We used CRDTs to implement efficient and performant synchronization among the nodes of a cluster. Using these data types, we were able to simplify our architecture and avoid creating a bottleneck by eliminating the need for a standalone service that is dedicated to storing the shared state. We also kept the latency low by avoiding remote calls on the critical path.

In the second part of this chapter, we analyzed how queues impact latency, and how we can apply load control policies to control latency. By benchmarking the trading strategy pipeline, we discovered the importance of applying back pressure and bounding queue sizes in order to reason about maximum latency. Unbounded queues will eventually lead to disastrous production performance. The formal name for the study of queues is a branch of mathematics known as queueing theory. Queueing theory, like monads, is a topic that deserves a more formal treatment. We focused on using empirical observations to drive improvements. Studying queueing theory will provide you with a stronger theoretical background and the ability to build models for system performance.

We extended the policy of rejecting work to interrupting work that is taking too long. In doing so, we explored a new functional programming technique in the form of the free monad. The free monad allowed us to maintain clean business logic describing what the pipeline does without focusing on how the pipeline accomplishes its goals. This separation of concerns enabled us to also add concurrency to the pipeline without complicating the pipeline description. The principles that we discussed enable you to write high-throughput and low-latency systems that remain robust when the system is at capacity, while retaining an emphasis on functional design.

Index

operation-based 230
operation-based increase-only counter 231
state-based 230
state-based increase-only counter 230
custom view
  constructing 147, 148, 149, 150

D

distributed automated traders
  about 223
  distributed architectures 224, 225
  first attempt 225, 226
distribution
  measuring 16

E

ExecutionContext 200
  used, for blocking calls 201, 202, 203
executor submissions
  used, for hampering performance 196, 197, 199

F

future
  and crazy ideas 187
  combining, with promise 206, 207
  exploring 183, 186, 187
  usage, considerations 189

H

HdrHistogram
  about 30
  URL 30
high-throughput systems
  list implementation 104, 105
  queue implementation 113
historical data analysis
  lagged time series returns 126, 128, 129
  multiple return series, handling 134

J

Java Mission Control (JMC) 35
Java Virtual Machine (JVM) 7
just-in-time (JIT) compiler 27

K

kernel optimization
  reference link 10

L

lagged time series returns
  data clean up 131
  Vector 130, 131, 132, 133, 134
latency 10, 11
latency benchmark
  coordinated omission problem 30
  final latency benchmark 31, 32, 33
  first latency benchmark 28, 30
  second latency benchmark 31
list implementation
  limit orders, adding 109, 110, 111
  list 105, 106, 107
  orders, canceling 112
  TreeMap class 108
ListOrderBook class 105
load-control policies
  applying 243

M

microbenchmark
  about 54
  order book 56
monads
  about 249
  free monads, exploring 256
  interpreter, building 250, 252
  program, describing 249
  task interpreter 253, 255, 256
multiple return series
  Array 135, 137
  Spire cfor macro, looping with 137, 138, 139
MV Trading (MVT) 21

O

Object Relational Mapping (ORM) 159
Option data type
  about 93
  bytecode representation 94, 95
  performance considerations 95, 96

Printed in Great Britain
by Amazon